The Child's Entry into a Social World

BEHAVIOURAL DEVELOPMENT:
A SERIES OF MONOGRAPHS

Series Editor
RUDOLPH SCHAFFER
University of Strathclyde
Glasgow, Scotland

Furnishing the Mind: A Comparative Study of Cognitive Development in Central
Australian Aborigines
G. N. SEAGRIM and R. J. LENDON

Acquiring Language in a Conversational Context
C. J. HOWE

The Child's Construction of Language
W. DEUTSCH

Pre-school to school: A Behavioural Study
N. RICHMAN, J. STEVENSON and P. J. GRAHAM

Theory and Practice of Observing Behaviour
G. FASSNACHT

Mothering in Greece
M. DOUMANIS

The Child's Entry into a Social World
H. R. SCHAFFER

BEHAVIOURAL DEVELOPMENT:
A SERIES OF MONOGRAPHS
Series Editor: RUDOLPH SCHAFFER

The Child's Entry into a Social World

H. R. SCHAFFER
*University of Strathclyde,
Glasgow, Scotland*

1984

ACADEMIC PRESS
(Harcourt Brace Jovanovich, Publishers)
London   Orlando
San Diego   San Francisco   New York   São Paulo
Sydney   Tokyo   Toronto   Montreal

ACADEMIC PRESS INC. (LONDON) LTD.
24/28 Oval Road
London NW1

United States Edition published by
ACADEMIC PRESS INC.
(Harcourt Brace Jovanovich, Inc.)
Orlando, Florida 32887

British Library Cataloguing in Publication Data

Schaffer, H. R.
  The child's entry into a social world.
  1. Child development   2. Socialization
  I. Title
  155.4'22   HQ767.9

  ISBN 0-12-622580-X
  LCCN 83-83430

Phototypeset by Dobbie Typesetting Service, Plymouth, Devon
Printed by St Edmundsbury Press, Bury St Edmunds, Suffolk

Preface

This book is concerned with the nature of children's social interactions in the early years and the way in which these change in the course of development. A very lively interest has recently been shown in this area, both by social scientists wanting to understand the roots of early development and by practitioners interested in optimizing the conditions under which young children are reared. As a result a great many findings have now accumulated; it is the aim of this book to bring these findings together in order to provide an overview and a common framework. This is particularly necessary as so much of the relevant data have been compartmentalized and treated in the literature under quite separate headings — headings such as mother–child interaction, socialization processes, preverbal communication, peer relationships, the development of conversational skills, and so forth. Yet all these topics refer to a common theme, namely the way in which mutuality between the child and his social partners manifests itself in the early years and becomes transformed in the course of development. It is the nature of that mutuality that will be described in the following chapters.

Even in the relatively short time that the field of social development has been subjected to empirical study, a number of trends can be discerned in the way in which investigators have gone about their task. There is, for one thing, the move from a purely individual based focus to a dyadic focus: instead of a concern in any one study with (say) mother *or* child there has been increasing interest in the mother–child interaction as such, with the consequent acknowledgement that new methods and concepts need to be developed to serve such a dyadic point of view. Even more recently the focus has come to be widened still further, with the realization that certain aspects of dyadic events cannot be fully understood without taking into account the social context in which they occur, with particular reference to the influence of other people's presence and behaviour on these events — hence a trend away from the study of dyadic groupings towards that of polyadic groupings. At the same time (and similarly motivated by a growing concern with the ecological validity of research results) there has been a move away from the laboratory as the physical setting of studies to the hurly-burly of the "real" world, where the influence of specific situational determinants is forcing investigators to make more allowance than was formerly the case for the particular circumstances under which social interactions take place. Such increasing complexity has also brought about a change in the conceptual approach to the phenomena examined: simple cause and effect explanations of what transpires between, say, a mother and a child are giving way to concepts that acknowledge the reciprocity of the influence process found both within the mother–child pair and between the pair and their context. And one further trend which can also be discerned refers to the fact that the rigid distinction between cognitive, social and emotional aspects of behaviour is at long last being abandoned: for certain purposes it may still be useful to distinguish phenomena in these terms, but the one-time tendency to treat them as wholly distinct and unrelated has given way to attempts to bring all three aspects simultaneously into the field of study.

One other change deserves special comment, and that is the move away from purely behaviouristic approaches to a willingness to take into consideration such intrapsychic phenomena as representations and intentions, acknowledging that these play a part in the social behaviour of even quite young children. It is unfortunate, however, that the pendulum appears sometimes to be swinging to the opposite extreme—from a refusal to recognize anything but overt response patterns to the endowment of quite immature infants with highly sophisticated mental processes that would enable them to participate in the most intricate social exchanges on more or less equal terms. Thus infants from the early weeks on have been attributed with feelings of shared understanding, theories of mind, notions of inter-subjectivity, communicative intentions and cooperative endeavours, with little attempt made to justify these concepts on the basis of unambiguous empirical observations. Such flights of fantasy distort the roles which the very young child and the parent respectively play in early interchanges; ascribing such phenomena to infants as "there from the beginning" merely prevents analysis of the development that eventually does take place in the child's competence to participate in and make sense of his social world.

This book is based on twin themes (see Chapter 1): first, that development is necessarily a joint enterprise of child and caretaker and that consequently any account of the child's progress through the early years must be as much concerned with the adult's as with the child's role; and second, that developmental progress is not so much a matter of gradual quantitative accretion but more one of sequential reorganizations that periodically overtake the child's mental life. Such transitions may well be initiated by forces stemming from the child's inherent programme; each level reached, however, stipulates sets of developmental tasks to which both child *and* caretaker must address themselves if the child is successfully to pass through that phase and progress to the next transition. Even intrapsychic phenomena develop in a social context, in that it is the child's exchanges with other people that play a crucial part in transforming potential into achievement and primitive behaviour patterns into increasingly sophisticated psychological functions. How other people play that part and how their contribution comes to be interwoven with the child's requires to be investigated for each step in the sequence.

Social development is thus basically an orderly process, in that it takes place primarily within the framework of sequential transformations common to all members of the human species. Our account will follow this sequence through the early years, beginning with the newborn child's psychological organization that equips him for social interaction in the first place, and then examining the various issues to which child and caretaker must address themselves consecutively in the course of these early years: the regulation of the child's internal states (Chapter 2), the coordination of mutual attention in face-to-face encounters (Chapter 3), the selection and sharing of topics (Chapter 4), the onset of reciprocal exchanges (Chapter 5), and the move from nonverbal to increasingly verbal exchanges (Chapter 6). At each level various new modes of adjustment need to be worked out between parent and child, and on the basis of the mutuality achieved the parent, as the more senior partner, is able to steer the child in particular socially desirable directions: socialization, that is, has to be seen as occurring in the context of social interaction (Chapter 7). Finally, the multi-person nature of the child's world must be acknowledged: dyadic exchanges occur against a background of other social relationships and may be influenced accordingly, and in addition the processes that characterize a child's participation in a dyadic group may not necessarily be those appropriate to his experiences in a polyadic group (Chapter 8).

This account stems from a programme of research into early social development that has been in progress at the University of Strathclyde over a considerable period of time. In this work I was joined by a number of colleagues: Christina Bryant, Glyn Collis, Charles Crook, Anne Hepburn, Christine Liddell, David Messer, Stuart Millar, Cathy Murphy, Meyer Parry, and Charmaine Whitehouse. I owe a considerable debt to the enthusiasm that all these individuals brought to our various projects and to the many discussions we held over the years; it is a debt that I acknowledge here with great pleasure.

March, 1984   H. R. SCHAFFER

Contents

1 Introduction: A Perspective

From birth onwards the child lives in a social world. He arrives with a number of physiological systems such as breathing, swallowing, elimination and temperature control which help him to survive, yet even these are of little avail to him in the absence of other people. Another person must provide food before his swallowing and elimination become functional; temperature control operates only within certain limits beyond which the child's caretakers must take the necessary measures for his protection; and breathing too may sometimes be endangered in the young baby without the timely aid of adults. And when it comes to other, psychologically more advanced, functions that enable the child to adapt to his physical and social environment, studies of children brought up under conditions of minimal social stimulation have shown only too clearly what tragically incomplete beings emerge when caretakers fail to compensate for the child's own deficiencies. Of necessity, the child is from the start embedded in a social world; without others he has no existence.

None of this means that the newborn infant's own awareness of others is as yet anything but rudimentary. As far as his parents are concerned, he may well be regarded as "one of us" from the moment of birth — if not before; to them he is already an individual to be respected as a full member of the family, and their own lives and relationships will be adjusted accordingly. From the child's point of view, however, birth is only an entry point; it is but the initial event that sets him on the course of acquiring, gradually and over a long period of time, that sense of group belongingness that is the ultimate hallmark of a social creature.

How the child progresses to this state, and particularly how he takes the earliest steps in this progression, has intrigued writers for a long time. Becoming a socially competent person is in many respects a life-long process, but it is in the early years of childhood that the most crucial developments occur, and it is with these that we shall be concerned here. But an account of social development needs to be every bit as much about the child's caretakers as about the child himself; on his own he is for a long time an incomplete being. Individuality, as Vygotsky (1978) argued so cogently, is a secondary phenomenon; social relationships are primary.

Paradigms for the study of social development

It is only relatively recently that speculation has given way to empirical research in explaining the nature of early social development, but already a considerable body of data has accumulated which provides us with insight into many features of this process. Not that there is one coherent theoretical framework as yet available within which one can do justice to all these diverse findings; in attempting to explain the child's first steps in becoming a social being writers at different times have laid emphasis on different aspects of this process, with changes in paradigm adopted perforce as new insights become available. Let us briefly consider the major paradigms that have appeared in the space of just the last few decades — each giving rise to a substantial body of findings, each abandoned as the accumulated knowledge forced investigators to adopt new perspectives, but each new one also assimilating the findings previously gained to fit in with its own particular orientation.

(1) Social development as the acquisition of individual competencies

Writers adopting this perspective focussed primarily on the child as an individual, without explicit reference to the social context in which he functioned. The task which investigators set themselves was to determine the types of behaviour which children, at given ages, display in inter-personal situations; no attempt was made, however, to relate the behaviour observed to those situations. A principal aim was to describe the various milestones of development that children reach at particular ages: the first smile, the appearance of fear of strangers, the beginnings of peer cooperation, and so forth. In this way the nature of individuals' social growth was to be plotted for the years of childhood. Thus little was said about the conditions under which the respective response patterns manifested themselves; the investigators' attention was on the child alone, the questions in their mind were whether that child was capable of such behaviour and how much of it he displayed, and little importance was attached to the way in which that behaviour was interlinked with the behaviour of the child's social partner.

As a result of the efforts by investigators such as Gesell (1940) a large body of normative data on early social development accumulated; the data were static in nature for they gave no indication of the child as involved in the hurlyburly of social intercourse; on the other hand they did provide much useful indication of the timing and sequencing of those aspects of social development that could be expected to appear in the repertoire of any child reared under normal expectable circumstances.

(2) Determination of environmental influences that shape development

One aspect to which the child-centred approach drew attention concerned the range of individual differences in the nature of social development. This was mainly confined to parameters such as the age at onset and the frequency of social response patterns, but variations even in these respects posed a problem that called for explanation. For such an explanation investigators, true to the then prevailing faith in the shaping influence of experience, turned to those aspects of the child's environment that could be expected to have the greatest effect on the course of development, namely the rearing practices of caretakers. Infant feeding methods, disciplinary techniques, the scheduling of rewards, maternal deprivation and father absence — these and many other aspects of the rearing environment were described, measured and related to the child's progress. Some of the studies adopting this paradigm have become classics in the developmental literature (e.g. Sears *et al.*, 1957); they provide a vivid picture of the great range of parental practices and of the way these varied across groups differing in class, education and culture; they yielded much insightful descriptive material and put forward various provocative proposals as to how the diversity of parental behaviour might account for the diversity of child development. However, as shown elsewhere (Schaffer, 1977), not only was this approach marred by a number of basic methodological and conceptual problems in the way it obtained and processed its data, but it has also become evident that on the basis of parental measures alone child behaviour and its development could not be predicted. As Bell (1968) has made clear, an approach based on the shaping of passive children by all-powerful parents was bound to fail in view of its one-sided emphasis on environmental influence.

(3) Social development as relationship formation

The need for an interactionist paradigm, which does justice to the characteristics of both child and parent, became evident from the shortcomings of the preceding approaches. In a sense it was already implicit in much of the earlier work: it was acknowledged that parental comforting and protection are geared to children's dependency needs; that mothers' feeding serves to satisfy infants' hunger; that adult discipline is required to check child aggressiveness. Yet neither theory nor empirical investigation have attempted to encompass both aspects simultaneously; the one was taken for granted while the other was being examined. It is one of the main achievements of Bowlby's (1969) attachment theory that it addressed itself equally to both child and mother, conceiving of them as a unit that has evolved together and in which the two stand in a continuing reciprocal relationship at all stages of the child's development. There has been some confusion as to whether the term "attachment" refers to an individual's characteristic or to a relationship; according to Hinde (1982) it is useful to distinguish between *attachment system*, designating an organization within an individual, and *attachment*, serving as a label for an affectionate bond and thus referring to a relationship between individuals. For our purposes, however, it is sufficient to note that Bowlby's emphasis on the mutual adaptedness of mother and infant has highlighted the need to examine social development in terms of what goes on *between* people, not just *within* individuals treated as isolated units.

(4) Social interaction as context for social development

Attachments are relationships, and relationships are enduring bonds that grow out of specific interactive episodes. It is, for example, widely agreed that a child's first attachments to particular individuals do not usually appear until the third quarter of the first year; whatever the precise cognitive and neurophysiological factors may be that make their appearance possible, they generally emerge from a history of many months of interacting, day in and day out, with the persons on whom the attachments come to be focussed. The relationship is thus the end-product of that history. We have learned much about the nature of that product: not only about the time of its appearance in the child's developmental timetable but also about its manifestation at various ages, the range of individual differences in the way it is expressed at any one age, the conditions under which it comes to be focussed on certain individuals, and most important of all (again thanks largely to Bowlby) about the way it should be conceptualized as a behavioural system of immense adaptive significance to human beings. But statements about relationships need constantly to refer back to the interactive episodes from which they are derived. There is, of course, a reciprocal association between the two levels (Hinde, 1979): on the one hand, social relationships arise through participation in social interactions; on the other hand, inter-actions take place in the context of formed relationships. However, the most concrete level at which one may observe social behaviour is that of interactions; any statement about relationships must take cognizance of this level; should it fail to do so, or should the knowledge base to which it refers be inadequate, it is in danger of degenerating into a mere exercise of building castles in the air. Much of the literature on children's dependency needs, inspired more by learning theory than by any observations of children, illustrates this danger only too vividly.

It therefore becomes important that the knowledge accumulated in recent years about early interactive development should be pulled together and examined. We need to find out what form the interactive episodes take at various ages and with different partners; the roles that adult and child respectively play in initiating, maintaining and terminating such episodes; the consequences that involvement in them may have for the child's development; and how young infants at the very beginning of life first become involved in interactive sequences. There is fortunately a growing body of research that has accumulated in recent years and that can now be consulted in the search for meaningful answers to such questions.

The concept of social interaction

To qualify as an interaction the separate activities of the participants must be coordinated in such a way as to form one unitary sequence. Thus the individual contributions, when considered together, need to have a coherence that entitles them to be considered as a single entity — a conversation, a game, a fight, a debate, or any other activity that is based on the mutual influence of the participants.

Social interactions have certain structural properties. These concern *inter alia* the number of participants, the length of interactive sequences, the number of individual turns in each sequence, and the balance of individuals' contributions. Such characteristics lend themselves easily to measurement and thus to comparisons of, say, mothers interacting with children of different ages or children with different kinds of partners. But structural properties alone tell one little about functional characteristics, in particular about the way in which the participants achieve mutual regulation of their separate activities. This is surely the most fundamental question to answer about interactions, and especially so with regard to those involving young children. As research with adults has made clear (e.g. Argyle and Cook, 1976), mutual regulation in face-to-face situations is a highly complex undertaking, involving a variety of smoothly executed skills carried out with split-second precision and generally without any conscious awareness. Each individual must coordinate not only his own various activities — speech, gestures, looking, bodily movements—into one integrated whole, but he must also synchronize these with the activities of the partner. Intra-personal synchrony needs to go hand in hand with inter-personal synchrony if the coming together of individuals is to have a "successful" outcome. How young children acquire such competencies, and how interactions are managed before children become fully able to play their own part in them, are the main topics to which research is currently addressed in this area.

There is also another sense in which questions can be asked about the *functioning* of social interactions, namely what are they for? Some of the consequences of interactions are immediate: a feeding situation results in the child's hunger being stilled; a joint play session may provide entertainment and relief from boredom. But there are also consequences of a more long-term nature, for it is in the context of interactions that the child gradually masters the techniques needed for social living: a particular way of communicating with others, notions of right and wrong, rules of hygiene, acceptable ways of eating and of dressing—in short, all those aspects that are involved in fitting the individual into a particular cultural framework. Socialization occurs in the context of social interaction; how it is accomplished is a topic of enormous interest about which we are still woefully ignorant.

(1) Levels of analysis: interaction and individual

That interactions, in the sense given above, occur from the earliest weeks on is evident to anyone who has ever watched a mother and her baby "talking" with each other: the to-and-fro of gaze and touch and vocalization, the mounting excitement carefully kept in check by the adult, the timing of each cue and its integration with cues of other modalities—all indicate a sequential exchange in which each response also functions as a stimulus for the other person and where a system of mutual influence thus comes to be established. No wonder such mother–baby sequences have been compared to a dialogue, a conversation or even to a dance, nor is it surprising that words such as smooth, integrated, enmeshed, synchronous and reciprocal are commonly used to describe them. Such words are often only metaphors and merely convey general impressions; they nevertheless indicate a widespread belief that even the earliest encounters already have an organization that in certain basic respects is analogous to more mature interactions. From the beginning (it is thus asserted) parent and infant can combine their separate streams of activity to form one coherent unit. What is in question is not so much the existence of such fundamental mutuality as its origins and nature, the relative contributions of adult and child, and the processes whereby it evolves in due course into more mature forms.

Statements about interactions are not, of course, statements about the individuals participating in them (Hinde, (1979), yet the two are frequently confused. An interaction may be "successful" (whatever the behavioural cues that give rise to such a judgment), but this does not by itself enable one to say anything about the skills and competencies of the individual partners. As we shall see, this becomes particularly relevant to understanding interactions involving participants of such unequal status as mother and infant; a beautifully integrated interaction sequence, such as seen in vocal dialogue where mother and infant appear to speak in turn with just the same precision as two adult interlocutors, gives no grounds for inferring anything about the skills that the individual infant brings to such an interchange. The success may be entirely a function of the more senior partner's ability to "carry" the child, of her willingness to fit in with his response patterns, thereby giving the semblance of a dialogue among equals which is in fact a pseudo-dialogue in that one participant does not as yet have the competence to play a proper part in maintaining the interchange. Much of the story of early interactive development concerns the way in which adult caretakers play out their pretence that the infant is in fact a fully qualified partner, able to take his turn and answer back as though aware of the rules of the game. A pretence it may be, yet there is also every indication that the eventual development of the child's competence to participate on equal terms occurs largely because of that pretence. The child, that is, acquires the skills of social interaction by being involved from the very beginning in such interactions by a partner willing to make up whatever his deficiencies may be, thus acquainting him with the hither and thither of person-to-person exchanges and gradually leading him on to assuming a progressively greater share of the responsibility for the interaction.

Variables derived from social events may refer either to the characteristics of the individuals participating in them (e.g. the child's activity level, or the mother's emotionality) or to the interaction as such. The concentration on individuality that has typified so much of our past efforts to understand human behaviour has meant that the latter kind of variable is still relatively infrequent; when it is used there is often disagreement about definitions (seen, for example, in the diverse ways in which terms like reciprocity and synchrony have been employed). Progress in evolving terms describing interactions has been painfully slow, yet the introduction of dyadic state variables (e.g. mutual gaze, or visual coorientation) shows that variables at this level can be operationally defined as clearly as those describing individuals and can serve to make statements that are unique to that level of analysis. It is, however, also important to remember that the distinction between the interactive and the individual levels is not an absolute one: terms such as a mother's sensitivity or a child's demandingness show that some variables can refer to individuals and yet have no meaning outside an interaction.

(2) Interactions as systems

Interactions may nevertheless be treated as units in their own right, with properties that cannot be deduced from an examination of the characteristics of individual participants. To describe all members of a group is not to describe the group—a point, as we shall see, with important method-ological implications. Conceptually, this accounts for the attraction of systems theory to many of those attempting to understand social inter-action (cf. Thoman, 1979), for the objective of this approach is to under-stand the properties and principles of wholes—be they solar systems or families, nuclear missiles or mother–child pairs. Any such unit may be regarded as a system with emergent properties that cannot be derived from a study of the component parts; the whole needs to be described in organ-izational terms, for it cannot be accounted for by isolating simple cause–effect sequences among the components. Accordingly, explanations of adult–child interaction are regarded as inadequate as long as they confine themselves to statements of the type "mother acts on child"; if the aim is to account for the child's behaviour such a statement fails to do justice to the multiplicity of interacting variables operative at any one moment of time, including the child's own actions upon the mother, the feedback effect of each partner's response, and the numerous characteristics of the context in which the inter-action takes place. Under these circumstances the immediately preceding behaviour of either partner may be a "cause" of the other's behaviour in only a very trivial sense.

Systems theory has no doubt served the useful purpose of stressing the organizational aspects of groups composed of interacting individuals. It sees the parent–child couple as an open system that is continually changing in the light of new circumstances, whether these refer to the emergence of maturationally programmed abilities or to the impact of environmental events. It has, furthermore, drawn attention to the importance of taking into consideration feedback effects resulting from the actions of either parent or child. And finally it has served as a useful antidote to simplistic explanations of children's development in terms of adults' impact or of critical period learning.

But all this does not rule out the need for causal explanation, for teasing out the contributions of specific factors within the whole—be they parental or child or contextual aspects. Identical dyadic conditions may, after all, be brought about in quite different ways: for example, a child's high compliance rate to parental demands may reflect either the naturally compliant make-up of that particular child or the specially appropriate manner whereby that parent expresses her demands. Observations of naturally occurring interactions may then no longer be sufficient; experimental procedures controlling relevant aspects of the interaction will need to be resorted to in order to isolate the role of individual factors. It may be noted that the recent interest in early peer interaction is, in part, motivated by just the same need to determine the role played by individuals; comparison of parent–child and child–child interactions can (roughly at least) indicate whether the "smoothness" of the former is largely due to the adult's willingness to fit in with the child's behaviour or whether the child already has certain skills that are evident in interacting even with individuals of equal developmental status who (unlike the adult) are unable or unwilling to compensate for the child's interactive deficiencies.

(3) Some methodological considerations

Methodologies employed in the study of social development are dependent on assumptions about the nature of that development. Thus most of the statistical techniques used in the past by investigators have been based on unidirectional causal models, where the assumption was made that children develop in particular ways because parents push them in those directions. If, on the other hand, the model assumes mutual influence of parent and child, and if moreover it tries to do justice to the influence of other simultaneously operative factors, measurement problems become vastly more difficult (Thomas and Martin, 1976).

In the study of social interaction two ways of using measures can be found: *monadic* and *interactional*. The difference lies not so much in the nature of the measure itself; the same index may be applied in either of these two ways. The difference derives rather from the investigator's focus: whether his attention is entirely on one participant and his aim is solely to make statements about that person as an *individual*, or whether he is simultaneously keeping an eye on both partners in a dyad (or on all members of a larger group) in order to study what transpires *between* them.

Monadic measures can be obtained in an interactive situation, but even when they refer to behaviour directed by one partner to the other they do not necessarily tell us anything about interactive processes. For example, the amount of a mother's speech to her child may be obtained from an observation session, but such a measure on its own is strictly about the mother as an individual and allows us to make no statement about the impact on the child. For that we require further information: whether the child is listening or not, whether he is able to comprehend what the mother says, whether her talk is related to what the child is interested in at that moment of time, and so forth, and our estimate of the mother's speech must then be related to that information. Monadic measures obtained from interactive situations do have uses; they allow us to assess individuals and hence to make such comparisons as the amount or type of attention fathers as opposed to mothers pay to their children, or the frequency with which first born children make requests for help compared with later born children, or the percentage of time that nursery teachers in contrast with mothers engage in conversation with children. But such measures do not tell us anything about the interaction—not even when they are collected from both participants at the same time and the totals then compared. To know that there is a positive correlation between the amount of mothers' speech and the amount of infant babbling gives us some idea of the congruence of these indices; it tells us nothing about the way in which the two sets of behaviour are mutually integrated. For that it is necessary to pay attention to the all-important temporal dimension along which interactions occur and to determine how the behaviour of both partners is interwoven along this dimension.

Interactive measures have three distinguishing criteria: (i) they require information about both participants in a dyadic session, (ii) that information needs to be obtained concurrently, and (iii) the two sets of individual data must be interrelated along a time base. Thus measures that in the first place refer to individuals become transformed through combination into indices at a higher, interactive level. The dyadic state variable of "mutual gaze", for instance, results from ascertaining the direction of gaze of the two partners separately and combining the data into one joint statement. Similarly, a bout of "joint involvement" is said to occur when the two individuals (say, mother and child) are both engaged with the same object at the same time. These two examples refer to simultaneously occurring events; however, the combination may also be sequential, referring to instances where the individuals' acts succeed each other, for example: child A offers—child B accepts; mother asks—child answers. Events combined on the basis of their simultaneous occurrence may, of course, also then be examined for their successive association with other simultaneous combinations; for example, one may ask whether the mutual gaze state of mother and child is usually succeeded by the dyadic state "mother only looking" (i.e. the mother is still looking at the child but the child is now looking elsewhere)—thus determining who is responsible for breaking mutual gaze. What soon becomes evident is that our vocabulary for describing interactions is far less adequate than that used for individual events; apart from such terms as joint involvement or mutual gaze, or terms like conversation or game that (rather more loosely) describe longer interactive sessions, we lack the necessary words and need to fall back on combination terms like "offers–accepts" or "asks–answers".

Studying interactive events thus involves paying attention to both the simultaneous and the successive combination of individuals' contributions.

At the recording stage this frequently calls for the use of tools like video- or film-cameras; for one thing, an eye may then be kept on both participants at the same time; for another, many different responses can be scored by repeatedly playing back tape or film; and finally, as many interactive events occur at great speed, slow motion facilities make it possible to detect phenomena that the unaided eye would not generally bring to consciousness, and interactive integration may then be examined at micro-analytic levels.

At the data analysis stage most attention has been given to the successive aspect of interactive behaviour, with a view to capturing the to-and-fro flavour of social interchange. In the past this has mostly been confined to examining very short sequences; in particular, analysis of conditional probabilities in sequences of events has been used to establish the contingencies between partners' immediately adjacent responses (Lewis and Lee-Painter, 1974). In this way one can ask, for example, if maternal vocalization is generally followed by infant vocalization or whether it is more likely to be succeeded by an infant smile. Such analyses have several limitations: for one thing, there is no guarantee that responses are elicited by the immediately preceding event rather than by something that occurred earlier on in the sequence; for another, the analysis assumes that behaviour is determined by single events instead of the multiple factors that one usually has to take into account; and in addition, this way of ordering the data fails to do justice to the hierarchical organization of behaviour which is instead seen in terms of simple chains, thus leaving aside such aspects as an individual's intentions or longer-term goals that may explain the form of particular sequences. Some of these disadvantages are now being minimized by statistical techniques such as lag sequential analysis (Sackett, 1978); it is still the case, however, that the questions asked about interactions have out-stripped the availability of methodologies suited to answer them.

Development as a joint enterprise

Accounts of psychological development have for the most part been individual-based. Their concern has been with the child as such; it is the child who is regarded as the basic unit of study, everything outside his skin being considered extraneous, even antithetical—forces that may have an impact on the child but that are not an inherent part of his developmental progress.

Such individual-based accounts fail to do justice to what is one of the most fundamental features of human development, namely its intimate dependence on the rearing environment. All psychological functions develop in a social context, and the younger the child the more important it is to regard him as part of a unit which inevitably includes the caretaker as a vital complement to the child's state of immaturity. Whatever strong genetic push may be responsible in the first place for the emergence of new capabilities and for the transition to new levels of functioning, a propensity cannot become reality unless the caretaker supports, maintains, completes and furthers the child's efforts. Development is a joint enterprise involving parent as well as child; the role of *both* needs to be specified.

(1) Sequential reorganizations in development

What the respective roles of parent and child are and how these change in the course of development are basic problems which need to be confronted. One thing is apparent, and that is that the nature of parental activities changes *pari passu* with the course of the child's development, in that the child's psychological organization as found at various stages elicits behaviour from the caretaker appropriate to that organization, helping to consolidate it and subsequently helping it to progress to new levels.

It is now increasingly recognized that psychological development is not a matter of slow and gradual quantitative expansion, but that it takes place primarily through periodic reorganizations of the child's mental life. As Piaget above all has shown, from time to time new capacities emerge which drastically alter the child's mode of adaptation to his environment, bringing into being patterns of behaviour that may well be based on previously established patterns and may even incorporate these, but that nevertheless signify qualitatively different ways of responding to and acting upon the world. Development, that is, turns out to be less a matter of steady accretion and more one of periodic and relatively sudden transitions to new levels.

Table 1. *McCall's scheme of developmental sequences in the first two years*

Stage	Age range (months)	Characteristic features
I	0–2	Endogenous control over behaviour
II	2–7	Knowledge of world completely subjective; actions not distinguished from external objects.
III	7–13	Ability to distinguish means and ends; explorations of objects goal-corrected
IV	13–21	Objects conceived as independent entities, child can operate on them mentally without the need for direct action upon them
V	21 +	Representation of relationships between objects; relationships may be symbolized and mentally manipulated

(Adapted from McCall *et al.*, 1977)

Take the scheme outlined by McCall *et al.* (1977) for the first two years of life (Table 1). Scores from infant tests, periodically obtained in the course of a longitudinal investigation (the Berkeley Growth Study) were subjected to factor analysis at each age and examined for changes in the item composition of the principal components. Where such changes occurred they were taken as evidence of discontinuity in the infants' developmental course. The major discontinuities found were located at ages 2, 8, 13 and 21 months; moreover, at these periods breaks also occurred in the pattern of longitudinal stability of individual differences. McCall *et al.* accordingly conclude that there are transitions in mental development which are located at these particular ages, revealing major changes in infants' psychological organization brought about by periodic restructuring. A stage-like progression is thus suggested, with consistency of behaviour within the stage but relative discontinuity between stages.

The location and nature of transition points is thus a matter of considerable importance, and especially so in the early stages of development when they are likely to be more frequent and to herald more profound changes than subsequently. Take two of the transitions listed by McCall *et al.*, namely those at 2 months and at 8 months respectively. These have been singled out by Emde *et al.* (1976) as involving particularly radical reorganizations. Thus the former is said to signal a shift from the infant's inner to his outer world: whereas previously the main concern was with the regulation of internal states of sleep and wakefulness, from 7 to 8 weeks on the infant becomes very much more receptive to external stimulation and oriented to events in the outer world. The transition is heralded by a cluster of psycho-biological transformations, observed in the onset of social smiling and of eye-to-eye contact with others, in changes in neural functioning such as reflected in EEG patterns, and in the greater regularity of state fluctuation. As a result the infant becomes more alert and more available to other people. The 8-month shift is also accompanied by a variety of behavioural and neural changes; its most marked expression (according to Emde *et al.*) is given by the onset of stranger distress, which is taken to indicate a new level of mental organization with wide-ranging implications for the child's emotional and social life.

The picture which these and other investigators paint of early development is that of a step-like course, where transitions to qualitatively different modes of behaviour occur from time to time, bringing about new modes of adaptation on the part of the child. Each break represents a period of instability; each new phase requires the consolidation of whatever achievements were ushered in at the point of transition. There is welcome agreement with regard to the location of some of the transitions (e.g. those at 2 and at 8 months); the existence of others is at present more doubtful. Even less certain are the precise factors that bring about the periodic transitions. The most probable explanation is that each reorganization is sequentially triggered by inherent forces that normally become operative according to some species-specific neurally based programme; it also seems likely that the cumulative effect of past experience is required to enable that triggering to take place.

(2) Interactive issues

Changes in the child's psychological organization, however they may be brought about, have implications not just for the child alone but also for his relationships with others and for the role that these others need to adopt. Take the afore-mentioned transition said to characterize the two-months period. If, as a consequence of preceding developments, the infant becomes able to turn away from inner preoccupations and appears suddenly to "discover" the parent, the quality of the interaction with her and the kind of treatment she offers him are likely to undergo marked changes. The developmental tasks confronting the infant respectively before and after this point are in some respects of a very different nature; given the impossibility for young children to cope with these tasks on their own the implications for the adult as well as for the child need to be considered. Whereas previously the infant's state regulation was the principal item on the agenda for child and parent, now the development of attentional processes means that the parent must be prepared to offer a different kind of stimulation—one that centres less on the child's inner condition and more on his emerging interests in the outside world. What is more, the infant would not have reached this point of transition if the parent had not been actively involved in helping him to master the task of state regulation; whatever maturationally determined neural processes may be playing a part, the input from the parent is also essential in getting him to the point where he can face the next developmental step. And once he has reached the new level of functioning the parent must again provide the necessary support, though that will now need to assume a different form corresponding to the child's new requirements.

Thus each stage brings a particular kind of developmental task that parent and child must jointly confront; the child is in certain respects a different being from what he was before and the relationship must therefore be renegotiated each time and placed on a different footing. The impetus that sets periodic reorganization into motion may well stem from the child's inner programme, establishing new goals; the pursuit of those goals, however, is a *joint* enterprise. Were it not so the child could not progress to more advanced levels; he acts as pacer but the parent is required to organize the child's world in such a way as to help him successfully to accomplish the tasks of that period. In time the parent's involvement becomes less direct as she is able increasingly to hand over responsibility to the child for tasks previously tackled jointly; at all stages, however, the nature of her interactive behaviour must change in tandem with his.

With the changing nature of the child, and with the corresponding changes characterizing the adult's behaviour, the interaction between them becomes periodically transformed as the pair face new issues. Parent and child may be regarded as a mutually accommodative interactive system, but how that accommodation is achieved varies from phase to phase according to the particular circumstances prevailing at that time. Of these circumstances the most marked are the new competencies that periodically emerge in the child; these refer to universal achievements evident across a wide range of child rearing practices, resulting in some specific extension of the child's ability to interact with his environment generally and the social partner in particular. They emerge more suddenly and succeed one another at a greater rate in the early years than subsequently, and their impact on the child and the challenge they pose to the caretaker are especially great at that time. Yet they can arise at all stages of development — witness the onset of puberty, a change with considerable interpersonal implications that in many societies is marked by special rites, following which the individual is allocated a new place in his community and treated as a different being.

The notion of *interactive issues* has been advanced to acknowledge the fact that the task confronting the parent–child couple varies from one developmental level to the next, and attempts have accordingly been made to produce lists of such issues as they arise in the course of childhood (Sander, 1969; Sroufe, 1979). Thus the list put forward by Sander refers to five sequential levels of adjustment that parent and child need to make during the first two years of life at various specified ages; that by Sroufe contains six such items for the 0 to 4½ year age range. Such attempts ought to be viewed with the following considerations in mind:

(1) The number and kind of issues identified is to some extent a matter of the level of analysis adopted. Thus Sander referred to the first three months as a period of initial regulation of biological processes, where the main task for parent and child is to achieve stability of basic physiological functions such as arousal and quieting states and waking-sleeping patterns. Als (1979), on the other hand, preferred to adopt a more molecular focus and as a result found three distinct aspects for the same period, representing different sequential steps to be taken by parent and child during this time. The identification of issues is thus determined, in part at least, by the particular orientation of the investigator.

(2) Yet another consideration strengthens the conclusion that finite,

universally applicable lists of interactive issues cannot be said to exist. While some changing circumstances may be brought about by forces common to all members of the species, others are of a more idiosyncratic nature affecting only certain individual parent–child couples or groups of couples. The common forces refer to the child's genetically determined developmental timetable, as a result of which certain new competencies mature periodically; being universal they tend to attract most attention. Yet the idiosyncratic forces must also be acknowledged: a severe illness in the child, a decision by the mother to take up employment, or a culturally imposed change such as starting school at some particular age—these are but some examples to show that all couples are likely to be confronted from time to time with problems specific to them that also urgently require some sort of re-negotiation of the relationship between parent and child.

(3) Different issues may arise at different times, but they do not necessarily constitute a neat sequence where each is the sole theme for the parent–child couple for a particular period, is then settled once and for all and disappears, to be replaced by another issue. It is, for instance, possible for any one issue to arise in different form at different ages: thus topic sharing (as we shall see) becomes of importance at 5 months when the child's newly developing interest in the world of objects requires techniques for mutual reference to be worked out with the caretaker—techniques which at that age involve various nonverbal devices but which need to be updated once more in the course of the second and third years when the child's developing verbal skills make possible new means of reference. As a result there is an overlap of this issue with others that have arisen since 5 months; certain themes may indeed continue to reverberate for years while others come and go comparatively speedily.

(4) Some issues arise quite suddenly; in infancy in particular there is generally little difficulty in assigning specific ages to transition points. Others, however, surface much more slowly and gradually; the onset of representational abilities to which we shall later refer provides one such example: as Piagetian accounts make clear, their emergence in the child's second year is a long drawn-out affair that does not necessitate the comparatively sudden readjustment which some other transitions require.

Despite these reservations, the concept of interactive issue is a useful one to adopt when describing the course of early development. It draws attention to the joint nature of the developmental task and to the fact that the child is part of a wider system than that defined by his individual make-up alone. It also serves to emphasize the changing nature of parental activity and the periodic realignment that has to take place in the relationship with the child. Whether the transition points represent periods of vulnerability when the child is especially susceptible to psychological and physiological stress—as has been suggested by Emde *et al.* (1976)—remains to be established; it is, however, these points that deserve particular attention in any description of development.

In the account below we shall single out various developmental periods and their attendant interactive issues, but without any claim of having produced an exhaustive list. We shall rather concentrate on those that have species-wide applicability and that seem to have especially profound implications for the child's developmental progress in the early years and for the parent's complementary role. The following will be referred to:

(1) *The immediate post-birth period*, when the most urgent requirement for parent and child is to regularize the infant's basic biological processes such as feeding and waking–sleeping states and to harmonize these with environmental requirements.

(2) *From 2 months on*, when largely as a result of changes in the infant's visual capacities a marked increase in attentiveness to the external world takes place, with particular reference to other people. The regulation of mutual attention and responsiveness in face-to-face situations accordingly becomes a central theme at that time.

(3) *At 5 months* newly emerging manipulative abilities bring about a shift of attention to the world of objects. How to incorporate these in social interactions and thus ensure topic sharing is the new basic issue which then confronts parent–child couples.

(4) *In the 8 to 10 months age range* some of the most profound changes take place; in particular, the emergence of relational and integrative abilities means that the child's behaviour now becomes much more flexible and co-ordinated. A more symmetrical relationship with the caretaker, based on reciprocity and characterized by intentionality, can thus begin to be established around this age.

(5) *Around the middle of the second year* the capacity for symbolic representation gradually emerges. From then on social interactions increasingly assume a verbal form; growing self-awareness leads the child to reflect more on his and other people's behaviour and to guide his actions accordingly; and verbal directives now become increasingly effective as a means of social control.

2 Initial Encounters

Mutual adjustment of parent and child is evident from the earliest inter-actions on. The assertion, sometimes made, that meshing of the two sets of behaviour increases over age as the partners gradually acquire experience of one another may at first sight seem a plausible statement; in practice, however, it is difficult to substantiate. There is no simple quantitative increase: meshing occurs at all ages, including the earliest. Mutual experience is, of course, important, but its most demonstrable consequence lies in the qualitative nature of the meshing process as it undergoes progressive modification with the child's growing social and cognitive competence and in the increasingly complex forms assumed by communication modes.

It would hardly be possible for mutual adjustment to occur so early on were it not for some degree of preparedness on the part of both caretaker and child which enables them to participate immediately in interaction with one another. Neither partner arrives with a blank slate; the urgency to engage in immediate, reasonably well-functioning interchange will not permit it. The child, for his part, needs to single out people as features of the environment that have a special significance to him and with whose behavioural characteristics he can readily synchronize his own; the parent, in turn, must be prepared to tune in to an individual of very different status from herself and be able to provide the appropriate treatment. It is therefore necessary to begin by considering the mechanisms whereby these initial encounters are established.

Infants' social preadaptation

Are children *born* social or *made* social? This is almost certainly a meaning-less question, though at one time it involved many a writer in heated controversy. What one does have to establish is whether the human newborn comes into the world specially equipped with certain structures that mediate interaction with the social environment — structures which are activated by corresponding stimuli from the parent and which in turn stimulate the parent to respond, thereby setting up behavioural interdependence from the beginning. There is in fact ample evidence to indicate that the neonate is in a number of respects already predisposed to respond to other people. The nature of such preadaptation can be seen in two main areas: firstly, in various inherent perceptual biases that predispose infants selectively to attend to other human beings, and secondly in a variety of response tendencies geared to mediate the child's interactions with others.

Perceptual selectivity

The impressive perceptual competence of newborn infants has been commented on repeatedly in recent years (e.g. Appleton *et al.*, 1975). A large body of knowledge is now in being which specifies this competence in detail and which demonstrates the considerable abilities even quite young infants already have in receiving and processing information from their environment. However, it is also now apparent that their responsiveness is far from indiscriminate. It seems rather that the infant is biased to respond more readily and more vigorously to some forms of stimulation than to others, and above all to stimuli associated with other human beings. In particular, people's faces and their voices have been found to elicit selective attention.

(1) Responsiveness to faces

An extensive literature (recently reviewed by Sherrod, 1981) demonstrates that, as a stimulus object, another person's face is one of the most attention-worthy features in the infant's environment. Even neonates (as Fantz, 1963, originally showed) are more interested in a disc with human features painted on it than in any other stimulus of similar size and shape, however brightly coloured or patterned.

Initially the source of attraction lies not so much in the realism of the stimulus as in a number of more primitive characteristics inherent in faces. Much research has gone into establishing the identity of these. Movement, contour density, complexity, solidity, symmetry: these and other character-istics have been the subject of much research. For instance, studies of infants' eye movements while scanning faces (Salapatek, 1975) show that attention tends to be concentrated on such borders as those between hair and forehead and between chin and clothes. The possession of strong contours is thus one characteristic that gives faces their initial attraction. Another is movement: Carpenter (1974) found that at the age of 2 weeks infants were much more attracted by moving than by stationary faces, and according to Girton (1979) 5-week-old infants are able to discriminate a schematic face with fast oscillating eye dots from a similar face with slow oscillating eyes, with preference shown for the greater speed. Complexity, though difficult to operationalize, is yet another aspect investigated: Haaf (1974), by varying the number of separate details presented in face-like stimuli, was able to show that the visual preferences of infants at 5 and at 10 weeks of age were determined by this aspect rather than by the degree of facial resemblance. And yet a further characteristic examined is solidity: Fantz (1966), by pairing a three-dimensional model of a female head with a similar flat form, obtained a strong preference for the former. In short, faces are highly salient to infants because they possess a number of characteristics that are precisely those to which the infant's perceptual apparatus is inherently attuned. Together they ensure that the child is visually oriented to its social partners from the beginning.

On the basis of this initial orientation the infant can proceed to learn about faces as proper human attributes. In so far as attention is initially so highly selective the visual world of the newborn is unlikely to overwhelm him. In time, partly as a result of a maturing sensory apparatus and partly though constant exposure to other individuals, the infant becomes increasingly capable of processing more information about people and, no longer bound to common stimulus properties, begins to discriminate among them. This developmental progression is well documented by studies of infants' visual scanning patterns. As Salapatek's (1975) detailed review shows, scanning movements in the first month of life are limited in the main to the outer contours of stimuli. In particular, those parts with the sharpest contours attract attention, with visual search concentrating just on single features within the whole. As yet the infant is insensitive to the total configuration. Around 2 months of age, however, a change in scanning pattern gradually occurs: now the infant begins to scan more broadly, taking in more features and attending to the internal as well as the external details of a form. Instead of examining only parts he now shows awareness of wholes. For instance, Maurer and Salapatek (1976) showed real faces to 1-month- and 2-month-old infants and filmed the eye movements of these babies during stimulus exposure. At the younger age fewer regions of the face were fixated than at the older, and these regions were confined mostly to the perimeter. By two months the infants were more likely to fixate features inside the face, with the eyes of the other person becoming particularly important — an observation which tallies with mothers' reports

(Wolff, 1963) that it is around this age that they find the infant for the first time begins to make "real" eye contact and so to treat the mother as a "proper" person. Once this has been achieved infants can proceed to ever-finer discriminations: for instance, by 3 months infants can not only distinguish the mother's face from that of a stranger but they can also discriminate between two different strangers and, furthermore, between such facial expressions as a smile and a frown (Barrera and Maurer, 1981). Thus, given the infant's initial preparedness to respond to this form of human stimulation, perceptual learning can take place relatively speedily and efficiently, making the infant soon capable of differentiating people in terms of the many subtle cues based on age, sex, expression and identity which are required for appropriate responding.

(2) Responsiveness to voices

Research on infants' auditory responsiveness, though of more recent origin, points in the same direction as that on faces. Here too there are indications that infants' perceptual sensitivities match the stimulus qualities offered by other people, singling them out from non-human auditory stimuli from the early weeks on. Two studies serve as examples.

In the first, Hutt *et al.* (1968) obtained electromyographic recordings from infants in the first week of life as a measure of responsiveness to various auditory stimuli. Comparisons of responsiveness to patterned, speech-like sounds (square-wave tones) and to pure (sine-wave) tones were of special interest. The findings show clearly that a considerably greater degree of responsiveness was obtained to sounds that have some of the same structural properties as human speech; the authors accordingly conclude that the structure of the human auditory apparatus at birth appears to be such as to ensure that the voice of others is from the beginning a prepotent stimulus. The second study supports and extends this conclusion. Molfese and Molfese (1980) investigated premature infants with a conceptual age of 35 weeks, recording auditory evoked responses from the left and right hemispheres to synthesized speech sounds and non-speech sounds. Recordings from the left hemisphere showed a clear differentiation of the two kinds of stimuli, thus supporting the idea that a mechanism sited in that part of the brain is even at this very early age already differentially tuned to speech. It appears that at least some of the perceptual mechanisms that are sensitive to language-related cues are lateralized before the infant even reaches term.

There are, of course, many cues in language that could be implicated in such early sensitivity. One of these refers to the temporal patterning of sounds. In a series of experiments Demany *et al.* (1977) demonstrated that infants aged 2 to 3 months were well able to discriminate sounds according to their characteristic rhythms and temporal patterns. Thus a succession of several sounds could be perceived as a unit and distinguished from other sequences. As the authors conclude:

> "This phenomenon of temporal grouping is, of course, not peculiar to rhythm perception. Language comprehension, for example, requires a similar process, since a semantic unit must be grasped as a whole despite its sequential character. In the results reported here, perceived structure rests purely on a temporal variable: the relative values of the intervals between sounds. These results indicate that skills of temporal analysis and synthesis, prerequisites for operating with the sequential dimension of language, are present well before the stage of speech" (Demany *et al.*, 1977, p. 719).

Some selective responsiveness to the human voice is clearly part of the neuronal organization with which the infant comes into the world. There is, however, not only differential attention to speech as opposed to non-speech sounds, but it has also become apparent that infants are already equipped to make certain distinctions *within* speech — distinctions that are meaningful to the processing of speech and that are operative long before the child himself is ready to use language. According to a series of studies by Eimas (1975), infants appear to have a preadapted capacity to segment speech sounds categorically, making the sort of phonemic discimations that are basic to all spoken languages. It has been known for some time that adults disciminate speech sounds in such categorical terms based on phonemic rather than acoustic information. Eimas *et al.* (1971) established that infants as young as one month listen to speech in just the same way: by habituating the sucking response to one sound and then determining whether they would dishabituate to another sound, it was possible to demonstrate that these infants were responding to speech in a linguistically relevant manner. Discrimination, that is, occurred only when the sounds belonged to *different* phonetic categories and not when they were acoustically spaced at similar intervals but belonged to the *same* phonetic category. In so far as category perception is not age-related or affected by experience an innate basis for this capacity seems most likely, based possibly on the existence in the brain of linguistic feature detectors that enable infants to process speech *qua* speech from a very early age on. Taken in conjunction with various other linguistically relevant distinctions that have been found in the first few weeks of life (e.g. Morse, 1972), it seems that infants are endowed with some "knowledge" of the phonetic structure of language long before they themselves begin to speak; they are thus prepared in due course readily to participate in one of the most important kinds of human interaction, namely verbal communication.

A further suggestion that the infant arrives in the world preadapted for linguistic interchange comes from the work of Condon (1977). Frame-by-frame microanalysis of films obtained of adult conversations has shown the existence of "self-synchrony", i.e. the occurrence within the same fraction of a second of units of both speech and body movement on the part of a speaker. In addition Condon also found "interactional synchrony", designating a similar correspondence between the speaker's units of speech and the listener's units of movement. Thus a precise isomorphism of body motion with the articulatory features of speech is said to occur at both intra-personal and inter-personal levels. The synchronies are of such split-second precision that they are quite out of the awareness of the individuals so engaged; according to Condon, however, they represent the basis on which verbal communication becomes possible.

This remarkable responsivity to speech, according to a study by Condon and Sander (1974), can already be seen in neonates. These authors found interactional synchrony of infant movement with adult speech to be evident from the first day of life on. The synchrony was observed in response to taped speech (thus ruling out the influence of visual stimulation); it was equally evident in English and Chinese; and it occurred only to natural rhythmic speech and not to such sounds as disconnected vowels or tapping. A primary entraining process of infant response to adult stimulation, fully functional from birth on, is thereby indicated. Such a proposal is, of course, fascinating, but it does present problems, and especially so with regard to the mechanism whereby speech and movement become entrained during particular interactions. Given the extreme rapidity of the entrainment process, a stimulus–response explanation is out of the question; similarly a predictive mechanism, operating at so young an age, also seems unlikely. Further work is clearly called for, directed in the first place at replicating the basic phenomenon of interactional synchrony itself.

An initial orientation to voices generally means that infants can quickly proceed to learn the discrimination of specific voices. According to some reports that learning occurs extraordinarily early on. In one study Mills and Melhuish (1974) gave three-week-old infants the opportunity to learn that by sucking on a non-nutritive nipple they could turn on a voice. The voice was either that of the mother or that of a female stranger equated for loudness. Both the total time and the rate of sucking per minute were significantly greater when the mother's voice could be produced by the baby. Similar results were obtained by Mehler *et al.* (1978), working with infants aged 4 to 6 weeks, though according to these findings the distinction holds only for normally intonated voices and not when the adults speak in an expressionless manner. And in yet another study deCasper and Fifer (1980) found the mother's voice to be recognized by infants within the first three days of life, having had at most 12 hours of postnatal contact with the mother. The explanation for such extremely early discrimination, if confirmed, may well be in terms of prenatal exposure. Most psychologists have, quite rightly, entertained the notion of prenatal learning with scepticism; however, it is known that three months before birth a child is already responsive to sound, and combined with the special sensitivity to speech described above it is not inconceivable that the human infant arrives in the world already accustomed to the particular voice to which he has had exposure. The alternative, that the first 12 hours of postnatal contact with the mother are responsible, must, of course, also be considered; in either case specific learning can take place so speedily because of an initial pre-disposition which (just as in the case of visual attraction to faces) orients the child to human beings by virtue of his inherent nature.

(3) Supra-modal models of people?

Faces and voices belong together; one and the same person is usually the source of both. It has generally been assumed that the infant does not initially have this knowledge, and that one of his developmental tasks is to learn that persons can simultaneously provide both visual and auditory stimulation. Piaget (1954), for instance, proposed that such knowledge can only come from experience: the child must *learn* to progress from a multi-modal to a unified modal world.

This view is not accepted by all. According to Bower (1974), inter-modal coordinations are built in; the child begins life in a unified world and his task is to learn the differentiation of the senses, not their association. The various kinds of stimulation which a mother provides through sight, sound and touch are thus automatically ascribed to the same source; voices are "known" to go with mouths, and any evidence of disparateness may consequently be disturbing to the young infant.

Unfortunately the evidence for this proposition is conflicting. In a study by Aronson and Rosenbloom (1971) faces and voices were experimentally rearranged. Infants saw the mother through a sound-proof window, but could only hear her through loudspeakers. When the voice came through a loudspeaker placed at the side, i.e. from a location away from the mother's face, infants of only 3 or 4 weeks of age were said to be disturbed: apparently the displacement of visual and auditory stimuli that normally go together was perceived by these infants and caused distress.

There are, however, a number of methodological shortcomings to this study, and accordingly McGurk and Lewis (1974) repeated the experiment under more controlled conditions and with a wider age range. Their findings fail to replicate those of Aronson and Rosenbloom: infants in none of the three age groups studied (1, 4 and 7 months) showed any undue distress to the displacement of face and voice. And similarly Condry *et al.* (1977), working with infants between 1 and 2 months old, found no indication that displacement was in any way regarded as "unnatural"; they too found themselves unable to support the idea that infants begin life in a perceptually unified auditory-visual world. As subsequent experiments with inanimate stimuli (McGurk and McDonald, 1978) have also failed to find evidence for a supra-modal type of perception in early infancy, it seems likely that vision and audition function independently at first; the realization that faces and voices belong together would thus not be inbuilt but would need to be ascribed to learned experience.

However, a more recent study by Dodd (1979) suggests that it would be wise for the time being to suspend judgment. Infants aged 10 to 16 weeks were presented with nursery rhymes spoken by an experimenter from behind a sound-proof window. The words came through a loudspeaker directly in line with the experimenter's face, and were delivered either directly in synchrony with the adult's lip movements or via a tape recorder that delayed the spoken words by 400 msec. and thus produced an out-of-synchrony effect with the lip movements. Two observers pressed buttons to record whenever the infants were not looking at the face. The results show that the infants clearly differentiated between the two conditions, paying significantly more attention when sound and lip movements were in synchrony than when they were out of synchrony. In view of the age of the infants one cannot, of course, conclude that awareness of mouth–speech congruence is definitely innate; however, as Dodd points out, it is noteworthy that neither age nor birth weight affected the results obtained, and that at the very least awareness of the association of the two forms of stimulation must develop soon after birth. Even this conclusion is challenged by McGurk and Lewis's negative results for infants as old as 7 months, though the discrepancy may well be explained by the very different methodologies employed by the two studies. The question of voice-face integration thus remains open.

Curiously, a similar issue arises in relation to the possibility of early imitation. To be able to match another's behaviour is to open up a most useful channel of communication between the two individuals; for the young child in particular this may have great developmental significance. Imitating, however, can involve some very sophisticated processes, and especially so when it involves the performance by the child of acts invisible to him such as mouth opening or tongue protrusion. To be able to copy such actions means converting visual images into their proprioceptive equivalent; it requires a degree of inter-modal integration not found in, say, imitating someone's hand movements. Thus a report by Meltzoff and Moore (1977), that imitation can be found in infants just 2 to 3 weeks old and that this applies to non-visible as well as visible actions, raised once more the possibility of a supra-modal form of perceptual organization that is present from birth. However, other workers (Hayes and Watson, 1981; Koepke *et al.*, 1983; McKenzie and Over, 1983) have failed to replicate the Meltzoff and Moore study, presumably because of a number of methodological shortcomings in that investigation. The Piagetian account of imitation, according to which this ability is tied to the use of accommodatory capacities that do not fully emerge until sensori-motor stage 4, i.e. about 8 or 9 months, remains the most likely, and the idea of an inherent supra-modal organization is thus still unsubstantiated.

Response organization

In addition to perceptual sensitivities the infant comes into the world equipped with a number of behaviour patterns specifically designed to bring him into contact with people. Some, in particular those concerned with food intake, have obvious survival value. By means of the rooting response, for instance, the infant automatically turns to the source of stimulation (usually the nipple) whenever his cheek is touched; this in turn is succeeded by such other innately organized responses as sucking and swallowing. Some other responses have a rather more general function; crying and smiling, for example, serve to attract the caretaker's attention and to maintain her interest in the child. Such social signalling systems offer compelling stimuli to parents, thereby ensuring their proximity and initiating interaction, be that for the alleviation of physical needs or for more playful purposes.

These responses are inbuilt, species-specific patterns that are mostly elicited by certain specific forms of stimulation, generally (but not necessarily at first) associated with other people. It is very much due to Bowlby's (1969) ethological theory of attachment formation that attention has been drawn to the role of such responses in mediating early social interaction. Attachment behaviour, according to Bowlby, comes to assume a highly complex and sophisticated form, but it has its roots in much earlier forms of behaviour—smiling, crying, rooting and sucking among them—that are present from the start and that emerged in the course of evolution because of their survival value. Their biological function is the protection of the young: all have in common the predictable outcome of promoting and maintaining proximity with conspecifics, in particular the mother, and they can therefore be classed together as attachment behaviours. They may thus be conceived of as innately determined fixed action patterns which are activated by stimulation emanating from human sources. In this sense the infant is genetically biased towards contact and interaction with other people.

(1) Biological rhythms

To understand the use of these fixed action patterns we must take note of one general behavioural characteristic, namely the temporal structure of action. Many of the infant's responses, it has been shown, are serially organized in time and occur in the form of predictable rhythms, and it is this periodicity in the infant's behaviour which enables other people to enmesh their own responses, also temporarily organized, with his. Social interaction, that is, has a time dimension which is based on inherent patterns.

There has been considerable speculation about the way in which social behaviour may be affected by innately determined temporal regularities. Byers (1975), for example, has drawn attention to one basic biological rhythm, manifested at a frequency of 10 cycles per second, that is to be seen *inter alia* in the alpha waves of normal EEG recordings and which he believes to underlie such subtle interactive phenomena as the pauses in conversations. This is highly speculative; biological rhythms nevertheless appear to play an important part in determining social responsiveness in the early months of life in particular.

Biological rhythms are endogenously determined cycles of activity that occur in a regular and predictable manner. The time basis over which cycling takes place varies between different rhythms. Some occur at split-second rates: sucking, for example, has been described as a "high-frequency micro-rhythm" which, in its non-nutritive mode, shows a pattern of bursts and pauses, with the bursts occurring at the rate of approximately two per second (Wolff, 1968). Other rhythms take place in approximately 24-hour cycles, such as the adult's waking–sleeping pattern; still others, like the menstrual cycle, take place over a much longer time period. Physiological functions like breathing and heart rate are perhaps the best known examples of rhythmical activities, and their relevance to the understanding of behavioural organization has been appreciated at least since Lashley's (1951) powerful plea for the study of temporal patterning in motor skills. Micro-rhythms in particular represent fundamental determinants of psychological functioning: In Wolff's (1968) phrase, "the rapid sequential arrangement of motor units is a fundamental property of all behavioural adaptations."

Some rhythms appear already *in utero*, as is evident from the cyclical nature of foetal activity. For other basic functions such as body temperature, urinary excretion and GSR measures, stability over the 24-hour cycle is not attained till some point during infancy, the age varying for different functions (Hellbrugge *et al.*, 1964). Cyclical activities are, to varying extents, open to external influence; however, the fact that they can appear spontaneously and with impressive regularity in the absence of peripheral stimulation is further proof of their endogenous origin. Thus Wolff (1966) has shown that various infant responses such as facial twitches, rhythmical mouthing, erections, startles and sobbing inspirations take place in rhythmical sequences, and that their occurrence in the absence of specific external or visceral stimulation shows them to be spontaneous discharge phenomena. Similarly in the case of non-nutritive sucking: Wolff (1968) found that infants suck on a pacifier at a rate which is almost identical in all normal babies. The fact that the same rhythm is found in spontaneous mouthing movements, without a pacifier, suggests that the temporal patterning is regulated by mechanisms in the central nervous system which are capable of instigating well coordinated actions independent of peripheral stimulation. Wolff also found that when the pacifier was removed right after the start of a burst of sucking the infant would generally continue to make mouthing movements up to the usual number of sucks per burst. Once a burst had been triggered it ran its course regardless of changes in peripheral feedback. In addition it was observed that the sucking rhythm of children with defects in their oral systems, such as cleft lip or palate, was the same as that of normal children, again indicating that sensory feedback played little part in regulating the temporal organization of the activity. Children with major congenital malformations of the brain, on the other hand, may produce various distortions of the sucking rhythms. These findings give support to Lashley's suggestion that autonomous oscillators in the central nervous system are the likely mechanisms for the temporal regulation of the micro-rhythms evident in motor behaviour. They produce highly similar sequential arrangements in the units of such behaviour in all normal members of the species, and only damage to the central nervous system can upset the predictable sequence.

In so far as biological rhythms are open to external influence the moment of birth, when the foetus is expelled into a completely new environment, involves some marked reorganization. For one thing, new rhythmical functions, such as breathing and elimination, appear which must be assimilated into the organism's repertoire. And for another, instead of the relatively limited environmental fluctuations that impinge on the foetus in the womb, the newborn infant is confronted with an environment demanding a far more complex set of adjustments. The child must now learn to adapt his timing systems to those prevailing in the outside world, just as his caretakers must also adapt their timing systems to his. Whatever the basic compatibility of adult and child may be, a great deal of mutual adjustment has to take place so that the two sets of behavioural streams are properly synchronized.

The details whereby such synchronization occurs have been examined with respect to various aspects of interpersonal behaviour. Some of these will be discussed later on; here we turn to one of the earliest tasks that faces parent and child, namely the regulation of the child's arousal states.

(2) Entrainment of states

The concept of state refers to an internal, spontaneously generated arousal condition that plays a large part in determining an infant's responsiveness to external stimuli. At least five qualitatively different states have been distinguished, stretching from deep or regular sleep through active sleep, alert inactivity, and alert activity to crying (Berg and Berg, 1979). Given a constant level of stimulation, they recur cyclically and mostly in predictable sequences. Here too a centrally located mechanism appears to be responsible for the rhythmical alternation, for in neurologically deviant infants impairment of the cycle may be found (Hutt *et al.*, 1969).

States fluctuate rapidly in early infancy. Thus a newborn tends to sleep for many short periods, randomly distributed throughout the day and interspersed with even shorter periods of wakefulness. It is therefore one of the earliest and most urgent tasks of the child's caretakers to establish a diurnal pattern that conforms to their own waking and sleeping patterns. Various aspects of this entrainment process have been investigated by Sander and his colleagues (summarized in Sander *et al.*, 1979).

On the basis of 24-hour automatic recordings of motility and crying, obtained from the day of birth on, supplemented by observations of state fluctuations and of caretaker interventions, Sander was able to trace the early changes in the waking–sleeping cycle. In the first few days following birth there is disorganization in the cycle: the occurrence and duration of the various stages are irregular, considerable crying and general motility are found, and intervention time by caretakers is substantial. By the end of the first postnatal week, however, a coordination is already apparent between infant state and caretaker activity. More than half of the longest sleep periods of the 24 hours now occur during the night, while motility and crying peaks have shifted to daytime periods. At the same time caretaking interventions diminish and, when they do occur, are successful in terminating crying and in settling the infant back to sleep.

This trend is not, however, a universal one. Sander found it when the infant was roomed-in with his own mother during the stay in the maternity hospital and when a demand-feeding regime was followed. Under these conditions, and also subsequently at home the mother is gradually able to "shape" the infant's activity cycle to conform to her own requirements. This may be done by, for instance, keeping the baby awake longer in the evening or waking him up early from an afternoon nap, so ensuring more sleep during the night hours. In the much more impersonal environment of the hospital nursery, however, where feeding and other interventions tend to be governed by the clock and not the infant's condition, the emergence of day–night differentiation did not take place so smoothly, and both restlessness and crying during the daytime were found to remain at a high level. When interventions did take place they were not as successful in calming the infant as those taking place under more personal regimes.

Given favourable circumstances, adaptation may occur with considerable speed. Moreover, after only one week following birth Sander found an individual specificity to the style of infant–caretaker adaptation, which he was able to demonstrate by means of a "cross-fostering" experiment. Infants awaiting adoption roomed-in with either one of two nurses for the first 10 days and were then changed over to the care of the other nurse. The change-over produced a marked upset in the crying and feeding patterns of the babies: having by now become accustomed to the temporal requirements of one person the change to another's interactive style disrupted the mutually adaptive pattern that had developed, and the learning process therefore had to begin all over again. As Sander emphasizes, the pre-empting task for all caretakers over the first few weeks of life is that of restoring the temporal organization of the infant and interfacing his periodicities with their own; however, the precise manner whereby this is accomplished is specific to each pair and leads to a unique and idiosyncratic set of adjustments.

There are other aspects to the initial coming together of newborn baby and adult caretaker, but the entrainment of states is a vital one for the satisfaction that the pair will derive from each other in the early weeks. Moreover, it illustrates certain general features; especially, it points to the way in which the infant's endogenous response organization forms the base on which the interaction develops, with particular reference to the temporal structure of that organization to which the adult needs to adapt her own response patterns. What we also see, however, is the considerable rapidity with which that structure in turn becomes adapted to the environment, i.e. to the demands made upon the infant by other people. It is this combination of inherent predictability and openness to the influence of experience in even the early weeks of life that sets social interaction on its course.

(3) The feeding situation

The same general features may also be found when we turn to what is one of the first structured encounters between mother and child, namely feeding. The success of such an encounter depends primarily on the proper coordination of maternal and infant actions; it is thus an example of a situation in which we can examine the nature of mutual adaptation at the very start of the child's life.

To make feeding possible in the first place there must be mutual orientation of the two partners. For her part the mother usually holds and supports the infant in such a way that he has easy access to breast or bottle. She generally remains facially oriented to him so that she can readily monitor his behaviour and adapt her own actions accordingly. But the infant too has to play his part in making the appropriate head and postural adjustments in order to commence feeding. This is seen particularly clearly in the use of the rooting response, in that either a single directed turning movement or rapid side-to-side movements provide an opportunity for the mouth to come into contact with the nipple (Prechtl, 1958). A tactile stimulus (such as that provided by the breast) delivered to a limited area around the infant's mouth usually elicits these responses. Occasionally the side-to-side movement may be so vigorous that the grasped nipple is lost again as the infant continues to turn; in those cases the mother will usually grasp the head and, holding it still, insert the nipple into the opened mouth. In hungry infants rooting may also occur in the absence of an eliciting stimulus; with increasing age, however, the infant becomes capable of employing rooting in a much more flexible and less mechanical fashion, able to guide his own mouth efficiently to the proffered stimulus.

Clearly the infant is far from inert in this situation; he is capable of increasingly flexible spatially oriented movements which, largely on the mother's initiative, will be interwoven with her own behaviour into a mutually coordinated action sequence. Blauvelt and McKenna (1961), in an observational study of newborns' orientational movements, found that these responses were generally so well coordinated with those of the mother that the two partners could very readily settle into a positional pattern conducive to further interaction — in particular, of course, feeding. Call (1964), also observing feeding sessions during the neonatal period, noted that already by the fourth feed after birth anticipatory approach movements could be seen when the infant was placed in a nursing position close to the mother's body but prior to actual contact. What is more, these responses quickly became adapted to the mother's specific feeding style, for when another person fed him the infant's pattern became disrupted and had to be changed according to that other adult's peculiarities.

The infant's feeding act is made up of a sequence of responses closely coordinated with one another: rooting, opening mouth, grasping nipple, sucking and swallowing. These components, sequentially organized and also integrated with the infant's breathing, form a total behavioural system that is innately adapted to cope with the task of food intake. Each component may, of course be studied in its own right, and sucking in particular has received a great deal of attention. As we have already noted, sucking can be regarded as a high-frequency micro-rhythm, in that it is innately organized to take place in temporal sequences that are similar for all normal, full-term infants, distinguished by various species-specific characteristics that differentiate it from sucking behaviour in other mammals (Wolff, 1968). The pattern is clearest during non-nutritive sucking (e.g. on a pacifier), consisting of bursts of sucks followed by pauses, with about 5 to 10 sucks per burst and pauses lasting between 4 and 15 seconds. The rate of sucking is generally fairly constant, being about two sucks per second.

In nutritive sucking the pattern is not as clear, for at the start of a feed bursts occur in a continuous stream. Subsequently, however, this also breaks up into the burst–pause pattern, though the pauses are shorter and the bursts are longer than those found in the non-nutritive mode. Also the rate of sucking is slower. If the milk supply is cut off, a rapid shift can be observed from the nutritive to the non-nutritive pattern: the regulating mechanism, it seems, is by no means immune from peripheral stimulation (Wolff, 1968). This can also be seen in the way in which the length of bursts or of pauses can be modified experimentally by making either the milk flow itself or the supply of extraneous visual or auditory stimulation contingent on the infant's sucking (Hillman and Bruner, 1972).

The mother's behaviour during feeding is in certain respects "driven" by the way in which the infant's sucking responses are organized. From observations of both breast- and bottle-feeding sessions Kaye (1977) has been able to isolate a "dialogue-like" pattern that can be distinguished in the behaviour of mother and infant. The pattern is based on the burst–pause structure of the infant's sucking, and becomes dialogue-like because mothers respond by fitting their own behaviour to the infant's in precise synchrony. During bursts the mother is generally quiet and inactive, so as not to interfere with the infant's sucking; during pauses, on the other hand, she jiggles, strokes or talks to the infant. Thus the cessation of sucking is interpreted by the mother as a signal for her to respond, and in this way she is able to insert her own activity into the intervals between the infant's action bursts. A turn-taking pattern thereby emerges, provided primarily by the mother's willingness to be paced by the infant and to fit in with his natural sucking rhythms.

Kaye's observation illustrates well the importance of temporal patterning in these early social interactions. The infant, by virtue of his endogenously determined rhythmic behaviour, provides the cues to which a sensitive mother then adapts. This she does by timing with considerable precision the stimulation she provides to coincide with those periods when the infant's attention is not taken up with the feeding act itself and when she is therefore likely to have greater impact on him. That, at any rate, is the ideal, but there are instances where the dialogue breaks down because of lack of clarity in the infant's cues. Field (1977a), in a study of 3½-month-old infants, found a similar pattern to that reported by Kaye, namely that maternal stimulation occurred mainly during nipple-out rather than nipple-in periods. However, among high-risk infants (such as prematures) a much less regular pattern occurred. In these cases the infants' feeding behaviour was less organized, the babies were more distractible, and the mothers had to spend more time coaxing them even during nipple-in periods. Where for organic reasons an infant's usual temporal patterning is disturbed he becomes less predictable to the mother, and "clashes" of behaviour are consequently more likely.

Mutual adaptation during feeding has endogenous components; it is, however, equally important to stress the extent to which mother and infant come to modify their behaviour in the light of their experience of one another. This is well illustrated in a series of reports by Thoman and her colleagues (Thoman *et al.*, 1970, 1971; Thoman and Olson, 1972). In a comparison of primiparous and multiparous mothers during the neonatal period a number of clear-cut differences emerged. Primiparous mothers took much longer over their task; they spent more time on extraneous, non-feeding activities and they interrupted the feed more often than the multiparous mothers. Thus the more inexperienced women had to persist more, and yet they were less effective in that their infants consumed not as much milk as those in the other group. When nurses were asked to feed the same babies it was found that they spent less time and had fewer interruptions than even the multiparous mothers. However, in following up these three groups of women over the first few days of the child's life it became apparent that the primiparous mothers soon began to change their feeding style, growing in efficiency and showing a marked decrease in the number of interruptions. The nurses, on the other hand, increased the time spent on the feed over the same period. It was also noted that there were marked differences in the way in which nurses interacted with individual infants, suggesting that the infants were providing cues to which the nurses responded. Inexperienced mothers, on the other hand, did not initially allow infants to express their individuality to the same extent: they interfered more with the interaction, dominating it and thus obscuring individual characteristics in the babies. In due course, however, they too showed the sensitivity seen in more experienced women.

Mutual adaptation in the feeding situation thus depends on two factors. In the first place, the infant provides an orderly temporal response pattern, arranged in sequences of activity and inactivity that enable his caretaker to intercalate her behaviour with his. The orderliness has an endogenous base, and being species-specific has somewhat limited variability among the infant population. At the same time it is not rigidly fixed but can vary from a very early age on according to the nature of the mother's stimulus input. And in the second place the mother's contribution lies in her ability closely to attend to the infant's behaviour, interpret his signals correctly and appropriately time her own responses. Such a repertoire of skills enables her gradually to adapt to the infant's individuality and in time produce the close "fit" that is necessary for successful feeding—and, as we shall see, for a wide range of other forms of interaction.

Responsiveness to people and to objects: two separate systems?

It can now be accepted that the infant is in a number of ways preadapted to interact with other people. A number of writers (Brazelton *et al.*, 1974; Richards, 1974; Trevarthen, 1977, 1979) have taken this conclusion a step further and proposed that the infant is equipped with two quite distinct modes of behaviour: one reserved for responding to people, the other for responding to objects.

This dichotomy is based on the differential responsiveness to these two classes of stimuli which has been found in young infants. For instance, Brazelton *et al.* compared infants' behaviour to the mother in a face-to-face situation with their behaviour when confronted with a toy (a 3½ inch furry monkey suspended in front of the child). Differences were found in a variety of respects, such as attention span, state behaviour, smiling and vocalizing. When confronted by the toy periods of attentiveness were long and concentrated, the body was tense and there were short bursts of jerky limb movements towards the object, until eventually attention became disrupted and the infant somewhat suddenly turned away. Attention span to the mother, on the other hand, was much briefer and the changes from looking at her to looking away tended to be smoother and less abrupt. The body was also more relaxed and the face considerably more mobile.

These two types of responsiveness are said to be detectable even in the neonatal period. Each type is augmented by further response patterns that appear in subsequent weeks, and Trevarthen (1977) in particular has provided some detailed descriptive accounts of behaviour sequences observed uniquely during interpersonal exchanges. One such pattern Trevarthen labelled "prespeech". This refers to a complex syndrome of expressive acts, consisting of a series of lip and tongue movements of a specifically "speech-like" nature, i.e. resembling in form the mouth movements of adults when speaking. These movements appear in bursts but need not be accompanied by any vocalizations. They are associated with particular kinds of head and trunk postures, and also with certain types of hand movements which Trevarthen considers to be "gesture-like".

The descriptive material provided by Trevarthen of infants' behaviour towards other people is some of the most detailed available and as such extremely valuable. The proposal regarding a "prespeech" syndrome, however, encounters a number of difficulties. For one thing, there are no controlled studies which show that the behaviour found is in fact elicited by the human-ness of the stimulus. This is indeed also the problem with the observations by Brazelton *et al.*: there is no guarantee that the various patterns of looking-at and looking-away are as specific to the two classes of stimuli as is claimed and are not merely due to experimental artifacts such as the novelty of the toy as contrasted with the familiarity of the mother. In addition, these studies fail to take account of a methodological safeguard to which Contole and Over (1979) have drawn attention, namely that judgments about differential behaviour should be made without knowledge of context, i.e. the source of the stimulation provided. Furthermore, Trevarthen's assertions are not backed by any statistical data to indicate that the various components of the prespeech syndrome are associated above a chance level; we have, that is, no assurance that they do constitute a syndrome. And finally, there is no indication that the behaviour observed bears the functional relationship to speech that is suggested by the use of the term "prespeech". Demonstrations of such a relationship are indeed difficult to provide; here we can but note that the argument rests on analogy rather than on proven continuity. As we shall see later on, the idea that language acquisition is in some way rooted in earlier forms of communicative behaviour has attracted a lot of attention and remains an intriguing one; it has yet, however, to move beyond the realm of guesswork. Trevarthen's assertion, that prespeech demonstrates a "clear commitment to intentional communication", is at present unsupported.

More generally, the proposition that two quite distinct modes exist for dealing with people and with objects respectively needs to be treated with caution. To quote Trevarthen (1979) again, the two kinds of responsiveness are in his view so different that one must conclude that the two classes of objects are distinct in the infant's awareness and used for quite different purposes: objects as sources of perceptual information; people as communicative partners. As applied to young infants, this is much too sharp a dichotomy; it neglects the fact that infants respond initially on the basis of particular kinds of stimulation rather than to stimulus objects as such. Visual attention, for example, is elicited during the early weeks of life by such qualities as movement, solidity and contour density and not by faces—though faces are endowed with these qualities. Any awareness of people as a category of stimulus objects in its own right develops later, succeeding an initial phase when attraction to others is governed by their possession of attention-worthy aspects but not yet by their human-ness.

This conclusion is supported by a recently published study (Frye *et al.*, 1983) which, by means of a signal detection technique, examined the ability of observers to distinguish the behaviour of 3- and 10-month old infants when confronted by the mother or by an object. The mothers and objects were either active or passive, with the activity taking a contingent form in one condition through spontaneous interaction or a non-contingent form (mother or object swayed from side to side) in another condition. In addition the infants were also observed when alone. It was found that the observers, viewing the videotapes of the infant without knowledge of the stimulus condition, were able accurately to judge whether infants of either age group were alone or not and, if not, whether the child was with something active or passive. Spontaneous interaction with mother or object compared to the swaying condition helped in making the differentiation, suggesting that contingence has an important effect on infant behaviour. The most significant finding was, however, that the observers were unable to determine if a 3-month-old was with mother or object, though they were able to make this distinction for 10-month-olds. Thus in the younger group such "communicative" responses as "greeting" and "withdrawal" were observed just as frequently in the object condition as in the mother condition, thereby throwing doubt on the claim that the object–person differentiation is manifested from early on. It appears rather to have a developmental course and to emerge later in the first year of life.

What is more, responsiveness to other people is by no means a homogenous category. Fogel (1979), comparing the behaviour of 5- to 14-week-old infants to the mother and to a peer, found various systematic differences: with the mother behaviour was smoother, more varied and more reliant on fine expressive movements; behaviour to the peer was more abrupt, more intense and contained more gross bodily movements — a pattern, let us note, very similar to that described by Brazelton for responsiveness to objects. Field (1979a) found differential responsiveness to each kind of an even wider range of individuals, i.e. mother, father, peer and stranger; yet one would not wish to claim that infants are endowed with separate response systems to deal with every one of these classes of individuals. Rather, the behaviour found is a function of the particular stimulus input experienced, so that in each case the infant responds in accord with the differential behaviour of the individual (or object) confronting him. Other people, as stimulus objects, do possess an attraction for infants not shared with the inanimate part of the environment; this does not justify the further claim that objects and people are separately represented within the infant, inherently linked to quite distinct sets of response systems that are used from the beginning for quite different purposes.

Maternal predisposition

The mother's readiness to provide appropriate care has already been commented on at several points in this account. As described elsewhere (Schaffer, 1977), the activities to which we attach the term "mothering" are extraordinarily numerous and varied, constituting a highly complex set of behavioural patterns. What is more, there are no indications that mothering is a role exclusive to the child's biological mother; on the contrary, unrelated females and also males show many of the same relevant characteristics. But whatever the activity performed or the identity of the caretaker, one theme remains constant, namely the impressive precision with which, under most normal circumstances, the stimulation provided by the adult matches the child's abilities to absorb and respond to that stimulation. This theme recurs with respect to every developmental phase and every aspect of the parent–child relationship, and we shall return to it repeatedly in this account.

Maternal care is complementary to the child's requirements from birth on; it would not be possible for the infant to survive were it otherwise. Using a term like "mother instinct" may be of little help in understanding the processes responsible for bringing about such a fit, but it does at least reflect the belief that the more basic aspects of mothering are just as much determined by endogenous forces as is the infant's social behaviour. A mother, that is, is genetically biased to provide certain forms of care that complement the infant's requirements.

Again it is largely due to Bowlby (1969) that maternal care has come to be viewed from such a perspective. According to Bowlby, a system of maternal behaviour has developed in the course of evolution that is reciprocal to infant attachment behaviour. The function of both systems is the protection of the young against predators, and while the infant employs responses such as crying and clinging towards this end, the mother reciprocates with a variety of retrieval responses whenever the child strays too far, as well as with the provision of food when he is hungry and of comfort when he is distressed. For both systems the predictable outcome is the attainment and maintenance of contact between mother and child. Contact in turn leads to affective interchange, and this is experienced as pleasurable by both partners and so furthers the process of bonding. The infant's social development thus proceeds because his mother provides him with a type of care that has evolved to achieve the same end as his own behaviour.

Whether Bowlby is right to assume that the basic function of maternal care is protection against predators is debatable. Maternal care has many functions, and to put all the weight on adaptation to predation is to neglect all those others, the sheer multitude of which may well account for the force and pervasiveness of this behavioural system. But this is a relatively minor matter: Bowlby's account, based on a biological perspective, has served above all to draw attention to the reciprocal nature of maternal and infant behaviour; such reciprocity has an endogenous basis and is evident from the very beginning of the child's existence.

(1) Hormonal influences on mothering

Whatever the biological origins of maternal care, more proximal determinants must also be considered. One such factor concerns the hormonal changes which accompany pregnancy and birth; these, it has been proposed, exercise a sensitizing effect on women, putting them in a "ready-state" to provide maternal care to the newborn child.

The evidence for this proposition comes mainly from studies with animals. Work on rodents (reviewed by Noirot, 1972) indicates that females who have just given birth will immediately show a variety of maternal care responses to their offspring; other animals require a more or less prolonged period of exposure to the pups before they overcome their wariness of the newcomer and also start to behave maternally. Taken together with evidence from studies that have induced maternal responsiveness by administering hormones to non-pregnant animals, one must conclude that the large hormonal changes associated with the birth process appear to be implicated in the very rapid establishment of maternal care in these species.

Two constraints must, however, be borne in mind. One is that the hormonal changes may account only for the initiation but not for the maintenance of maternal behaviour; for the latter, stimulation from the offspring experienced during interaction with it is also required. There is thus a temporary period following birth when maternal behaviour is under hormonal control, but this is quickly followed by a phase when such behaviour is dependent on stimulation provided by the young. And in the second place it seems that in higher mammalian species experiential factors come to play an increasingly greater, and hormonal control a correspondingly lesser, part. As Poindrou and Neindre (1980) have shown in the case of sheep, primiparous ewes have far greater difficulty initially in providing appropriate care than multiparous ewes, and only after a period of "practice" will they too behave in the maternal manner that the previously experienced animals show straight away.

It may well be that in humans this balance between experience and hormonal control has tilted even further in favour of the former. There is in fact little direct evidence available for human mothers, partly because one obviously cannot experiment as with animals and partly also because of the confounding effect of social pressures on mothers to behave in particular ways. On the whole it seems unlikely that hormonal factors *per se* play a significant part; the ability of adoptive parents to provide love and care of a generally excellent standard (Tizard, 1978) argues against relying on hormonal mechanisms to any great extent. And it is also pertinent that Berman (1980), in reviewing the evidence for human sex differences in responsiveness to the young, found no unequivocal support for such differences and concluded that cultural factors are probably more important in determining whatever differences do exist between males and females in this respect than are hormonal factors.

(2) Neonatal contact and maternal effectiveness

The experiential factors that influence the kind of care offered by the human mother are no doubt many and varied. As yet, however, the evidence as to their identity is scarce. One possibility that has gained credence is that the mother's own upbringing will affect her subsequent effectiveness as an adult to rear children: in particular, it has been suggested that deprived children may in turn become depriving parents, setting up a cycle that is often difficult to break (Rutter and Madge, 1976). To substantiate such a claim is, however, no easy task; in consequence this particular claim remains a hunch rather than a properly supported conclusion.

Another proposal stems from the work of Klaus and Kennell (1976). It is based on a series of studies of two groups of mothers, differing in the amount of contact they had had with their baby in the neonatal period. One group had experienced the rather limited amount of physical contact that tends to be customary in Western maternity hospitals, whereas mothers of the other group were given 16 hours of additional contact during the first three days. Seen again on a follow-up visit to the hospital one month later both sets of mothers were observed during an examination of the infant and during bottle feeding, and were also given a standardized interview. A number of differences emerged: the extended-contact mothers remained closer to the baby during the examination, they showed more soothing behaviour, engaged in more eye-to-eye contact and in more fondling, and reported greater reluctance to leave the baby with someone else.

In further follow-up observations the differences between the two groups were maintained. Seen when the children were one year old, the extended-contact mothers still remained closer to the baby, soothed it more readily and appeared to be more preoccupied with it. At age two records of the mothers' speech to the children in an informal play situation showed the extended-contact group to use more questions, more adjectives, more words per proposition and fewer commands than the control group mothers. The verbal output found in the former group was thus said to indicate greater variety and elaboration. At age five the children of the extended-contact group were found to have a significantly higher IQ and more advanced score on two language tests than the children of the control group.

These findings led Klaus and Kennell to suggest that just a few hours of extra contact with the infant during the neonatal period can bring about a considerable enhancement of maternal behaviour—an effect that one can still observe several years later. They propose therefore that a sensitive period exists in the first few hours of life during which it is necessary for the mother to have close contact with the newborn baby if later development is to be optimal. Lack of such contact interferes with the bonding process; it prevents the proper growth of the mother's attachment to the child. The immediate postpartum period is thus of crucial importance in shaping maternal behaviour; experiences at that time will have long-term implications for the relationship with the child.

The studies by Klaus and Kennell have had one very positive effect: they have drawn attention to the rigid procedures adopted by many maternity hospitals and to the need to support a mother's confidence in handling her new baby from as early a time as possible. Where mother and baby are separated for most of the day other than for feeding periods, or where the separation is especially severe and prolonged as in the case of special-care infants kept in incubators, it is plausible that the mother's caretaking abilities will be affected *at the time*. Changes in hospital routines that lead to an improvement in the opportunity for early contact are without question all to the good. The long-term significance of these early experiences, on the other hand, are much more questionable.

This point is given weight by the failure of other research workers to replicate the Klaus and Kennell findings. Whiten (1977), for instance, found some differences in maternal behaviour between an extended-contact group and a control group one month after birth; two months later these differences had disappeared. Carlsson *et al.* (1978, 1979) observed differences during the neonatal period; six weeks later these were no longer evident. Grossman *et al.* (1981) separated out the effects of early contact (i.e. immediately postpartum) and of extended contact (several hours daily of rooming-in for the first week), and found at the end of the neonatal period only a few temporary effects associated with early contact, and even these were for some reason restricted to mothers who had planned their pregnancy. No connection emerged between either early or extended contact and the quality of the relationship to the mother one year later. And in a particularly well controlled study Svejda *et al.* (1980) randomly assigned mother–infant pairs to either routine care or to a programme of 10 extra contact hours in the first 36 hours of the child's life, having ensured that no mother knew beforehand of her participation in a research study and thus avoiding "Hawthorne" effects. Videotaped sessions of free play and breast feeds 36 hours after birth were scored blind for 28 discrete response measures and 4 general response categories: no differences were found in any of these.

In view of the very small and atypical sample investigated by the Klaus and Kennell group (the mothers were mostly very young, unmarried, black and from disadvantaged backgrounds), replication is especially important. Some of the additional studies concede the possibility of short-term changes; none give an indication that the effects are anything but temporary and that the quality of mothering is affected on a once-for-all basis by events occurring during a highly specific period immediately following birth.

There are a number of methodological shortcomings in the Klaus and Kennell studies which might well account for their findings. Double-blind procedures, the elimination of Hawthorne effects and random assignment to conditions are clearly essential if one is to have confidence in results from group comparisons, and these safeguards were not always adequately applied. In addition, various problems arise from the way in which measures were used and interpreted. For one thing, most measures were derived solely from the mother's behaviour and not related to the child's condition at the time: for instance, fondling during feeding should be related to the infant's ongoing behaviour before it can be regarded as "appropriate" rather than as "interfering". For another, results are often discussed in value-laden terms: a lot of touching of the infant, for example, is regarded as something desirable when it could just as easily be interpreted as "over-stimulation" and therefore undesirable. And finally, some of the measures seem to reflect the mother's relationship to the investigator rather than to her child: thus standing near during the child's physical examination could well reflect the greater confidence which some mothers felt in the presence of the doctor. Such considerations may all play a part in favouring the extra-contact group.

But a more fundamental point is that the model of the mother–child relationship adopted by Klaus and Kennell is an unduly rigid and deterministic one, based on the now largely discredited notion of critical periods. The idea that the future behaviour of an organism—be it mother or offspring—is determined by particular experiences encountered at some highly specific period of life is no longer tenable (Clarke and Clarke, 1976). The claim that the future course of the mother–child relationship can be predicted from knowledge of events occurring within a few hours or days after birth offends the model of this relationship which has emerged in recent years, i.e. a transactional model (Sameroff and Chandler, 1975), according to which the relationship must be regarded as an ever-open system in which mother and child mutually and progressively modify each other's behaviour and remain malleable with respect to external influences. The critical period model, on the contrary, sees the relationship as a system that is essentially closed except for that very brief period immediately after birth; when applied to the nature of mothering such a view would condemn all adoptive parents, all mothers too ill after the birth immediately to care for their child, the mothers of all incubator-reared infants, and presumably the vast majority of fathers as well. There is in fact no evidence whatsoever to suggest that such consequences exist.

Conclusions

Two questions may be asked about the initial encounters of parent and child: by what means are they brought about in the first place, and what are they principally used for.

As to the first question, it is apparent that in a number of ways the child arrives in the world preadapted for social interaction. He is equipped with a perceptual apparatus specially tuned to respond to human-like stimulation; faces and voices in particular have attention-attracting qualities of considerable potency. Thus prepared the infant can learn to make discriminations among his social partners; according to some reports such learning is already evident very early on in life. Moreover, the infant is endowed with a response organization specifically adapted to initiating and maintaining contact with others. In particular, the temporal regularities which characterize many early response patterns make the infant's behaviour predictable to other people and enable them more easily to enmesh their own behaviour with his. Thus infants are programmed to stimulate their caretakers in certain specified ways; adults in turn are programmed to be susceptible to such stimulation and to respond in an appropriate manner.

The use to which these early encounters are put relates primarily to the infant's endogenous organization. As has been pointed out by various authors (Als, 1979; Sander *et al.*, 1979) the most urgent requirement during the first few weeks is to regulate the infant's basic biological processes of feeding, sleeping and arousal. Behaviour in the first two months or so following birth is governed substantially by endogenous factors; it is necessary to stabilize these before the infant can freely attend to the outer world. The main issue for parent and child during this period is how to bring about such stabilization. Much of this is achieved in the context of social interaction, where the parent provides support to the periodicities of the infant's behaviour by coordinating them with her own caretaking patterns. In some cases this task will be more difficult than in others: for example, dysfunctions of the nervous system may bring about irregularities in the infant's temporal organization and thus cause problems for his caretakers (Alberts *et al.*, 1983). In general, however, the entrainment process enables the adult to help the infant gradually to consolidate his own internal regulatory mechanisms; at the same time it also allows her to ensure that the infant's behaviour patterning begins to conform with her own characteristics and expectations. The child's socialization is thus set in motion at the very start of life.

3   Face-to-Face Interactions

Around the age of 2 months infants reach one of the major transition points encountered in the course of development. Having with the aid of the parent successfully coped with the task of regulating inner states, they can now increasingly turn to the outer world. This is seen most notably in the reorganization of visual behaviour (Bronson, 1974; Haith, 1979): infants now become capable of accommodating their visual fixations to the distance of objects; the fixations become less fleeting and more systematic; changes in scanning patterns occur in that attention is paid to small internal details of objects instead of only to external features and sharp contours; and in general the speed and efficiency of visual information processing improves sharply, becoming less reactive and more "volitional".

As a result the child's behaviour towards other people also changes: direct eye contact is made with the partner; periods of prolonged gaze ensue; and the first externally elicited smiles appear. Thus, having earlier achieved some degree of stability over the infant's somatic condition, the task of adaptation confronting the parent–child couple shifts accordingly. The child's interest now centres on salient features of the environment; he spends increasingly more time in an alert state, undisturbed by internal matters, and he can thus more easily attend to the most salient environmental feature of all, his caretaker. Interactions come to take place primarily in the context of face-to-face encounters, in which the exchange of looks and gestures and vocalizations predominates. The main theme for adult and child now becomes the regulation of mutual attention and responsiveness.

Even in the preverbal period face-to-face exchanges are of a highly intricate nature. They involve a considerable variety of signals—visual, vocal and bodily—that are integrated into coherent patterns of communicative significance to the other person and that additionally need to be synchronized with the response patterns of that other person if some meaningful interchange is to result. The child needs to acquire the means of actively participating in such a to-and-fro; he must become able not merely to respond but also to initiate; he has to develop the ability to regulate the interchange so that he is provided with an optimal level of information; and at the same time he has to learn to adapt to the specific interactive styles of different partners. The adult needs to support the child in this task: she has to be aware of his as yet very limited abilities and be prepared to compensate for them accordingly; she needs to deploy devices to maintain the child's attention and yet know when to withdraw in order to prevent overload; and she must present stimulation to the child in an orderly, predictable and easily assimilated manner. The easiest way of doing so is with her own face; its versatility is such that it can readily be adapted from moment to moment according to her reading of the child's requirements. Thus both partners must learn how to engage each other in mutually satisfying exchange patterns.

Mutual gazing

Gazing is probably the most versatile of all interactive responses. Its on–off cycles can take place with great rapidity, and it functions both to take in information from the other person and to send signals to that person. As we have seen, gazing at faces begins very early, the face being such a potent stimulus to infants. Even during feeding the infant's gaze will be on the mother's face, not on breast or bottle. From 2 months on this response system plays an increasingly important part in inter-personal situations; subsequent developmental changes in it reflect well the changing nature of early social interactions.

(1) Establishing "en face"

From their very first encounter with the newborn baby mothers attempt to bring about mutual gazing. They do so by aligning their face in the same vertical plane as the infant's, so that the two sets of eyes can meet — a position known as "en face". Thus when confronted by her baby the mother is continually manoeuvering her head to keep it at the optimal distance and in the optimal plane, adjusting it to stay centred in the infant's visual field and thereby (quite unconsciously) ensuring maximum impact in the light of the infant's limited visual abilities.

It has been suggested (e.g. by Klaus and Kennell, 1976) that mothers behave in a highly stereotyped manner when they are first confronted with the infant after birth: gingerly exploring it with their fingertips, working from the periphery inwards — as though they are checking that everything is there. Just how universal or, for that matter, important this phenomenon is remains a matter for conjecture; there can be no doubt, however, that mothers do show an intense interest in the eyes of the newborn infant. More attention is probably paid to the eyes than to the rest of the body, and frustration is expressed when the eyes are closed. It is as though open, moving eyes are a sure indication of life, never mind what the rest of the body is doing. Through them the infant shows that he is indeed a person: they are the "windows of the soul".

Yet mothers are not content merely to see the eyes; they also want to establish mutual gaze as soon as possible. Manoeuvering into the "en face" position can be seen from the beginning: if the infant is lying in its cot the mother aligns her face accordingly; if she is holding him in her arms she will turn her head sideways in an attempt to establish visual contact. There are indications that fathers behave in just the same way: they too show an intense interest in the newborn infant's eyes, and they too will adopt the "en face" position whenever possible (Parke, 1979; Rodholm and Larsson, 1979). At first, however, the parents' efforts to bring about mutual gaze are likely to meet with frustration, for in the early weeks of life infants' looks are fleeting and "empty" — as though the child sees right through the other person and finds nothing meaningful to fixate. This changes around the second month of life, and Wolff (1963) has described well the impact that the change has on the mother. It is as though the infant now becomes "real" to her, as though mutual recognition of each other's existence and identity can now be found. The emergence of the ability to sustain visual contact (often also accompanied by a smile) thus seems to mothers a vital milestone in the relationship, when she and the child become persons to each other.

There is some evidence that for infants too mutual gaze represents a meaningful, sought-after type of stimulation. Papousek and Papousek (1977) showed 5-month-old infants two films of themselves, one which allowed eye-to-eye contact with their image and another (otherwise identical) which excluded eye contact. The films were shown simultaneously on two TV monitors in a visual preference set-up. Significantly more visual attention was paid to the film that permitted eye contact: in one experimental session it elicited twice as much, in another session nearly three times as much looking as the other film.

It appears that there is an urge on the part of both adult and child to establish eye contact. It is often a necessary prelude to further interaction: smiles are exchanged, the two vocalize to each other, bodily games occur. Mutual gaze can function as a "setting" stimulus: thus K. Bloom (1974) found it to be necessary as a context within which infant's vocalizations can be socially conditioned. But it also exists in its own right, without any further motive: as every lover knows, staring into the other's eyes can in itself be an intensely moving and pleasurable experience.

(2) Infants' looking patterns

The visual system is at birth developmentally ahead of all other sense modalities and is thus well suited as the primary channel for communication in the child's early encounters with other people. In addition it is also extraordinarily versatile, for its on–off nature means that, by a simple motor act, the individual can orient to or avoid whatever stimulus events are occurring in his visual field. Moreover, given the rapidity of eye opening and shutting and of head turning, he can do so with great speed and efficiency.

There are, however, certain regularities in infants' visual behaviour towards other people which underlie this versatility. As Stern (1974) has pointed out, infants do not gaze steadily at the mother when they are attending to her; nor, for that matter, do they steadily maintain gaze aversion when they try to avoid visual contact. In both cases alternation between gazing-at and gazing-away continues—only the length of the individual periods of attention and avoidance varies. The rate of fluctuation, however, shows certain regularities: according to Stern, any increase in gazing-at is normally relative to a decrease in gazing-away, producing regular cycles from the onset of one attentive period to the onset of the next. The distribution of gaze-to-gaze intervals thus remains stable and uninfluenced by the interest-value of visual input. This suggests that there may be biologically given limits to the infant's visual behaviour: gaze alternation itself is an intrinsic process that the infant brings to social interaction, and its temporal patterning is further constrained by common physiological factors.

The extent to which an infant is able to maintain visual attention to the other person depends in part on his arousal state, being greatest during "alert inactivity" (Wolff, 1965). Inner stimuli are then least likely to interfere with attentive processes. In the early weeks of life state fluctuations occur with considerable rapidity, and periods of sustained attention are therefore likely to be brief. In any case, the visual system at that age is still not sufficiently mature to cope with changes of distance and place; only with the improvements that occur during the first few months in visual accommodation and tracking abilities will infants be able to maintain contact even when the mother's face is not in the optimal position. This is shown by the two developmental curves for visual attention which Papousek and Papousek (1977) found to correspond to two different situations: first, when the infant was held by the mother in a position optimal for visual contact; second, when the mother was 1·5m away from the infant (see Fig. 1). Attention to the mother in the second situation improves with age; attention during close contact, on the other hand, declines as he becomes aware of more distant objects in the environment which also capture his attention.

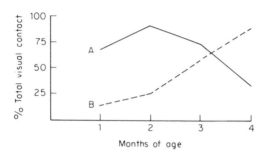

Fig. 1. *Visual contact with mothers in infants one to four months of age being held by mothers (A) or 1·5m distant from mothers (B). (Papousek and Papousek, 1977).*

In general, the amount of attention which the infant is able to pay to the mother increases with age over the first few weeks of life. This is demonstrated by Carpenter *et al.* (1970), who measured the amount of looking at three stimuli (the mother, a manikin, and an abstract form) in the course of a longitudinal study over the first 8 weeks. A sharp increase occurred during this period in attention to all three stimuli, reflecting the infant's increasing control over the visual apparatus. What is also significant about these findings is the consistently lower amount of attention paid to the mother's face compared with the other two stimuli. This, Carpenter *et al.* believe, is due to the incongruity of the mother's still face during its presentation — a condition imposed by the procedure but found disturbing by the infants, who consequently responded by actively avoiding the stimulus through repeatedly looking away.

Such active avoidance is a characteristic feature of visual behaviour which can play a significant part in social interaction. The on–off nature of vision means that the individual can exclude stimulation that is too stressful and that makes demands which, for one reason or another, he cannot meet. There is evidence that this is indeed the function of infants' gaze avoidance. In a study of both normal and premature infants aged 3 months, Field (1979b) measured the amount of looking and of heart rate changes when confronted by the mother or a doll. The mothers were requested to behave either spontaneously or merely to imitate whatever the infant did — the latter condition producing less animation and activity on the part of the mother than the former. The continuum of animation was extended further by presenting the doll in either a mobile or an immobile condition. The results show a definite relationship between the degree of animation and the amount of looking: the greater the animation of the stimulus the *less* the infants looked at it. However, as the heart rate measures make clear, the more animated stimuli also elicited a *greater* degree of arousal. It can therefore be conjectured that looking away served the purpose of modulating arousal level: thus, during the spontaneous-mother condition, an overload of information could only be prevented by looking away for longer periods— as if infants needed time-out to process the information and return to more acceptable levels of arousal. As Field points out, the looking-away periods were not characterized by passive disinterest or active search for other stimulation; rather, the infants showed expressions of concentration as though they were still trying to absorb the stimulus. The effect was particularly marked for the premature infants who might well have been even less able to assimilate arousing stimuli.

A stimulus can be warded off by suitably varying the length of gazing-at and gazing-away periods. In Field's study, for instance, the ratio of looking/looking away varied across stimulus conditions in line with the other two measures: periods of looking decreased and periods of looking away increased with the animation of the stimulus. However, the nature of the visual system permits even more subtle distinctions than those given by on and off periods, for it can vary the extent to which a stimulus is at the centre or at the periphery of the visual field. Thus Kaye and Fogel (1980), who found that the time spent directly gazing at the mother declined during the age span 6 to 26 weeks, stress that the difference was made up by peripheral head direction and not by looking away. During peripheral looking the infant can attend to other stimuli and yet remain oriented to the mother, ready to turn to her if the occasion arises. Beebe and Stern (1977) indeed suggest that the infants have a considerable repertoire for modulating experience and that it may be useful to think of this in terms of gradations along an "engagement–disengagement" spectrum that contains steps such as "facing and looking", "side looking", and "visual checking" at one end and "fuss/cry" and "turn to environment" at the other. It seems highly likely that, with increasing age, infants become a great deal more sophisticated in their visual strategies for dealing with social stimulation: the rate of gaze-on/gaze-off has been found to double in the first six months, indicating the infant's growing ability to free himself from a stimulus and yet readily return to it; at the same time there is an increasing use of peripheral vision as a means of remaining in contact (Kaye and Fogel, 1980).

(3) Parental interactive repertoire

Quite unconsciously, parents do their very best to make it easier for infants to attend to them. During the neonatal period they manoeuvre themselves into the "en face" position; in subsequent months they continue to adopt strategies designed to capture and hold an infant's attention.

What mothers do with their faces, voices and hands when interacting with young children has been carefully described by a number of investigators (Brazelton *et al.*, 1974; Stern, 1974, 1977; Stern *et al.*, 1977; Trevarthen, 1977). Basing their descriptions on film analyses, these writers have shown how "deviant" a mother's behaviour is in comparison with behaviour towards another adult. Interacting with an infant involves a highly idiosyncratic style containing three main features: exaggeration, slowing down, and repetition.

(a) Exaggeration. Facial expressions are the most striking example. Take Stern's (1977) description of a mother's often seen "mock surprise" expression:

> "Her eyes open very wide, her eyebrows go up, her mouth opens wide, and her head is raised and tilted up slightly. At the same time, she usually says something like 'oooooh' or 'aaaaah'. This expression is fairly stereotyped but has innumerable minor variations: the mouth may form a smile, or form a large circle with or without pursed lips or even stay closed; the head may move towards the baby rather than up and back, or it may tilt to one side; and of course the entire fullness of display may vary from a mild displacement of facial parts in space to a full-blown facial display where each part is displayed to its maximal position — that is, eyes as wide open as possible, eyebrows as high as possible, and so on" (Stern, 1977, p.19).

Were such an expression directed to an adult it would be regarded as quite bizarre; towards infants it is commonplace.

There are a number of such exaggerated expressions that mothers frequently use: thus Stern (1977) also describes the frown, the smile, and the "Oh, you poor dear" expression of concern and sympathy — all specific to interactions with infants. At the same time the mother's voice changes: though mostly of a higher pitch, she may suddenly drop it to an unusually low bass and so cover a much wider range than is normal in adult conversation. Changes in loudness and intensity are also exaggerated, again covering an unusually wide range. Together with a peculiar pattern of stresses, these paralinguistic features put maternal speech to infants into a class entirely of its own.

(b) Slowing down. Not only the nature but also the tempo of maternal

behaviour is highly distinctive. As Stern (1977) points out, facial displays are generally slow to form and are then held for a long time: thus the mock-surprise expression "grows slowly almost as if the mother were performing in slow motion, gradually but dramatically building to the fullest degree of the display and then, once 'there', holding the achieved position for an extremely long time (relatively speaking). At other times, mothers speed up their behaviours in an exaggerated way, and at other times they 'play' with the speed and rate of behaviour flow, varying it with changes of pace and unexpected spurts and runs" (p.18). Again speech is also affected: occasionally exaggeratedly speeded up but mostly slowed down, particularly with regard to vowel duration. The pauses between maternal utterances are also considerably longer than one would normally find in adult-directed speech.

(c) Repetition. Listening to a mother's speech to her infant makes readily apparent that it contains a great deal of redundancy. The same phrases are repeated again and again, the same nonsense sounds and noises are made over and over.

Yet microanalysis of the structure of maternal behaviour suggests that repetition extends even further. According to Stern *et al.* (1977), this structure can best be described in terms of the following three units (illustrated in Fig. 2):

(a) The *phrase*: a single utterance or burst of movement, generally lasting less than one second.

(b) The *run*, formed by a series of phrases similar in content or duration.

(c) The *episode of maintained interaction*, which is a series of runs, generally lasting a minute or two, during which a definite tempo is maintained.

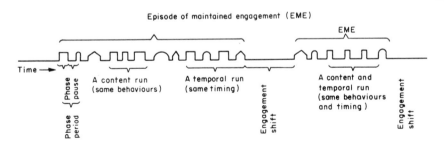

Fig. 2. *A schematic representation of different structures within a sequence of caregiver behaviours. The sequence is illustrated as consisting of only three "types" of behaviour represented here as:* ⊓,∩,⌒. *(Stern et al., 1977).*

This hierarchical arrangement provides a "theme-and-variation" format for maternal behaviour. During each episode the mother keeps the tempo of her behaviour within specific limits; at its end she reappraises the interpersonal situation in the light of the infant's state and then pitches the next episode accordingly. A gross re-tuning thus occurs during the interval between episodes; yet all along the mother monitors the infant's behaviour in readiness to change the content or tempo of her own responses. Finer re-tuning can go on at the level of the run: the same stimulus is presented repeatedly, yet can be provided with slight variations in order mildly to violate expectancies and thus to maintain attention. A fine balance between repetition and change needs continually to be struck: on the one hand the repetition of phrases similar in content and/or tempo provides the infant with a highly ordered stimulus world in which he can be fairly certain as to "what comes next." And on the other hand the mother ensures that the infant remains attentive to her by suitably changing her behaviour from time to time, thus providing variation on the basic theme. Fluctuations occur, but they are kept within limits. Only when the infant's behaviour indicates the need for change of a grosser nature will the mother reset the stimulation she is providing.

There are probably a number of reasons why maternal behaviour takes such a "deviant" form. For one thing, it is designed to ensure that the infant's attention will be attracted to and held by the mother's face. Whatever the infant brings to the social interaction that makes the face so attractive to him, he does need further help—particularly so in the early weeks of life when the visual apparatus is not yet fully mature. This help a mother provides: having first obtained his orientation towards her by putting her face in the right place, she then does her best to maintain the infant's attention towards her—and for that her exaggerated expressions and vocalizations are uniquely suited. Given the biological importance to the child of the social partner and the need to establish interpersonal communication, it is clearly necessary to bring about as soon as possible the first step in communication, namely mutual orientation. The combination of infant preparedness and maternal idiosyncracy achieves this remarkably well.

A further function of maternal infant-specific behaviour is to present the child with a predictable world. A large part of early stimulation is of a social nature: the mother is still the single most frequent stimulus the infant meets, and even his encounters with the rest of his environment are largely mediated by the mother. By thus restricting the range of stimulation the mother helps to prevent any overload on the infant's ability to assimilate new experiences, and just the same point applies to the way in which the mother packages her own behaviour. Again this represents a highly restricted selection from her total range: were she to present her full behavioural repertoire from the beginning it would only cause bewilderment and disregard. Instead, the constant repetition of a few but highly salient experiences gives the infant the opportunity to learn about social interaction at an easy pace and in a confident mood.

A related point also takes into account the infant's limited information processing ability. It refers especially to the tempo at which the mother's behaviour is set. Stern *et al.* (1977) point out that the phrases provided for an infant are only half the length of those provided for an adult, while the pauses that separate them are almost twice as long. The mother, that is, acts as though the infant can take in much smaller chunks of information at any one time than an adult, and as though he needs more time to process each before receiving the next.

From the infant's point of view the way in which mothers behave is most helpful in getting to grips with the social world. It enables him to acquire the first steps in the communicative act, in that the way in which the mother presents herself is uniquely suited to his attentional and learning capacities. As so often in this account, such maternal behaviour is by no means unique to mothers: fathers talking to their infants, children talking to younger children or to dolls—indeed almost anyone naturally and quite unconsciously adopts the communicative style outlined above. Experience with children may improve it, but most people adopt it quite automatically as part of the "right" way of talking to a young child.

(4) Temporal regulation of mutual gaze

Both mother and child bring particular characteristics to the face-to-face situation. These two sets of individual characteristics are formally adapted to each other; in practice, they need to be interwoven for a dyadic encounter to occur.

There are a number of ways in which the interweaving of a mother's and an infant's gaze differs from that found among adults. The usual situation in adult dyads is marked by symmetry: both partners take responsibility for the regulation of the interaction; the on–off looking patterns of the two individuals have similar characteristics; and the initiation and termination of mutual gaze episodes tends to be determined by both to the same extent. In mother–infant pairs there is visual asymmetry: the infant, initially at least, still operates very much within the limits of his inherent biological organization, whereas the mother is capable of far greater flexibility and accordingly is much more ready to let the infant set the pace and follow him.

Take a typical mutual gaze episode. The mother is looking intently at her infant, face still and waiting. The infant's head is turned sideways and his gaze is averted. After a while he turns to look at her, and at once the mother's repertoire of infant-specific behaviours comes into play: she greets his attention with great delight, her face approaches his and becomes contorted, she smiles, she touches and she vocalizes in the manner specifically reserved for him. The infant watches quietly at first; then he too stirs into activity, smiling and gurgling and bringing all four limbs into action. Very soon he may then look away again, though perhaps only for a fraction of a second before he attends once more to his mother's antics. Eventually a rather longer look-away will appear, as though the infant has for the time being disengaged himself. The mother too will then quieten; her watchfulness, however, is maintained — all ready for the next engagement.

The extremely long gazing periods on the part of mothers found in such sequences have been described by several investigators (e.g. Fogel, 1977; Schaffer *et al.*, 1977; Stern, 1974). In adult–adult interaction such prolonged looking at the other person is usually inappropriate and disturbing, for the to-and-fro of gazing acts as a signal to the other person that helps to smooth the interchange. In the interactions with the infant, however, mothers' prolonged gazing stems from the primary responsibility they bear to maintain the interaction, and the watchfulness is required so that they can immediately respond to every new attentive sign made by the infant. As Fogel (1977) has put it, the mother's continuous gazing provides a "frame" within which the infant's gazing may cycle to and fro.

This asymmetry in amount of looking also entails an asymmetry in the responsibility for initiating and terminating mutual gaze episodes. As Stern (1974) has demonstrated, the probability of the mother being the first to look is far greater than that for the infant; having begun to look she will continue until the infant looks back; and subsequently she is reluctant to be the first to break the contact. The mother, that is, appears to be almost constantly ready for interaction; it is up to the infant to determine whether interaction in fact takes place.

The mutual gaze patterns of mothers and infants show a number of regularities, though microanalytic techniques are required to demonstrate them. Changes in visual behaviour can, after all, take place with great rapidity, even in infants. In one study (Schaffer *et al.*, 1977) the mean length of looks of 12-month-old infants directed at the mother during a play session was 1·33 seconds, with few looks lasting longer than two seconds. What is significant is that the integration of the looking patterns of the two individuals also takes place with such rapidity: as Stern (1977) has put it, mother and infant interact in a split-second world, where social signals are perceived and responded to more rapidly than we realize. The speed of interpersonal synchronization is in fact so great that a stimulus–response model could not account for all interactive sequences. It seems rather that the temporal integration one sees within a dyad may be based on a shared programme — Stern (1977) uses the analogy of a waltz, where both partners know the steps and thus move in synchrony, though they are also able to react to each other's cues in stimulus–response fashion in order to reset their general direction.

This sharing may be brought about because both participants — indeed all human beings — have in common a particular way of functioning in social interactions that is based on some universal, wired-in characteristic. It has been suggested (Jaffe *et al.*, 1973) that there are certain mathematical regularities in the gross temporal pattern of mother–infant gazing, that these are identical to the regularities found in adult verbal conversations, and that they may therefore describe a basic property of all human communication which is first seen in the attention regulating behaviour of mother and infant. This is a fascinating but highly speculative suggestion; what does seem probable is that visual interaction is not a random combination of two separate sets of visual events: the co-occurrence of gazing-at, as shown by the two individuals, is inevitably greater than chance.

Whatever the role of inherent factors, there is little doubt that a shared programme does depend to some extent on the mutual expectancies which develop through experience. Mother and infant must learn about each other, and in particular about each other's temporal characteristics. If a face-to-face interaction is to be maintained, a mother must develop a sensitivity to the cyclic nature of her infant's attentive capacity. It is, after all, primarily her responsibility in the early months of the infant's life to ensure that interactions can take place. The mother does this partly through her watchfulness, which enables her to respond immediately to the infant's overtures; she must also, however, respect the infant's need to disengage from time to time and not bombard him with unphased stimulation. Brazelton *et al.* (1974) have described the on–off cycles for a number of mother–infant pairs, and have illustrated the considerable variations that may occur between individuals in the extent of such cycling. A mother needs to learn to adjust her rhythm to that of the infant, so that she can appropriately increase or reduce her own activity in the light of the cues the infant provides. We can but speculate, but it may well be that the extent to which the infant experiences sensitively timed stimulation in his early dyadic encounters will determine how soon he too will enter the dialogue as a fully participating rather than merely receiving partner. It is certainly one of the main tasks of the mother to ensure that a temporal organization for which she was primarily responsible in the early stages becomes in due course a *joint* venture.

That the interchange does become more symmetrical as the child gets older is neatly illustrated in Kaye and Fogel's (1980) study. These authors followed-up a group of mother–infant pairs and recorded their face-to-face interactions when the children were 6, 13 and 26 weeks old. The results show how effective the mothers' use of exaggerated facial expressions was at the youngest age as a device for holding and maintaining the infants' attention. At the two older ages, on the other hand, the infants were no longer totally captured by this stimulus but had sufficient control over their own behaviour to be able to stop attending and look away. In addition, a greater symmetry appeared in "greeting" behaviour: at all three ages mothers usually acknowledged the infants' onset of attention to them by smiling, head bobbing and facial expression; at the older ages, on the other hand, the infants were less and less likely to wait for the mother's greeting before they themselves greeted her. A shift from merely responsive to increasingly spontaneous behaviour is indicated, with the infant becoming less dependent on the mother's initiations and more capable of setting in motion an interchange himself. Being one of the unfortunately rare examples of an attempt to investigate age changes in face-to-face situations, this study may be regarded as particularly valuable in documenting the growing skills of infants to participate in a gradually more balanced manner in such exchanges with an adult.

Vocal interchange

Among adults verbal exchanges provide the means *par excellence* of communication. Speech is an extraordinarily versatile tool for this purpose, and interest in its ontogenetic beginnings during the early years reflects the importance attached to this function. Vocal interchanges between infants and mothers during the preverbal stage have therefore most frequently been investigated in the hope that they would shed some light on the way in which speech first emerges. This is given extra force by the possibility that there may be some "natural" association between vocal input and vocal output: according to Freedle and Lewis (1977), infants' vocalizations are more likely to be responded to by mothers' vocalizations than with any other form of behaviour, and similarly mothers' vocalizing is more likely to elicit a vocalization from the infant than any other type of response. The scene is thus set for a lifetime of conversation.

The use of the vocal mode for mutual communication lags well behind the visual mode during infancy. Whatever its eventual sophistication, vocal expressions for most of the first year of life reflect the infant's inner condition; not until the end of the year are there firm signs of its communicative use. Until then it is largely a one-way system, in that it is left to the mother to act *as if* the infant were trying to communicate. Yet the very fact that from the beginning she attempts to involve her infant in dialogue-like exchanges based on the vocal mode makes it important to investigate these if we are to understand the development of early sociability.

(1) Infants' vocalizations

In the early weeks a great variety of non-cry vocalizations appear, and these quickly become increasingly distinct both from each other and from crying sounds (Kaplan and Kaplan, 1971). From 3 or 4 months on babbling can be heard, when clearly articulated vowel-like and consonant-like sounds are combined into syllabic constructions of marked intonation. Babbling sounds merge into patterned speech by the end of the first year.

There is no agreement yet as to the continuity or discontinuity between the babbling stage and speech. What is apparent is that the initial occurrence of babbling sounds is not dependent on the auditory experience of hearing either oneself or others; the continuation of babbling, on the other hand, does depend on such experience. Thus deaf infants start babbling at the usual age and make sounds no different from hearing infants; by 8 or 9 months, however, they gradually stop babbling (Lenneberg, 1976).

The sheer amount of vocalization varies greatly and shows only tenuous relationships to any of the variables so far investigated. According to Jones and Moss (1971), the infant's state determines vocal responsiveness to some extent, in that most vocalizing occurs during alert inactivity. The same investigators also found that infants aged 3 months vocalized more when alone than when with other people, a warning against regarding this response in the early stages of development as "social" (in the sense of being exclusive to the presence of other people). However, Anderson *et al.* (1978) found a rather more complex relationship between the amount of vocalizing in 3-month-old infants and maternal presence or absence. They differentiated four distance conditions between mother and infant, and measured the percentage of session spent vocalizing in each (given here in brackets): mother holding the infant (9·2%); mother being near but not touching (19·2%); mother being further away but still in visual range (11·4%); mother out of the room (16·6%). The greatest amount was found in the "near" condition—more than twice as much as in the "holding" condition. This leads Anderson *et al.* to suggest that a somewhat "distanced" partner seems to be the most helpful condition for eliciting vocalizing, and that physical contact may in fact inhibit such behaviour—as opposed to the facilitating effect it has on visual exploration (Korner and Thoman, 1972). However, the relatively large amount of vocalizing that occurred when the mother was out of the room is also noteworthy.

Some sort of relationship of vocal output with social stimulation does seem likely—one need only consider the oft-reported quietness of institutionalized infants lacking the usual amount of contact with other people (e.g. Provence and Lipton, 1962). That vocal responsiveness can be increased by the action of another person has been known since the study by Rheingold *et al.* (1959), in which each vocalization by an infant was followed by adult social stimulation. The resulting increase in vocalizing was attributed to conditioning, and in a further study Weisberg (1963) went on to demonstrate that this effect could only reliably be obtained with *social* reinforcement: following each infant vocalization with the chime of a bell, for instance, did not increase responsiveness. There is some doubt, however, as to whether the effect can be attributed to conditioning: more recently K. Bloom and Esposito (1975) have found non-contingently delivered social stimulation to be just as effective in raising the vocalization rate of 3-month-old infants as contingent stimulation. The adult's social behaviour, in other words, serves to *elicit* the infant's vocalizations rather than acting as a source of reinforcement. In addition K. Bloom (1974; K. Bloom and Esposito, 1975) has also made the interesting observation that this effect can only be obtained if the infant can see the adult's eyes: where these are not available such other social actions as smiling, talking and touching are ineffective. The adult, with particular reference to his eyes, therefore acts as a "releaser" of vocalizations in 3-month-old infants.

Developmental changes in vocal responsiveness have been suggested by M. M. Lewis (1959). He proposed the following three stages:
(1) at 3 to 4 months infants respond to spoken speech with a high rate of vocalizing;
(2) subsequently vocal output decreases considerably, as the infant is absorbed in attending to the other person's speech (having presumably realized that such sounds carry meaning);
(3) from about 10 months on an increase in vocal activity takes place again, as infants "respond" to the speech they hear. There is some support for this scheme in a study by Roe (1975): naturalistic observations of infants 3 to 15 months old indicated no change over age in the percentage of time spent vocalizing. However, in sessions where mothers were asked to try actively to elicit a vocal response from their infants Roe found a great many vocalizations around 3 and 4 months, a considerable dip at about 9 months, and a subsequent increase from 11 months on.

It is apparent that we are still very ignorant as to the precise conditions under which vocalizations in infants occur. One problem is the narrow age range that has been investigated by past studies: nearly all have concerned themselves with 3 or 4 month old infants, for at that age responsiveness is easily elicited, the strangeness of the experimenter is as yet no obstacle, and artificial experimental conditions can more easily be administered than subsequently. As long as interest focussed on such issues as the condition-ability of the infant this choice of age was understandable; as new issues come to be raised, however, attention will have to be switched to other ages. This applies particularly to the communicative use of vocal behaviour, where the most fruitful age range to cover in relation to the emergence of this ability is the end of the first and the beginning of the second year. A study by Harding and Golinkoff (1979) is one of the rare examples of such a focus. These investigators observed infants in the age range 8 to 14 months in a number of interaction situations with their mothers, in order to plot the onset of intentional vocalization. By operationally defining intention according to such criteria as making eye contact with the mother and persistence until the goal was achieved, Harding and Golinkoff were able to show that infants do not use vocalization in an intentional manner until they have achieved a particular level of cognitive sophistication, i.e. Piagetian causal stage 5. Only at that point will an infant realize that his behaviour can be used as a means to obtain an end—a cognitive realization with far reaching social implications (see Bates *et al.*,1975). It seems evident that, once this stage has been reached, an infant's relationship with the mother may undergo profound changes—a general point to which we shall subsequently return but which has particular consequences for vocal communication.

(2) Parental vocal input

We have already referred to the exaggerated manner with which mothers use their voice when interacting with infants, and at a later point we shall also consider the particular linguistic style ("motherese") used in talking to children. Here our concern is mainly with the temporal features that characterize mothers' vocalizations during infancy.

Let us first note one perhaps surprising fact, namely that people do speak to infants—even the very youngest, who may still be many months away from beginning to comprehend speech. Rheingold and Adams (1980), in an observational study of personnel in a maternity hospital nursery, found not merely that people do speak to newborn infants but that they speak a great deal. Most of the activities that the nurses carried out (feeding, changing, medical procedures, and so forth) were accompaned by speech—most of it in well-formed sentences, much of it in the shape of instructions or questions to which the adult obviously did not expect an answer. Thus from the very beginning speech forms an integral and constant part of a child's environment.

The adult's speech is, however, not to be regarded as just a monologue—a unidirectional flow arbitrarily imposed on the infant. For one thing, the content of speech is closely related to whatever the infant is doing at the time; hence comments are mostly about his yawning, defecating, kicking, grimacing, looking and other such ongoing activities. It is as though the mother starts from the infant's point of view and tries to ensure that her remarks concern whatever is likely to be closest to his interest. For another, mothers time their speech to coincide with the infant's state of alertness: there is obviously little point in talking to a sleeping infant, but, as Jones and Moss (1971) have shown, mothers' speech also varies according to type of waking state, with the greatest amount being found during maximal alertness. And finally, at a rather more detailed level of timing, mothers appear to adapt the temporal characteristics of their vocalizations to the infants' capacity to absorb them. Stern *et al.* (1977) report that the mean duration of mothers' vocal phrases was found to be 0·47 seconds, while the duration of the pauses between the phrases was 0·91 seconds. This may be compared with values of 1·42 and 0·60 seconds that have been reported for speech to adults (Jaffe and Feldstein, 1970). It appears that infant-addressed speech arrives in much briefer chunks of information, interspersed by pauses that are much longer, giving the infant more time to process the stimulation just presented.

Individual differences in the extent to which mothers set up face-to-face dialogues deserve far more attention than they have received. There are some intriguing social class differences that have been reported in this respect (Kagan and Tulkin, 1971): middle class mothers spend more time talking to their infants in face-to-face situations than working class mothers; the former also provide a greater number of distinctive vocalizations under these circumstances than the latter. Whether the difference stems from the value placed by mothers on this type of contact, or whether it merely reflects the time available to a housewife with many other duties, the result might well have implications for the varying rates of children's verbal development associated with social class. A finding by Jones and Moss (1971) is relevant: the amount of mothers' verbalizations that were contingent on the infant's own behaviour correlated significantly with the extent to which the infants vocalized; there was, however, no such correlation with the total amount (whether contingent or not) of maternal verbalization. To be meaningful, speech must be delivered to infants as a *personalized* form of stimulation, not as something unconnected with their own activity and certainly not as just a background noise of radio, television and adult conversation.

(3) Coaction and turn taking

For certain types of dyadic interaction it is essential that the roles of the participants alternate. This applies particularly to verbal conversations, for it is virtually impossible to talk and listen at the same time. One individual must therefore remain quiet while the other takes the floor; meaningful communication would otherwise not occur. Periodically the two participants exchange roles: the listener takes the floor while the speaker in turn becomes a listener. Such an exchange must be accomplished smoothly; should both individuals simultaneously claim the active role their behaviour will clash and disrupt effective communication. Procedures for regulating the exchange of roles must therefore be available to both participants.

In the conversation of adult dyads a multiplicity of cues may function as turn taking signals (Duncan, 1972; Kendon, 1967). Syntax, pitch, intonation, shift of gaze and gesticulation are among the more important mechanisms that make smooth changeover possible and prevent overlapping and clashes of role. These cues generally function so effectively that turn taking is an almost inevitable part of conversation (a linguistic universal, as Miller, 1963, was moved to call it). The question arises whether it is specific to *verbal* interaction, where listening to the content of the other person's speech is, of course, essential, or whether it antedates the onset of language and is already a formal characteristic of vocal interchange between mother and infant in the preverbal period.

(4) The prevalence of turn taking

A number of observers (e.g. Brazelton *et al.*, 1974; Trevarthen, 1977) have commented on the "conversation-like" quality of mother–infant interactions in face-to-face situations, with turn taking as the main characteristic giving rise to this impression. Thus Bateson (1975), from an intensive study of one infant's interaction with his mother between 1½ and 3½ months, concluded that vocalizing tends to occur in alternating form—a "proto-conversation", as she called it, in that the vocal exchange functions to affirm and maintain social contact rather than deriving its meaning from content.

Not everyone agrees, however, that turn taking is the predominant mode of vocal interchange in those early months. Stern *et al.* (1975) found that the mothers of 3-month-old infants were *more* likely to begin vocalizing when the infant was already vocalizing than when he was silent, and to continue vocalizing while the infant was doing so. Infants too tended to begin to vocalize more readily during maternal vocalization than in silent periods, though their continuing did not seem to be influenced by the mother's activity. Thus a strong tendency for a "coactional" pattern appeared, i.e. mother and infant vocalized in unison. A similar picture emerged from a study by Anderson *et al.* (1978), also working with 3-month-old infants: they too found both mother and child to be more likely to start vocalizing when the other one was already doing so than during silence; again the mother's ceasing to vocalize was related to the infant's silence, whereas no such relationship emerged for the infant.

Such findings have led Stern *et al.* (1975) to propose that two types of early communicative behaviour can be distinguished: a coactive and an alternating mode. They occur under different circumstances, in that coaction is to be found mainly during periods of high arousal, e.g. at times of "fun" when playing games, or on the contrary, on occasions of negative affect when the child is upset. The alternating mode, on the other hand, is found at times of low arousal, as during task performance. The two modes, according to Stern *et al.*, both emerge early on in life, but initially coaction is the more prevalent pattern, giving way only subsequently in the course of development to turn taking as the predominant mode.

Just how prevalent the two modes are at different age points, and indeed whether they deserve to be regarded as distinct types of communicative interchange, remains a matter of controversy. A study by Hayes and Elliott (1979) of infants aged 12, 14 and 16 weeks produced contradictory evidence to that obtained by Stern *et al.* and Anderson *et al.* In their sample simultaneous vocalizing occurred for only 2% of the total session, whereas mothers vocalized alone between 34 and 41% in the three age groups and for a further 3 to 4% infants vocalized alone. The probability of mutual vocalizing following either the mother or the infant starting to vocalize alone was found to be low: there appeared to be no clear tendency on the part of either individual to join in with the other. A similar picture emerges from a study by Davis (1978), though on a rather wider and older age range, i.e. 6 to 16 months. Only 1% of maternal utterances in this sample occurred while the child was vocalizing; only 0·3% of child utterances interrupted a maternal utterance. Turn taking was thus the predominant interactive mode.

This was also found in a study by Schaffer *et al.* (1977), in which preverbal 12-month-old children were compared with verbal 24-month-old children. Turn taking characterized the exchanges of the younger children with their mothers just as much as it did those of the older group. Overlaps, i.e. both partners vocalizing simultaneously, occurred rarely and with no greater frequency in the younger than in the older group. Such overlaps were mostly very brief and were as likely to be caused by the mother interrupting the child as by the child interrupting the mother. Some appeared to be genuine clashes, i.e. a breakdown in the predominant turn taking arrangement; others resembled Stern's description of coaction, in that they occurred on such high arousal occasions as laughing, crying, and "chorusing" (i.e. mother and child deliberately joining in "oooohs" and "aaaahs"). In several respects the vocal interchange, at the younger as much as at the older age, resembled the precisely coordinated temporal patterning of adult conversations. Speaker-switch pauses, for instance, were mostly very brief—generally less than one second; the point of transition from speaker to listener was thus managed with the competence one expects among mature participants.

There are several reasons why different studies may have come up with such apparently divergent findings on coaction and turn taking. One concerns the different ages of the children studied; another refers to a variety of methodological differences. Clearly, if a developmental trend is to be described it becomes important to include both younger and older infants in the same investigation rather than compare age groups across different studies, each employing its own procedures, definitions and data analyses. This has been done by Collis, Bryant and Messer (in preparation), in a study that compared infants aged 4 months (the age when Stern *et al.* claimed coaction to be the norm) and 12 months (when Schaffer *et al.* found a prevalence of turn taking). The average number of overlapping vocalizations in mother–infant dyads turned out to be very similar in the two age groups, in both of which they occurred relatively infrequently. However, variability in the incidence of overlaps was considerable within each group, and this was largely a function of the extent to which the particular context associated with overlaps happened to arise in each dyadic session. Turn taking, that is, may be the more usual pattern, but departures from it are very much influenced by purely temporary factors that prevail at the time of the interaction.

Whatever the final verdict on the prevalence of turn taking, there can be little doubt that it antedates the appearance of language in the child. Vocal exchanges, well before their information content becomes important, are already characterized by the form required for successful verbal communication to take place. There seems little reason why infant coos and babbles on the one hand and maternal nonsense talk on the other should each be listened to in silence—unless it is in preparation for the exchange of speech that will eventually follow.

(5) Mechanisms of turn taking

Turn taking is an interactional phenomenon, i.e. it characterizes the relationship between individuals rather than the individuals themselves. Its occurrence within a dyad does not on its own justify any statements about the "ability" of the participants to take turns; in particular, the fact that an infant under certain conditions takes turns with the mother does not necessarily indicate that the infant actually possesses this social skill.

There are at least three ways in which turn taking can be brought about. In the first place, both partners may be acting jointly and in full cooperation because both are conversant with the rules and are thus equally responsible for ensuring smooth interaction. In this sense, they both may be said to possess the necessary social skill. There is no doubt that socializing agents do exert pressure on children to develop this skill—mothers are frequently heard to tell their pre-school children that they "must not interrupt while someone is talking!" Thus in the course of development consciousness of this rule is fostered and becomes one device for regulating social interactions. It is improbable, however, that this occurs already during infancy.

The second possibility is that turn taking is at first brought about entirely by the mother's action. The mother, that is, inserts her vocalizations between the sounds the infant makes at will. She is highly attentive to his behaviour, and times her interventions in such a way as not to interrupt him. The interaction is thus based on the infant's burst–pause pattern on the one hand and the mother's sensitivity to this pattern on the other, rather as we have described for interactions during feeding. In both instances the mother allows herself to be paced by the infant and thereby takes major responsibility for setting up a dialogue.

There are a number of indications that mothers do behave in this way during vocal interchanges. For one thing, speaker-switch pauses when the mother follows the child are considerably shorter than those when the child follows the mother (Schaffer *et al.*, 1977; see Fig. 3)—a difference that most probably reflects the readiness of the mother to reply to her child. For another, Stern *et al.* (1975) found that the effect of the mother's vocal state (whether she is vocalizing or silent) on the infant's behaviour is not as strong as the effect of the infant's state on the mother. It seems therefore that it is primarily the mother who is responsible for the particular temporal patterning of the interchange. And finally, mothers keep their vocalizations very brief, with plenty of pauses, thereby giving the infant every chance to join in. Should he not avail himself of the invitation, the mother can then continue with further brief bursts of her own.

While there is plenty of evidence of the mother's important role in sustaining the interchange, it would nevertheless be a mistake to regard the infant as entirely oblivious of the mother's ongoing behaviour. The third possibility for bringing about turn taking is accordingly that some mechanism is present from the beginning which makes production of vocalizations and listening to other sounds inherently incompatible. During stimulation of six-month-old infants with vowel or consonant-vowel sounds Webster (1969) found a significant reduction in the infants' own vocalizing (and especially in the particular sound to which they were listening). A subsequent study (Webster *et al.*, 1972), using high pitch and low pitch sounds, confirmed the suppressant effect on the infants' vocal production, but also indicated an increase in vocal activity immediately following stimulus offset. A possible mechanism for turn taking is thereby indicated, providing a suppressant effect during stimulation on the one hand and a facilitating effect immediately after stimulation on the other. Such a relationship may well be confined to certain types of auditory stimuli, in particular to human speech—a highly attention-worthy sound. It would therefore be the act of attention that inhibits vocal production—a possibility supported by a study

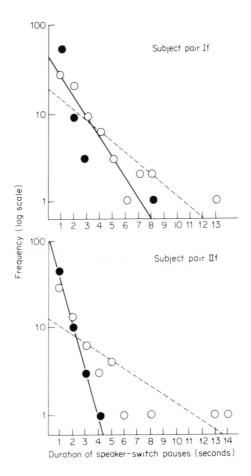

Fig. 3. *Speaker-switch pause distributions for two subject-pairs.* ●————● *child–mother pauses;* ○————○ *mother–child pauses. (Schaffer* et al., *1977).*

in which Barrett-Goldfarb and Whitehurst (1973) compared the effect of mothers' and fathers' taped voices on the vocalizations of one-year-old infants. Not only was the suppressant effect of such stimulation confirmed, but it was also noted that the effect was particularly marked for the preferred voice. As these authors point out, the suppression of babbling when presented with important sounds has obvious adaptive significance. There is no more important sound than the voice of another person, and this may especially apply to the voices of certain significant people. These people need to be listened to, and an inbuilt mechanism that ensures this may well exist.

(6) Integration of vocalizing with looking

More often than not communication is multi-modal. Visual, auditory and proxemic signals are sent and received simultaneously in one coherent whole, avoiding contradiction and ambiguity. This applies particularly to the synchronization of looking with speaking: as the work of Exline and Winters (1965), Kendon (1967), Argyle (1972) and others has shown, looks are not distributed randomly during a conversation but occur at particular points and exercise specific functions. One such function is to regulate turn taking, in that it is one of the cues sent to the listener that the speaker has finished and is willing to exchange roles. Looking thus plays a significant part in coordinating verbal dialogue.

The interactions of mothers and infants present a different picture. As we have already seen, mothers tend to look at the child almost continuously in face-to-face situations. This does not vary according to whether they are speaking or listening—in contrast to adult conversations where looking is more closely associated with listening than with speaking. There are, as we have also seen, good reasons for such attentiveness: if the mother is primarily responsible for keeping the dialogue in being she must be watchful for the cues the infant provides as to his own state of attentiveness. She must time her responses to come in at appropriate points of his activity; she must not interrupt the infant's ongoing behaviour; and she must allow him plenty of time to emit actions that she can then treat as "replies" to her own. No wonder that such intense watchfulness appears to be the norm for mothers' gazing.

Rather less is known about the way in which infants' looking is related to vocalizing. It does appear, however, that the integration of these two behaviour patterns is initially absent and does not emerge until the second year of life. In their study of 12- and 24-month-old children Schaffer *et al.* (1977) found signs of integration only in the older group: looks at the mother by these children were initiated primarily during or immediately following the child's utterances rather than the mother's. In the younger group no such pattern was evident; looks were distributed randomly throughout the interaction. However, even in the older group there was no indication that the children's looks served a regulatory purpose in turn taking—indeed the sole cue that was consistently available for this purpose was silence. It should be emphasized, however, that this particular study took place in a play situation, where the presence of toys clearly complicated the observed looking pattern. Sustained face-to-face situations in children older than 8 or 9 months are difficult to arrange; nevertheless, it is likely that in such a situation a clearer pattern might become evident at an earlier age. It does seem, however, that in the interim we must conclude that the integration of looking with vocalizing is a developmental phenomenon and not present from the beginning.

Interactive style

Our emphasis so far has been on generic characteristics. Yet it is readily apparent to the most casual observer that, within the common framework, there are considerable variations in the manner and style which characterize the interaction of particular adult–infant pairs. Not a lot is as yet known about the nature, origin and consequences of such individual differences; what there is suggests this to be an extremely fruitful area to explore.

(1) Some cultural variations

Interpersonal behaviour takes place in a cultural context. The influence of this context on child rearing methods has been documented extensively (Le Vine, 1970), for the variations in the way in which adults execute such basic tasks as feeding and toilet training are not only fascinating in their own right but are also thought by some to shed light on the antecedents of personality development. Most of this material has been of a globally descriptive nature, documenting (for example) the customary age of weaning, the amount of verbal stimulation provided to infants, or the way in which caretaking arrangements are distributed among adults. A more process-oriented, detailed analysis of the interactions within which culture-determined variations in such practices occur is only now beginning to emerge.

The manner whereby mother and child mutually regulate their behaviour may be examined at various levels. The way in which sleeping–waking behaviour becomes patterned in accordance with the requirements of the infant's social group is an example from the more macroscopic end of the continuum. In Western samples studied, sleep rapidly becomes pushed into the nocturnal part of the 24-hour day in the course of the first few months of life, so that already by 4 months the average longest sleep episode is almost 8 hours (Parmelee *et al.*, 1964). Among the Kokwet in Kenya, however, Super and Harkness (1982) found no such trend: sleep periods remained relatively short and were not concentrated into "right" times for at least the first 8 months of life. Given the sleeping arrangements of the Kokwet (the baby remaining in skin-to-skin contact with the mother throughout the night, ready to suck at the breast the moment it wakes, while the father is sleeping elsewhere), night waking is experienced as far less of a disturbance than in Western households. In all societies mutual adaptation of mother and child must occur, but its content may differ radically to fit in with the particular family circumstances prevalent in each society.

At the more microscopic level of face-to-face interaction, culturally associated differences are also evident. Among the Mayan Indians of Mexico Brazelton (1977) found the extent of interaction through smiling, vocalizing and even looking very much reduced in comparison with Western norms. During feeding, for instance, the mother's glances at the baby tend to be perfunctory and without expectation of response. The infant's own social overtures are rarely responded to; it is as though the mothers consider a quiet, undemanding infant as the desideratum and thus do their best to avert a demand–response pattern from developing. Presumably a passive personality type has social value in this particular setting; the style of mothering adopted to achieve it, however, has considerable implications for our ideas about maternal sensitivity. As we have seen, the norm that has emerged from Western studies stresses the very great watchfulness of mothers in the presence of their infants, so that they are constantly ready to intervene at appropriate times and provide relevant stimulation. Whether the reduced watchfulness described for Mayan Indians (as well as for various African societies, see Leiderman *et al.*, 1979) is analogous to a depressive condition, with similar consequences for the child, or whether there are compensating means of communication through alternative channels (kinaesthetic in particular) remains a fascinating problem for future work.

The emphasis on different communicative channels is certainly one of the more obvious points that emerges from cross-cultural studies. One example is the work by Caudill on the differences between Japanese and American mothers (Caudill and Schooler, 1973; Caudill and Weinstein, 1969). Among Japanese mothers a far greater emphasis is placed on physical contact with the infant: in comparison with American mothers they spend more time in close proximity to the child, providing more rocking, carrying and soothing, even during the child's hours of sleep. The preferred mode of communication is physical rather than verbal; vocalizations by the infant, that are greeted with joy and encouragement by the American mother, are responded to much less readily, and similarly there is far less spontaneous verbal stimulation by the Japanese mother in the form of "chatting". Thus two distinct styles of child rearing can be seen: on the one hand the American mother encourages her child to be active and vocally responsive; on the other hand the Japanese mother sets out to soothe and quiet her infant. Again cultural expectations provide the context for these different patterns: the American mother aims to produce an active, vocal and independent being; the Japanese mother, on the other hand, tries to foster a verbally and physically restrained type of individual who can be drawn into increasingly interdependent relations with others.

These cultural comparisons all relate to differences in the amounts of stimulation that are provided by different means. They do not indicate that there are differences in the actual structure of interaction, i.e. in the temporal regularities that we examined in previous sections. There may be greater reluctance to engage in mutual gaze or in vocal interchange in some societies than in others; there is, however, no indication that the interactions which do occur differ in any formal way from those described for Western samples. The temporal characteristics are universals; they define the process of interaction itself. It is only in the content of interchange that individual differences are to be found.

(2) Individual couples

Each participant in a social encounter brings along a set of characteristics that will help to determine the nature of that encounter. This applies to the youngest baby as much as to an adult: both contribute to the outcome of the interaction which may thus—in certain respects at any rate—assume a character unique to each dyad.

There are certainly plenty of indications that differential social behaviour can be found at quite an early age. According to Yogman *et al.* (1976), infants as young as four weeks show differentiated behaviour to mothers, fathers and strangers respectively; the mutual rhythm of limb movement that these writers found to exist between mothers and infants could not be detected in the interaction with fathers and strangers. Thus infant and father engaged in abrupt and staccato movements with each other; with the stranger, on the other hand, the interaction was marked by cautious approaches and withdrawals: for instance, the stranger engaged in long silences and occasional tentative touches, as if confused by the infant's cues, and sent confusing cues in turn. Fogel (1979), comparing infant-mother and infant-peer interactions, also found that behaviour with the mother was smoother, more varied, and less abrupt and intense than with the peer. Field (1978), on the other hand, studying four-month-old infants in face-to-face interactions, found few differences between mothers and fathers—if, that is, the parent observed was the child's primary caretaker. Instead, differences did emerge between primary and secondary caretakers, irrespective of the parent's sex—a finding which appears to point to the differential amount of experience with the child as the crucial factor.

These studies have looked at variation amongst classes of individuals (mothers, fathers, etc.); comparisons within classes that hold such factors as sex and experience constant are even fewer in number. One strategy is to examine the same mother's behaviour with several of her own children—an approach illustrated by Stern's (1971) study of a mother's interactions with each of her three-month-old twins. The two interactive patterns turned out to differ radically in a number of respects: in the amount of face-to-face contact, in the pattern of initiating and terminating interactions, in the duration of avoidance of contacts, and so on. These differences were found in all the interactions observed, and appeared to represent stable features characterizing each pair.

Such a strategy, and also that based on cross-fostering, are promising approaches to the study of dyadic uniqueness. The manifold ways in which this uniqueness shows itself remains to be established. It has been suggested (e.g. by Stern *et al.*, 1977) that the modality whereby interactive behaviours are expressed in adult–infant encounters is of less consequence than the temporal patterning of the stimulation—in particular, that vocal and kinaesic acts are presented in similar chunks of time, and that the interactive patterns established by each pair derives from the particular rhythm which characterizes their interactions. Each pair thus work out a mutual pattern in which both duration and latency of activities are matched. Stern (1977) has described such rhythmic matching with respect to mother's and infant's head movements in a face-to-face situation. Such movements, he believes, show a striking temporal relatedness: the infant's head-turns away from the mother occur predominantly as she approaches the infant, and head-turns towards the mother occur with her withdrawals. The matching generally takes place within the same split-second, providing a closely synchronized mutual approach–avoidance pattern. The pattern cannot be explained in terms of reaction times; a predictive model based on the partners' previous experience of one another may be more appropriate. For the infant such previous experience may involve only the last few seconds; for the adult knowledge of the infant's preferred tempo of interaction is more likely to be derived from a much longer period of acquaintance.

It is apparent that there are a great many gaps in our knowledge with regard to the individual differences that characterize dyads. Their manifestation, their stability over time, the mechanisms whereby they become established and their functional continuity with similar phenomena described for adult interactions are some of the problems to which attention must be given if we are to view dyadic differences as in any way significant. Individual differences can be found in pretty well any aspect of human behaviour: their meaningfulness needs to be established.

Disturbances in early interactions

We have seen how each adult–infant dyad can normally be expected to establish some kind of mutuality in the course of the early weeks of life. Various processes, some inherent and some involving experience, ensure that the infant can interact with the other person in a functionally meaningful manner that leads to food, social learning, and just sheer pleasure. But what if the normal process of interaction is interfered with?

There are two sorts of data presently available which bear on this question. In the first place, a number of studies have experimentally interfered in the interaction by altering the adult's usual behaviour and so providing a distorted stimulus input to the child. The source of the disturbance, that is, stems from the adult's behaviour. The second body of work refers to interactions that are distorted through some form of pathology in the child. We shall examine these two kinds of studies in turn.

(1) Experimentally induced distortions

The intricate enmeshing of mother's and infant's responses generally found in dyadic situations is largely dependent on the mother's ability to provide appropriate stimulation — appropriate, that is, in terms of rate, amount and contingency. The infant soon builds up expectations as to the nature of this input, and it is these expectations that experimentally induced distortions are intended to disrupt.

One such distortion is achieved by asking the mother to remain blank-faced while seated opposite her infant. Such a request is in fact extraordinarily difficult for a mother to follow, such is the compulsion of the infant's own changing expressions. Asking the mother to fixate a target to the side of the infant does not make the task much easier, for the temptation to steal glances at the infant's face is often quite overwhelming. However, both Trevarthen (1977, 1979) and Tronick *et al.* (1978) have described the effects on infants of mother's immobile face, the latter in the following terms:

"As in the normal interaction, the infant orients toward the mother and greets her. But when she fails to respond, he sobers and looks wary. He stares at her, gives her a brief smile, and then looks away from her. He then alternates brief glances toward her with glances away from her, thus monitoring her behaviour. He occasionally smiles briefly, yet warily in less and less convinced attempts to get the interaction back on track. As these attempts fail, the infant eventually withdraws, orients his face and body away from his mother with hopeless expression, and stays turned away from her.''

Tronick *et al.* found this sequence typical of all infants from the earliest age studied, i.e. from one month through to four months. The disturbance, moreover, spilled over into a subsequent normal interactive condition, in that the infants generally showed an initial period of wary monitoring of the mother.

Trevarthen's (1977, 1979) report confirms this picture: the infants observed by him also showed wariness and unhappiness, as their continuing efforts to elicit a reponse from the mother failed again and again. The infants withdrew or became overtly distressed—a response naturally difficult for the mothers to resist. It appears, however, that it is not just immobility of the mother's face that gives rise to such behaviour. Trevarthen, by a rearrangement of lighting either side of a partially reflecting window, had mothers talk with another adult while still apparently facing the infant. Again infants showed strong reactions of puzzlement and unhappiness as the mother's behaviour became non-contingent to their own.

The importance of these observations lies in their demonstration that the infant's socially directed behaviour quickly becomes linked to particular kinds of maternal responses, that it is sustained by them, and that their failure to appear in the usual manner or at the usual time has disruptive effects. Experimentally induced distortions must, for ethical reasons, be extremely brief; their study may, however, throw light on more permanent distortions such as found in cases of maternal depression or insensitivity. In this connection it is interesting to note that Stern (1977) finds the same withdrawal syndrome in infants under naturally occurring conditions of maternal over-stimulation as that described above for experimentally induced conditions: again there is a ''turning-off'' as though the infant is no longer able to cope. The nature of infant defence mechanisms in the face of distorted maternal behaviour has been the subject of much speculation, primarily by psychoanalysts; there is an enormous potential for moving this topic from the speculative to the empirical realm and throwing more informed light on disturbances in the mother–infant relationship.

(2) Child pathology

The disturbances considered above originate in the mother's behaviour; they may also stem from some pathological condition in the child which interferes with communicative behaviour.

Probably the most severe of such conditions is autism, for this syndrome centres on the child's gross inability to communicate with others in the normal way—through gaze or language or gesture. Autism is rarely diagnosed till after infancy, and data about behaviour during this period depend therefore usually on mothers' retrospective accounts (Schaffer, 1971). A report by Kubicek (1980) on a four-month-old infant, who was diagnosed two years later as autistic, is therefore of particular interest. Both this infant and his fraternal twin were filmed in face-to-face interactions with their mother. Marked differences occurred between the two sessions. For one thing, the autistic twin showed a much more limited range of social responses than the normal twin, in that he used primarily those responses which effectively limit social contact and ward off the mother's approaches (such as looking away, turning of head, increasing bodily tension during maternal stimulation, and so on). And for another, the autistic twin rarely varied the intensity of the responses he did use, maintaining instead a set, neutral expression throughout the interaction, and in this way failing to provide his mother with the positive feedback which one would normally expect. A structured interaction did occur, but it was based on a maternal approach–infant avoidance pattern that rarely varied.

In most cases of autism one finds virtually all channels of communication severed. In other cases of infant pathology just one such channel may be unavailable, and it becomes of interest to determine the extent to which alternate means can be used to compensate for the blockage. The tragic occurrence of infant blindness provides one such example, and thanks to the sensitive observations by Fraiberg (1977) some insight into this condition is available. As Fraiberg makes clear, blindness in the child makes enormous demands on a mother's adaptive capacities. The absence of eye contact *per se* represents a considerable communicative barrier, for mothers tend to interpret it as a state of "no interest". The blind infant is, of course, unaware of the many facial, gestural and bodily signals which are continuously emitted by his social partner; the comparative paucity of spontaneous vocalizations in blind infants may well be due to being cut off from such a rich source of eliciting stimuli. It is, however, not only the child's receptive but also his productive communicative abilities that are affected, for the absence of eye language prevents him from sending those visual signals that let a mother know when a child is attending to her and ready for her contribution. The bland facial expression so often found in the blind is similarly a communicative barrier that makes the interactive task so difficult for the mother.

Yet despite these obstacles and despite the very great reliance normally placed on visual exchange, Fraiberg's follow-up descriptions make clear that mothers can overcome these problems—either spontaneously or with professional help. Alternate channels of communications are resorted to: mothers learn, for instance, that gross tactile or kinaesthetic stimuli can be used to elicit smiling—stimuli such as bouncing, tickling, nuzzling, and so on, which come to have the same effect that normally the sight of the mother's smiling face has. And to compensate for the lack of the infant's facial expressiveness, mothers learn to attend to the child's hands: when presented with a toy, for instance, the blind infant's facial expression suggests that he is "bored"; attention to his hands, on the other hand, tells a different story, for they may be very busy exploring the toy and giving every indication of interest. Once the mother learns to shift her attention from face to hands she can, as Fraiberg put it, "read an eloquent sign language of seeking, wooing, preference and recognition, which becomes increasingly differentiated during the first 6 months."

Whatever part vision normally plays in early social interaction, its unavailability need not prevent communication. No one particular modality is a *sine qua non* for human interaction. This point is emphasized in a study by Adamson *et al.* (1977) of a sighted infant reared by blind parents. Admittedly, a number of interactive problems were evident in this case: for instance, the mother's tendency to seek information about the infant during feeding by lightly running her fingers over his face elicited inappropriate rooting responses and so disrupted the feed; in face-to-face interactions the infant came to avert his gaze from the mother's bland expression in the same way that we described above for experimentally induced blandness. Nevertheless, mother and child soon learned to establish contact by other means such as body games (patting the infant, playing with its fingers, and eventually more complex reciprocal games) and, from the second half-year on, through the medium of objects that could be incorporated into playful interactive sequences. This picture of normality is confirmed by Collis and Bryant (1981) in the case of somewhat older children. As shown by case studies of four families, each with at least one blind parent and one sighted child in the age range 9 months to 2½ years, social interactions were remarkably little affected by the parent's handicap. Such families develop routines, based on sound and touch, that circumvent the lack of vision and, at least within this early age range, provide the children with social experiences that do not deviate too drastically from the norm.

Child pathology can, of course, take many forms, varying in severity and in the type of problems presented to the mother. Take the case of preterm infants (Brown and Bakeman, 1979; Field, 1979b; Goldberg *et al.*, 1980). Such children are characterized at birth by lowered responsiveness and poor behavioural organization: during feeds, for instance, their sucking patterns are less likely to show the on–off regularities found in term infants; they are more restless and distractible and provide the mother with fewer unambiguous cues as to their state and requirements. Considerable demands are thereby placed on the abilities of their caregivers, and no wonder that these are often overtaxed. Field (1977b), for instance, noted that mothers of preterm infants tended to provide stimulation during feeds that was not only excessive but also inappropriately timed in relation to the infant's behaviour. As Field (1980, p.115) put it:

"The picture emerging from these analyses . . . is one of a vicious cycle of the infant being relatively inactive and unresponsive, the parent trying to engage the infant by being more and more active or stimulating which, in turn, leads to more inactivity and unresponsivity on the part of the infant. Although the parent's activity appears to be directed at encouraging more activity or responsivity in the infant, that strategy, in fact, is counter-productive."

A similar picture emerges from descriptions of other forms of infant pathology. Rosetti Ferreira (1978), for instance, points to the problems faced by the mothers of malnourished infants, who (mainly because of lethargy) provide far fewer cues on which to base appropriate stimulation. And equally difficult is the task of the mothers of Down's Syndrome infants as described by Jones (1977): these children tended to emit vocalizations quickly on top of each other, with little room in between for the mother to respond. In consequence far more vocal overlapping was found, and the development of dialogues characterized by turn taking was thus considerably slowed down.

It should not be thought, however, that child pathology inevitably leads to an aberrant dyadic pattern. Take an observation by Sorce and Emde (1982) on Down's Syndrome infants. Noting that these children were considerably less emotionally expressive than normal children, these authors went on to describe how the mothers were much more likely to react even to low-intensity emotional signals than mothers generally do—as though they had recalibrated their responsiveness threshold to ensure that the child was not deprived of interactional experience as a result of an inherently depressed level of signalling. Mothers of normal infants confronted by the same Down's Syndrome children did not respond so readily, suggesting that the recalibration depended on experience with these children. Thus mothers can learn to compensate for infants' diminished or deviant capacities to participate in social interaction, thereby providing a clear illustration of the way in which the parent–child system as a whole may continue to function satisfactorily despite some deficiency in one part, thanks to adjustments being made in another part.

Whatever problems there may be, it should not be thought that the vicious cycle will inevitably become a permanent feature of the parent–child relationship. As Sameroff and Chandler (1975) have pointed out, the existence of an initial condition in the child, such as prematurity, does not in and by itself enable one to predict long-term developmental outcome. That depends on how the condition impinges on the particular caregiving environment into which each individual child is born. In some such environments the initial difficulties may be exaggerated, in others attenuated, and if remedial help is to be provided it clearly becomes important to identify the specific child–environment combinations that are at risk. There is certainly plenty of evidence to show that people do escape from the vicious cycle: thus Goldberg *et al.* (1980), following up preterm infants to the end of the first year, found that the interactive disturbances present early on tended to diminish with time in the sample as a whole. Early pathology, it is clear, does not inexorably lead to later pathology.

Nevertheless, one should not underestimate the considerable burden placed on the caregivers of a child who is in any way deficient at birth in his capacities to fit into the social environment. A lack of predictability is the common feature of such cases. When the partner fails to respond as expected, the other person can adjust within certain limits. Parents in particular, by virtue of their greater maturity, can compensate for the infant's deficiencies, retune their own behaviour and find alternate modes of access. Infants too are surprisingly adaptable; yet for both adult and child there are limits beyond which mutuality can no longer be achieved, and it is these that define the area of dyadic pathology.

Conclusions

Around 2 months of age the child appears to "discover" the social partner, and for the next few months great fascination is shown in other people as stimulus objects. Face-to-face interactions thus become particularly satisfying experiences for both child and parent. The adult is, however, more than just a static source of interest; she is an individual almost continuously in action as she busily sets up, maintains, monitors and guides the to-and-fro with the child. An enmeshing of her responses with those of the child is therefore required; how to bring about such interweaving of action sequences in face-to-face situations is the principle interactive issue for the couple at that period.

Dyadic interchange is a highly intricate process, which adults generally carry out so smoothly that they are not even aware of the diverse skills they require to bring it about. Infants' skills are far more limited: no aspect of their behaviour at this age period suggests that they are as yet able to view their actions as helping to set up jointly constructed events. Nevertheless, the dyadic interchanges in which they are involved appear in many respects as integrated and orderly as those among more mature individuals — a tribute to the willingness of the parent to assume the responsibility of ensuring that an interaction does proceed. It is up to her to compensate for whatever interactional deficiencies the child still has — hence devices such as slowing down and repetition in order to make allowance for the child's limited information processing ability; hence also the mother's watchfulness in order constantly to adjust her behaviour in the light of feedback from the child; and hence also the ability (within limits) of recalibrating her input when confronted by an unresponsive child.

A picture of most impressive sensitivity on the part of the parent thus emerges, illustrated strikingly by her near-constant responsiveness that is reported by many studies of early face-to-face interaction. There is, however, one important reservation to bear in mind: most of such studies have been carried out under laboratory or other specially set-up conditions where there is little to distract the parent and where she is thus free wholly to devote herself to the child. There have been few investigations of the influence of other contexts; however, we shall return to this theme in a later chapter when we consider how adult–child interaction is affected by such possible distractions as the presence of other people.

One other point also needs stressing, and that is that the effectiveness of dyadic interchange does not in itself allow one to make statements about the respective skills of the individual participants. As has already been pointed out, conclusions about *interactions* are different from conclusions about *interactants*; yet, on the basis of the former, some authors have been tempted into ascribing considerable competence to individual infants, describing their behaviour in terms of "primitive intentions", "expectations", "communicative skills", "readiness to share", and so forth. Such terms are highly interpretative: rarely have the respective contributions of adult and child first been separated; where they have there is every indication that, at this early age, interchanges proceed so smoothly because of the supportive role played by the adult. There is no doubt, of course, that parents generally impute motives, skills and intentions to their infants, making them thus more "human" in their eyes. However the fact that parents think children start life as real persons tells us something about parents, not about children.

Nevertheless, even in the short period between 2 and 5 months infants are already acquiring some of the competence required for social interaction. There have been very few studies that have traced changes over age and our knowledge is therefore still limited; it does appear, however, that interchanges gradually become more symmetrical during this period, that children's actions become less responsive and more autonomous, that memory of previous encounters begins to exert its influence, and that infants generally become more competent in handling the information presented by the other person with speed and efficiency. It seems plausible that the precise nature of interactive experience provided by the child's caretakers will determine the rate at which the child acquires such competencies, for example that the more sensitive the parent is in interlinking her responses to his the sooner he will learn to participate as an active partner. However, as yet there is little evidence to substantiate such expectations.

4   Topic Sharing

Around the age of 5 months a marked change takes place in the nature of social interactions. From now on the child's encounters with other people increasingly occur around objects—third parties, as it were, that form the focus of the encounters. While much of the first half year was concerned with the regulation of mutual attention between parent and child, now the basis of mutuality shifts as environmental features come to be incorporated into the interaction. Rattles, buttons, spoons, blocks, bits of paper—these and any other object that the child can lay his hands on and explore come to form the content of the interaction; they are the topics which the participants must learn to share if meaningful encounters are to occur. How to structure the interaction around such external topics is the main issue to which adult and child must now address themselves.

In a sense, every interaction has a topic. In the early months of life, however, the topic arises from within the dyad itself: it is the mother's funny face which she pulls to amuse the infant and keep him attentive, or the child's toes that she repeatedly wiggles for him, or the vigorous movement sensations that she provides when bouncing him on her knee. Such personal topics remain; increasingly, however, they come to be supplemented by topics introduced from outside the dyad on which the child can directly act and which he can control himself. For a time it seems as though the child switches from a fascination with human beings to a fascination with objects, and during this period it is, as we shall see, largely up to the adult to convert the child's object play into a social situation. It is as though the child can attend to only one thing at a time, person or object, and so, having familiarized himself with the parent in the early months, he now turns to the world of things and, even during a joint play session, devotes his attention mostly to toys rather than to the parent. Flexible coordination of attention to both person and object comes later; until then the parent must take primary responsibility for any sharing of topics that is to occur.

The factor mainly responsible for relocating social interactions on this new plane is the development of manipulation in the child. The onset of this ability around the age of 5 months is, of course, preceded by a developmental history that goes back a considerable time: as Bower (1974) points out, all of the components involved in reaching and grasping can be found in foetus at a conceptual age of 14 to 16 weeks. But such components initially appear in isolation; thus the infant in the early weeks of life is already capable of visually orienting to an object, reaching for it, contacting it or grasping it, yet eliciting any one of these responses will not, as later, bring about the whole sequence (White, 1971). The child may look without reaching; he will touch without wishing visually to inspect. It is the infant's achievement around 5 months that the constituents can now be put together and form an integrated behaviour pattern: the child, that is, can now reach for and obtain objects under visual guidance. Manipulative behaviour at that age is, of course, still a long way from being the precisely adjusted, economically executed activity that it will eventually become; it has nevertheless advanced to a point where it becomes relatively suddenly one of the most prominent features of the child's behaviour, enabling him vastly to extend his direct actions upon the environment, to supply his own stimulation, and to discover the varied potential of objects by varied actions upon them. No wonder the child's interests appear to switch from humans to things. In their longitudinal study of face-to-face interactions Kaye and Fogel (1980) found a drop in visual attention to the mother from 70·1% of the session at 6 weeks of age to 32·8% at 26 weeks; the mothers moreover reported that they no longer felt the face-to-face situation to be appropriate at the older age, wanting instead to incorporate objects into their play and to share with the child reactions to external events.

How to bring about such sharing is thus the new issue confronting parent and child. A number of devices have evolved whereby mutual attention to an external topic can be brought about: direction of gaze, gestures such as pointing, object contact and referential language. The last of these has probably received most attention: words can stand for things, and by introducing them into the dialogue one person can share with another his particular interests. Joint attention thus achieved is the basis on which further discussion can then take place (Bruner, 1977). Long before the onset of language, however, routines for achieving joint reference have already appeared. Given the child's newly developed interest in the world of things the parent needs to home in on the same attentional focus, and for that matter the child too will in due course want to ensure that he can draw the adult's attention to particular features of the environment. There must therefore be procedures which enable the individual to communicate his interest of the moment to other people, and it is the development of these procedures during early childhood that we need to examine.

Gaze direction

In face-to-face interaction looking at the other person has obvious communicative significance—even, as we have seen, in infancy. What has been less discussed is the communicative significance of seeing another person's gaze directed at some other feature of the environment. And yet we need only consider the familiar example of seeing somebody in a crowded street craning his neck and staring at a building opposite: we automatically follow his gaze in an attempt to identify the focus of his interest and—in common with most other passers-by—thereby share whatever he is attending to. This everyday example illustrates, first, that another person's visual behaviour can have interactive significance and secondly that the ability to identify the focus of interest represents an important social skill. Joint visual attention entails topic sharing and may constitute the first step in a whole sequence of further interaction.

(1) Visual coorientation

While mutual gaze refers to two individuals attending to each other, the term "visual coorientation" indicates joint attention to some specific aspect of the environment. It can be observed among infants and their mothers at quite an early stage and it plays an increasingly important role in their inter- actions.

Collis and Schaffer (1975) recorded the behaviour of mothers and infants (aged 5 and 10 months) in a laboratory observation room which contained a number of large, prominent and brightly coloured toys. Otherwise the room was bare, except for a chair on which the mother sat with the infant on her knee. Analysis of video recordings indicated two main findings. In the first place, it was noted that there was a strong tendency for both mother and child to be attending to the same toy at the same time—the phenomenon of visual coorientation. And in the second place, when examining how this was brought about, it emerged that almost invariably it was the infant that led and the mother then followed. In other words, the infant visually took the iniative by spontaneously looking from one toy to another while the mother, closely monitoring his behaviour, immediately followed his gaze and looked at the same toy. The infants, in this particular situation, rarely followed the mother's gaze (see Table 2).

A number of points can be made about these observations. They illustrate, in the first place, one way in which mutual reference to an external topic comes about between mother and infant. The infant's gaze clearly exercises a powerful effect on the mother: it is a signal to which she responds readily. Attention is a function generally treated as a purely individual, within-the-person phenomenon; here we see, however, that it also has interpersonal significance in that one individual's attentive behaviour may give rise to predictable consequences in the behaviour of other individuals.

Table 2. *Visual following of partner's gaze to a specific target by infants and by mothers.*

Mother-infant pairs	Total number of mother's looks	Number followed by infant	Total number of infant's looks	Number followed by mother
A1	61	6[a]	44	11[b]
A2	79	3	41	7
A3	26	0	16	6[a]
A4	57	2	23	9[b]
A5	109	1	18	14[b]
A6	61	1	37	15[b]
A7	79	3	52	18[b]
A8	69	3	117	43[b]
B1	45	2	24	12[b]
B2	69	6	74	21[b]
B3	40	1	8	2
B4	109	4	82	54[b]
B5	51	8	49	27[b]
B6	94	13	99	48[b]
B7	101	6	16	4[c]
B8	72	0	32	10[b]

[a]$p < 0.01$, [b]$p < 0.001$, [c]$p < 0.05$. (From Collis and Schaffer, 1975)

In the second place, the observations highlight the role which the mother's sensitivity to her child's behaviour plays. Given the rapidity of changes in gaze direction, a very precise sense of timing on the part of the mother is required if she is to home in on the same target as the child. There is, of course, no suggestion that mothers follow each and every one of the infant's looks; a sufficient number are, however, followed to convert the infant's experience into a joint experience. Once more emphasis is laid on the temporal parameters of the interactive episode.

However, visual coorientation is important not only in its own right but also because of its consequences. Sharing a mutual topic is not an end in its own right; it is rather the focus around which further interaction can occur. In the above study, for instance, it was frequently noted that a mother not only looked at the same object as her infant but that she would then elaborate upon their mutual interest by pointing to the toy and verbally labelling and commenting upon it, and thereby providing a potential context for semantic learning. What is more, by monitoring the infant's focus of attention the mother is given information about the likely future course of the infant's behaviour, enabling her to take anticipatory action by, say, removing out of harm's way the precious vase which so intrigues him or, on the contrary, bringing nearer some desirable but innocuous object.

The mother's use of visual coorientation as a context for further input is illustrated in a study by Collis (1977). By examining the temporal contiguity of this dyadic state with various features of maternal speech, Collis was able to demonstrate that labelling of particular features of the environment coincided with the infant's (and mother's) attention to them. Naming of objects, that is, was introduced in the context of the infant's own spontaneous attention to them: the coordination of visual and vocal inputs, ensured by the mother's careful timing, thus gave the infant the opportunity to extract from the situation information concerning the relationship between certain words and their referents. For purposes of naming the mothers appeared to select visual coorientation as the appropriate context; for other sorts of speech, on the other hand, this particular context was not necessarily regarded as the best. The coincidence of child attention and adult input is one to which we shall return: the tutorial function performed by the adult of ensuring such coincidence is a constant factor in understanding the outcome of many kinds of early interactions.

(2) The infant's ability to follow gaze direction

So far we have considered situations in which visual coorientation was achieved as a result of the *mother* following the infant's gaze. Other studies have concerned themselves with the *infant's* ability to appreciate the significance of another's gaze direction, mainly in order to determine at what age this ability first becomes evident.

Scaife and Bruner (1975) tested infants in the age range 2 to 14 months by confronting them with an experimenter who, having made eye-contact with the infant, turned his head 90° to the left or to the right. The proportion of infants giving a positive response on at least one of the two trials given was found to increase steadily with age. Collis (1977), however, in discussing these results has pointed out that it is necessary to take into account the chance level of responding, and by calculating this has concluded that it is not till 8 months that Scaife and Bruner's subjects performed significantly better than chance. Certainly by 12 months there is unequivocal evidence that gaze following takes place, though, as Butterworth and Cochrane (1980) point out, success depends on such situational factors as the position of the target relative to the infant: anything outside the infant's peripheral visual field presents considerable difficulties at this early age. Even at 18 months infants frequently failed to locate the adult's locus of interest when it was in the area behind the infant. By the age of 2, on the other hand, children seem to be much more adept: Masangkay *et al.* (1974) placed toys to the right and to the left of children and also above them and on the floor just in front. More than half the 2-year-olds correctly responded when asked to identify the toy looked at by an experimenter seated opposite.

It is highly likely, as with so many developmental functions, that there is no *one* specific age of onset for this skill, but that the age at which one can first detect it depends greatly on the particular task demands of the test situation employed. These refer not only to the location of the target but also to the precise cues which the adult provides when fixating that target. Such cues include the turning movement of the head towards the target, turning the eyes, the orientation of the head and the orientation of the eyes. In an attempt to determine the role played by these various cues, Lempers (1979) employed three conditions: (1) the experimenter turned head and eyes while the child was watching; (2) the experimenter's head and eyes were oriented towards the target, having turned while the child's attention was elsewhere; (3) only the eyes of the experimenter turned, his head remaining still. Results from three age groups, namely 9, 12 and 14 months, are summarized in Table 3. Due to the small number of subjects, conclusions must be tentative. It does seem, however, that at 9 months following another person's gaze was low under all conditions tested, and that at the two older ages rather more successes were obtained in the first condition, i.e. when the cues of both orientation and movement were present.

Table 3. *Number of children performing correctly or incorrectly under three conditions of eye gaze (for description see text).*

	9 ms.	12 ms.	14 ms.
Condition (1)			
Correct	3	10	11
Incorrect	9	2	1
Condition (2)			
Correct	0	6	5
Incorrect	5	3	3
Condition (3)			
Correct	0	5	5
Incorrect	4	3	5

(Adapted from Lempers, 1979)

One can conclude that by the end of the first year another person's gaze direction is becoming a meaningful signal to the infant. The onus for topic sharing from then on rests no longer exclusively with the mother: now the infant does not just attract but is also attracted by another's interest, and the relationship becomes a more balanced one in consequence. There is still a great deal to be found out about the precise mechanisms responsible for bringing about visual coorientation; for the time being we are at least able to draw attention to this phenomenon and the role it plays in bringing adult and child together.

Pointing

Of all the ways of indicating one's own interest and attempting to induce another person to share that interest pointing is most likely to come to mind. It is a highly visible gesture, and in comparison with gaze direction it is less subtle and ambiguous in its intention. It is found in all cultures and everywhere takes the identical form: the arm extended (though not necessarily fully) and one finger (always the appropriately named index finger) extended from the hand. As Werner and Kaplan (1974) describe it, pointing is the most "specialized motoric means for the expression of reference." To study its beginnings we must consider not only the child's use of the gesture but also his comprehension of other people's pointing.

(1) Comprehension

As with the ability to follow gaze direction, it would be misleading to give one particular age when a child first becomes capable of correctly comprehending the meaning of pointing, i.e. of visually following the direction of another person's pointing finger to its target. It is true that at a very early age infants show no appreciation whatsoever of the significance of this gesture: their most likely response is to look at the extended hand but not beyond it. At a much later age there is also no doubt that children have acquired the meaning of pointing and that they are able correctly to determine the target so indicated under virtually all circumstances. In between, however, there is a developmental period during which they may perform correctly under some circumstances, but not under others. Assessment of their ability then depends to a large extent on the particular task requirements to which they are subjected.

Success during this transitional period depends on at least the following situational factors: (1) the relative position of infant, pointing finger and target, (2) the distance of the target from the infant, and (3) the precise cues which the other person provides in performing the gesture.

The way in which the first of these factors affects infants' responses is illustrated in a study by Murphy and Messer (1977). Infants aged 9 and 14 months were placed in a high chair, with the mother seated on a stool alongside. They faced a one-way window, suspended in front of which were three toys well separated from each other. The mothers were asked to draw the infants' attention to these toys in any order and in any way they wished, with the one constraint that they remained seated. The behaviour of each mother–infant pair in the course of a five-minute session was recorded by a videocamera stationed behind the one-way window.

The infants' ability visually to locate the particular toy to which the mother pointed was found to vary according to the orientation of the toy relative to the infant and the mother. Three types of point were distinguished (Fig. 4): *across* the infant to the toy on his side, *forwards* to the toy in the middle of the array, and *away* from the infant to the toy on the mother's side. At 14 months there was no appreciable difference in the ability to follow in any orientation: for the most part all three types of point elicited successful following. At 9 months, on the other hand, success rate varied systematically according to the type of point: only when the mother pointed in the *away* direction were infants able to follow at a rate significantly above chance. A few infants were able to follow the mother's points *forwards*, but points directed *across* the infants' midline caused greatest difficulty.

The reason for the younger infants' differential performance is most likely to be found in the spatial separation of the pointing hand from the

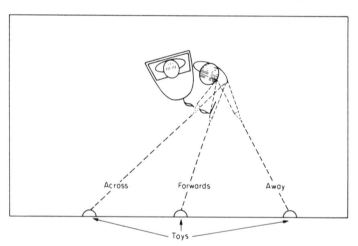

Fig. 4. *The three types of points that occurred during the observational sessions. (Murphy and Messer, 1977.)*

target. In the *away* position hand and toy are in the same visual field, and it takes only a slight shift of gaze by the infant to go from one to the other. The shift of gaze required is much greater in the case of the other two positions, and particularly so for points *across* when the infant must move his gaze through an angle of 90°. Under these circumstances the infants usually looked at the mother's arm in front of them, often then catching sight of the toy just behind the arm, i.e. the middle one which the mother was not in fact pointing to.

It appears therefore that at 9 months there is as yet no true understanding of the indicative meaning of the pointing gesture. The infant's attention is attracted by the hand, and he will look at the target only by chance when it happens to appear in the same visual field into which the moving hand has drawn him. As Millar and Schaffer (1972, 1973) have shown, younger infants have great difficulty in integrating behaviour to spatially separate stimuli: their attention to one stimulus appears to preclude responding to another that is outside the immediate visual field (part of the "out of sight, out of mind" phenomenon). To use the pointing finger as a signal to go beyond the visual field of that finger is therefore not yet within the younger infant's ability. As Murphy and Messer (1977) put it:

"The development of the infant's ability to follow points in a variety of circumstances probably takes place through a progression from the 'easier' points, when he stumbles from the hand to the relevant object, to the more 'difficult' points which entail an ability to perceive that the finger is an important directive cue which is directing the infant's gaze away from the visual field of the pointing hand. It is likely that the infant's awareness of the importance of the finger as a directive signalling device develops out of his success in following points where the relevant toy is not far removed from the finger. Concurrently, the infant may start to generalize his looking response so that points where there is a larger angle between the object and the hand are now followed. This progression is facilitated by a certain amount of redundancy in the environment. There are a limited number of salient features in the surroundings to which the mother points and thus the accuracy which is required of the infant as he attempts to work out the specific direction of the point is considerably reduced" (Murphy and Messer, 1977, p.352).

The second situational influence which we listed, namely the distance of the target being pointed at, was examined by Lempers (1979). Infants aged 9, 12 and 14 months were administered a series of tasks to assess their comprehension of pointing. In one task the object pointed to was only about 50 cm from the adult's finger, while in another it was at least 2½ metres away. As Table 4 shows, the *near* condition was substantially easier than the *far* condition: even at 9 months the majority of infants were able successfully to follow the pointing finger to a target only 50 cm away. In fact these results can be explained in the same terms as those obtained by Murphy and Messer: nearness of finger and target means that the infant can fairly readily see both simultaneously, and it is therefore quite likely that his gaze meets the target accidentally. A distant target makes it more likely (though not inevitable) that it is not located in the same visual field as the pointing finger, and to succeed under these conditions requires the child to understand the symbolic meaning conveyed by pointing, i.e. that he must search in the direction indicated by the finger.

Table 4. *Number of children performing correctly or incorrectly, targets pointed at either near or far*

	9 ms.	12 ms.	14 ms.
Near condition			
Correct	9	0	0
Incorrect	3	12	12
Far condition			
Correct	1	8	9
Incorrect	11	4	3

(Adapted from Lempers, 1979)

We should note, however, that distance introduces one further complication, namely the likelihood of other objects intervening between finger and target. In the two studies just referred to, both conducted under laboratory conditions, such distractions had been removed; in real life, however, the environment is never that tidy. It then becomes necessary not merely to follow the general line of regard indicated but to select rather precisely which one of various alternatives is the correct object of attention. The closer the objects are to one another the more sophisticated the individual has to be in being able to follow the precise direction of the point, and no doubt some developmental progression occurs in this respect. Beyond a certain limit, however, pointing ceases to be of help as a referential device for even the most sophisticated subject and then, as we shall see, the much more precise means of verbal reference becomes a necessity.

The third situational factor which appears to affect comprehension of pointing refers to the cues provided by the person performing this gesture. Again the study by Lempers (1979) illustrates this aspect. In one task the adult first engaged the child's attention and called his name; then, when eye-to-eye contact had been established, he extended his arm in the direction of the target while continuing to look straight at the child. In another task the adult extended his arm while the child's attention was diverted away from him, and only then did he call his name. Thus in both tasks the adult's gaze towards the object was eliminated as a cue, but only the second task eliminated the movement of the hand being extended. When the target was nearby the success rate achieved under these two conditions did not differ: it appears that the orientation of the hand was sufficient under these circumstances to direct the child's attention appropriately. However, with a more distant target a difference did emerge, at least for 9-month-old infants: these do require the additional movement cue for success, while infants of 12 months and older can respond appropriately on the basis of hand orientation alone.

Taking the gesture to pieces in order to study the role played by each separate cue inevitably gives rise to somewhat unnatural situations. For instance, it is highly unlikely that the adult would steadily fixate the child while extending his hand to the object of interest: as Murphy and Messer (1977) have described, mothers nearly always look up at the target as they begin to point and only then will they turn to look at the child. However, for the sake of understanding gestural communication such experimental analysis is justified; let us also remember, though, that under natural conditions the adult will provide the child with considerable redundancy of cues: he will look towards the object, point to it, refer to it verbally, and if need be make manipulative contact with it by tapping, shaking, etc. Under such circumstances children are likely to succeed at a higher rate and at an earlier age than under laboratory conditions, thus again highlighting the importance of thinking of this ability as initially tied to a particular set of conditions. The folly of expecting it to emerge in full-blown, all-or-nothing fashion at some particular age is obvious.

(2) Production

The last conclusion applies equally to the development of the child's ability himself to produce this gesture. There has been much argument as to the age when pointing first emerges: Lempers *et al.* (1977), for instance, review some of the divergent findings of the early "baby biographers" as to age of onset of pointing, and in similar vein some infant developmental tests attempt to provide a specific age as the norm for the first appearance of this skill. Again, however, it is more fruitful to think of an age range within which pointing may appear under some conditions but not under others.

In the study by Murphy and Messer (1977) pointing was found to be rare among their 9-month-group. Three of the 12 infants in this group pointed, but with only 5 points between them. In the 14-month-group 8 out of 12 infants spontaneously pointed, producing 2 to 28 points each. A further infant was seen to point outside the testing session. Results by Lempers (1979) on spontaneous pointing indicate a comparable picture. At 9 months three out of twelve infants were observed to point, at 12 months six and at 14 months 11 infants out of groups of 12 pointed. Similarly Leung and Rheingold (1981) found that the proportion of infants who spontaneously pointed to interesting stimulus objects increased from 1 out of 8 at 10½ months to 9 out of 16 at 12½ months, 12 out of 16 at 14½ months, and to all 8 infants at 16½ months. In all these studies distal objects, mostly of considerable salience, were employed, while an interested adult remained close to the child. Under these circumstances pointing appears to be rare before 10 months and increasingly common after 12 months.

When pointing first appears, however, it differs in a number of ways from the more mature form. For one thing it may be ambiguous with regard to its target: as Murphy and Messer (1977) noted, in comparison with the mothers' gesture pointing, even in their 14-month-group, was often ill-directed and vague. In addition these authors found that some children, after pointing at the object, would look away leaving the pointing finger still directed at the toy in which they were clearly no longer interested. But much more significantly, it appears that pointing at first emerges in a non-communicative fashion. Bates *et al.* (1975) provide a detailed description of one infant, Carlotta, whom they observed over a period of some months. At 13 months of age this child was first found to use pointing as a clearly communicative gesture:

> "This is all the more surprising, since a pointing gesture has been available in non-communicative sequences for several weeks, in examination of small book figures, and in orienting toward novel and interesting sounds and events. However, these earlier pointing sequences never involve a search for adult attention. Carlotta may use them while alone in a room and unaware of our observation; when others are present she does not point and then turn around or look toward the adult, seeking confirmation or approval. In fact, when Carlotta finally does use the pointing gesture to communicate with adults, she passes through a peculiar transitional period that looks very much like a rough effort to put two previously separate schemes together . . . She would first orient toward the interesting object or event, extending her arm and forefinger in the characteristic pointing gesture while uttering a breathy sound 'ha'. Then she would swing around, point at the adult with the same gesture, and return to look at the object and point toward it once again. This series of steps — point at object, point at adult, point at object — puts together in chained form the components that eventually form the smoother deictic act of simultaneously pointing at the object while turning to the adult for confirmation." (Bates *et al.*, 1975, p.217).

We shall return later to the suggestion that children learn to combine object schemes and person schemes into one communicative activity. Here let us note that Carlotta's behaviour fits in well with the proposal made by

Werner and Kaplan (1974), that a stage of pointing-for-self occurs before pointing-for-others. They believe that the gesture, when it first appears, is indicative of the child's newly found ability to distinguish self from object, knower from known, and that it thus facilitates the psychological distancing between the child and the object of reference. Pointing is therefore initially an attentional mechanism for the development of "objects of contemplation"; sharing with others only comes later.

This view contrasts with that put forward by Vygotsky (1966), who believes pointing arises from social transactions and is initially a gesture for others and only later one for the child himself. The developmental origins of pointing, according to Vygotsky, are the infant's unsuccessful reaching for objects to which the mother then responds by giving him the object:

> "In the beginning the pointing gesture is merely an unsuccessful grasping movement . . . The child tries to grasp too distant an object but its hand reaching for the object remains hanging in the air and the fingers make grasping movements . . . Here for the first time arises the pointing gesture in itself . . . When the mother comes to the aid of the child and comprehends his movement as a pointing gesture the situation essentially changes. The pointing gesture becomes a gesture for others. The child's unsuccessful grasping movement gives rise to a reaction not from the object but from another person. The original meaning to this unsuccessful grasping movement is thus imparted by others. And only afterwards, on the basis of the fact that the child associates the unsuccessful grasping movement with the entire object situation, does the child himself begin to treat this movement as a pointing gesture" (Vygotsky, 1966, p43).

Vygotsky is thus placing the onset of pointing into his well known developmental scheme, whereby behavioural phenomena first appear in an *intermental* context and become *intramental* only subsequently. That mothers do a tremendous amount of interpreting of infants' behaviour and that, by completing the child's action they provide him with feedback as to its interpersonal significance, is not in doubt. However, as far as the relation between reaching and pointing is concerned, there is little convincing evidence. Murphy and Messer (1977) observed *both* reaching and pointing to occur towards distal objects; what is more, reaching increased with age as did pointing, and the only infants in their younger group who pointed were also the only ones who reached. There is thus no indication that pointing took the place of reaching — at least within the age range covered. It is also significant that Leung and Rheingold (1981) found reaches, unlike pointing, to be accompanied by "demand" vocalizations; it seems therefore that the two kinds of response serve rather different functions — "give me" and "look at that" respectively.

A rather more convincing explanation of the origins of pointing emerges from the descriptive account given by Shinn (1900, quoted by Lempers *et al.*,

1977) of the way in which pointing first manifested itself in the ninth
month of one particular infant:

> "The power of communication was considerably increased in this month by the
> acquisition of one exceedingly useful sign. The way in which it was developed
> is an interesting example of the evolution of such signs. First the baby began to
> use her forefinger tip for specially close investigations; at the same time she
> had the habit of stretching out her hands towards any object that interested
> her—by association, no doubt with touching and seizing movements.
> Combining these two habits, she began to hold her forefinger separate from
> the others when she thus threw out her hand towards an interesting object;
> then, in the second week of the month, she directed this finger alone towards
> what interested her; and by the third week, the gesture of pointing was fairly in
> use." (Lempers *et al.*, 1977, p.219.)

It may well be that pointing to distal objects develops out of exploring close
objects; where the latter are small or two-dimensional (as in picture books)
the specialized innervation to the forefinger ensures that a more economical
movement is used than a whole-hand response. Certainly close objects elicit
more pointing than more distant ones; thus Murphy (1978) found a group of
9-month-old infants to produce a total of 43 points between them while
looking at a picture book, whereas a comparable situation but containing
distal objects produced only five points (thereby again highlighting the
influence of situational factors on the nature of the findings obtained). To
what extent one-finger exploration of near objects indeed developmentally
precedes pointing to distant objects, and the functional relationship
between these two patterns, remains an open issue. Most studies of pointing
have either involved cross-sectional designs or been based on tiny samples
or (as in the case of Vygotsky and of Werner and Kaplan) lacked altogether
an empirical base. Questions about the developmental origin of this gesture
(and also about the relationship between the onset of comprehension and
production) need detailed longitudinal studies before firm conclusions can
be reached.

(3) Pointing in a dyadic context

One can study pointing from either an individual or an interactive point of
view—that is either as a skill which individual children acquire and which
enables them to use and comprehend this gesture, or as a form of behaviour
that is embedded in the to-and-fro of the communicative interchange of two
or more people. So far we have discussed pointing largely from the former
point of view; we now turn to discuss how it is actually used within dyadic
exchanges.

Let us first consider how mothers set about getting the infant's attention by this means. In fact mothers of infants younger than about 9 months seem to know perfectly well that this is a useless gesture, as yet well beyond the child's comprehension (Murphy and Messer, 1977). Attention attracting devices are of a more immediate nature: the object is tapped, shaken, or (wherever appropriate) brought to the child. Distance cannot yet be spanned, certainly not by gestural means; the infant needs more active help in picking out the particular object which the mother wants to share with him. When Murphy and Messer asked mothers of 4 to 6 month-old infants to attract their attention to distal objects they found these women to adopt a very distinctive style. A lot of time was first spent by the mother waving her hand in front of the infant's eyes or clicking her fingers, and only when the mother was sure that she had the child's attention focussed on her finger would she then slowly extend her arm towards the object. The mother, that is, broke down the gesture into its component parts (attention being obtained first to the speaker, then guided from there to the target), executing each part in slow motion in order not to lose the child, and then spanning the distance by bringing the finger into the same visual field as the target. Even so these young infants often failed to follow—whereupon some mothers would then simply, in apparent desperation, physically twist the infant's head in the desired direction!

The mothers of the older infants observed by Murphy and Messer also frequently first made sure that the child's attention was on them, though a quick tap on the arm was usually sufficient. In all instances, however, mothers carefully monitored the effect of their behaviour on the child, precisely synchronizing their looking towards both the object and the child with their pointing (See Figures 5 and 6). In most cases the onset of pointing was accompanied by starting to look at the toy within the same 0·1 sec., and then, within approximately one further second, the mother looked back at the infant. In this way she could assess the effect of her gesture and take appropriate further action.

It is the look back at the other person which, as far as infants are concerned, has been used to distinguish between pointing-for-self and pointing-for-others. Lempers (1979) found that up to 12 months of age the majority of points were unaccompanied by such looks, and that only from 14 months on did the majority of infants appear to check the effect of their behaviour on the adult. Caution is, however, required in "diagnosing" infants' communicative competence by this means: in a book-reading situation, where infants sat on their mothers' laps, Murphy (1978) observed hardly any direct looking at the other person—not even by two-year-olds, nor for that matter by the mothers themselves. The spatial arrangement was such that it did not lend itself easily to direct gazing; the partners could, however, show awareness of each other by other means. To classify pointing as communicative or not solely on the basis of accompanying looks without consideration of situational constraints is clearly not justified.

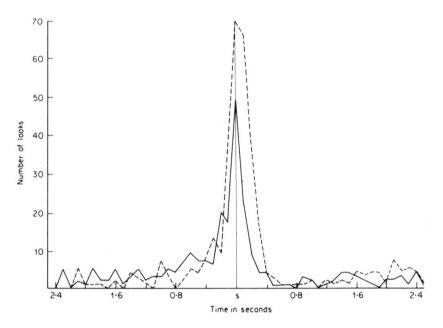

Fig. 5. *Looking patterns of mothers of nine- and 14-month-old infants towards the toy at which they are pointing. The total number of looks by each group is plotted against the time at which a look started. S indicates the start of points; figures to the left of S indicate time before the point and those to the right of S time elapsed since the onset of pointing.* — — — — *Nine-month group;* ———— *14-month group. (Murphy and Messer, 1977.)*

Murphy's (1978) study provides a good illustration of the way in which pointing is used in the context of an ongoing dyadic interaction. Infants aged 9, 14, 20 and 24 months, and their mothers, were videorecorded while looking together at picture books. This is a situation which lends itself particularly well to studying the way in which the participants share their interests in the various topics (i.e. the pictures), the means that they use to attract the other person's attention, and the way in which they elaborate on the topics. As seen in Table 5, with increasing age an increase occurred in the incidence of pointing by both mothers and children. Infants' pointing rose particularly sharply between 14 and 20 months: at the former age the children had just discovered the joys of page turning, and were so busy practising this new skill as an activity in its own right that they spent relatively little time examining the pictures. The mothers, realizing this, also concentrated less on pointing and joined the infants' page turning activities. By 20 months the infants had become thoroughly competent at page turning and the mothers were consequently left free to concentrate on pointing, while at 24 months the rather frenzied page turning was no longer evident, the children appeared to be genuinely interested in looking at the pictures,

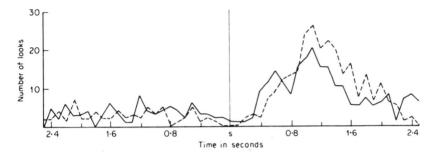

Fig. 6. *Looking patterns of mothers towards their infants (nine- and 14-months) before and after pointing. The total number of looks by each group is plotted against the time at which a look started. S indicates the start of points; figures to the left of S indicate time before the point and those to the right of S time elapsed since the onset of pointing. ————— Nine-month group; ————— 14-month group. (Murphy and Messer, 1977.)*

Table 5. *Incidence of pointing by mother and children in a picture book situation.*

	9 ms.	14 ms.	20 ms.	24 ms.
Mothers' points:				
Mean number	27.13	22·38	35·63	47·38
Range	2-56	12-37	13-66	10-85
Childrens' points:				
Mean number	5·38	6·38	40·25	27·50
Range	0-75	0-19	14-73	1-67

(Adapted from Murphy, 1978)

and the mothers again took a more active role in drawing attention to particular features. The manner of pointing also changed with age: both infants and mothers began increasingly to combine discrete points into "pointing strings", with anything up to 15 points strung together without any break between them. This is most likely a function of the infants' ability to take in more information as they get older: whereas the young infant would point to a cat and regard the picture as "done", the older child appreciates that the cat has ears, eyes, whiskers, etc., and marks his attention with a series of rapid points to all these details. The mothers adapted to this increasing competence of their children and also produced pointing strings as part of their commentary on the pictures.

The way in which mothers adjust to their children's behavioural characteristics is particularly well illustrated by the nature of their speech which accompanies pointing. Speech in general was found by Murphy to accompany pointing to a far greater extent than non-pointing activities; there were, however, also systematic variations according to type of speech. At 9 months the mothers did not verbalize a great deal; at 14 months, on the other hand, a considerable amount of naming went on, in that a large number of pictures pointed to by the mother were labelled at the same time. To a lesser though still significant extent this applied also to the infants' pointing: again the mother used such occasions of shared attention for tutorial purposes by introducing the verbal label of the object that the child was examining. By 20 months, however, the incidence of labelling had sharply declined, and instead mothers now mostly produced wh- questions. In other words, at the beginning of the second year, when the children were just learning to comprehend language and to acquire a vocabulary, the mothers concentrated on supplying verbal information. By the end of the second year, when the children had acquired a fund of labels, the mothers' speech was designed to demonstrate the child's knowledge by means of questioning him ("Who is this?" "What is that?", etc.).

Among the children, an association between pointing and vocalizing was not found in this study in the two younger age groups. Only from 20 months on was pointing a special occasion for simultaneous vocalizing. This was mainly a matter of naming, often in response to the mother's requests to supply the label. Gestural and linguistic means of reference thus came to be associated, and as a result one began to see in the children what was evident all along in the mothers, namely the use of multiple, simultaneously occurring cues when referring to particular environmental features. Communication, that is, had become multi-modal: initially an infant may only look at an object, subsequently he becomes capable of also indicating it by means of pointing, and then finally he is able to add speech as well with which to communicate to others the focus of his interest.

Pointing is an activity that in adults is unlikely ever to occur on its own. Instead, it is usually found in association with such other activities as looking and vocalizing with which it is closely synchronized. In young infants such synchronization is initially far more limited; they tend to perform one response at a time rather than perform a coherently integrated multi-response whole. Thus when pointing emerges it will first be performed on its own, without looking at the other person and without simultaneous other-directed vocalizing. Only with increasing age (and presumably practice) will it become possible to combine these previously disparate acts into communicative patterns distinguished by the sort of redundancy that makes for effective transmission of messages.

Manipulation

A much more immediate way of indicating one's interest in a tangible topic is by being — literally — in touch with it. It is more immediate than gazing or pointing because no physical distance is involved; it is also not a gesture but a direct action on the object in question. It is thus considerably less ambiguous than the other two devices mentioned, and in consequence it is the principal means used by parents to attract the attention of very young infants.

(1) Fostering social interaction through object manipulation

Waving, shaking and tapping a toy are all devices that an adult may quite deliberately employ in order to attract a child's attention to that object. Yet even when an individual contacts an object for no other reason than that he himself is interested in it, with no intention of influencing other people thereby, it may still have this effect and thus facilitate the occurrence of social interaction.

A study by Eckerman *et al.* (1979) illustrates this point. One-year-old infants observed an unfamiliar adult behave in three contrasting ways with toys in a laboratory observation room. In one condition the adult approached and sat down beside a toy, in another she not only approached but also manipulated the toy in a repetitive fashion, and in the third her manipulation of the toy was of a varied nature. A marked difference in the infants' behaviour was found between the first and the other two conditions. For one thing, toy manipulation elicited more attention than merely approach: the infants watched the adult for 93% of the time while she was handling the toy, as opposed to only 62% of the time during the approach condition. For another, the adult's manipulation of the toy markedly facilitated contact by the infant of the same toy, occurring on over 55% of trials and usually within 30 seconds of the time the adult first touched the toy. There was also a marked tendency for the actions performed by the infant to duplicate those performed by the adult. And finally, an increase in the incidence of such social responses as smiling and vocalizing to the adult suggested that not only attention to the toy but also the child's willingness to interact with the adult was affected.

These results illustrate the interpersonal significance of object manipulation. The type of manipulation, repetitive or varied, appeared not to matter; the mere fact that the adult was doing something with the toy attracted the child's attention and drew him towards it — and, for that matter, towards the adult. Eckerman *et al.* regard the child's approaching and contacting an object which another person is manipulating as a basic social skill, in that it may constitute the opening move in a series of interactions, all based on the child's ability to share the other person's focus of attention.

The magnetic quality of object manipulation can be seen especially clearly in peer interaction. Mueller and Rich (1976), during observations of a playgroup composed of five 1-year-old boys, were struck by the way in which toys — or, to be more precise, the actions performed on toys — could bring children together and keep them in contact for a short while at least. They documented the nature and frequency of children's "clusters", operationally defining these as periods of at least 10 sec. where three or more children focussed their attention on a single object or activity. These clusters were clearly not just an opportunity for several children to gather around the same toy at the same time; they were also perhaps the single most important mechanism whereby the children were brought into active contact *with one another*. And once in contact they were able to exercise and develop other, more direct, skills involved in social interaction. The very fact of being brought into proximity with other children in this way provided each child with an opportunity to expand his social repertoire and learn to integrate object play with person-directed responses. Object-centred clusters, that is, formed a context for social learning.

(2) Object manipulation and maternal speech

We have already seen that episodes of joint attention, brought about through visual coorientation or through pointing, are used by mothers as occasions for the introduction of speech, particularly of referential speech. A report by Messer (1978) illustrates that object manipulation functions in a similar manner.

Messer observed infants aged 11, 14 and 24 months in a free-play session in which the mothers were encouraged actively to participate. Two kinds of data were extracted from the videotaped sessions, namely toy manipulations by either partner and the verbal references to the toys made by the mothers. In checking the co-occurrence of these two kinds of responses, Messer found that between 73% and 96% of verbal references (depending on age and the type of reference) were to the particular toy that was at that moment being manipulated by either the mother or the child. The mothers, that is, showed the watchfulness we have already seen to be so characteristic of interactions with young children and consequently were able closely to synchronize their speech with ongoing manipulative activities.

Certain types of manipulation were especially closely associated with verbal reference, in particular one designated "mother brings and holds" — an action generally used to introduce a toy to the infant and attract his attention to it. Thus, timing their verbal responses in such a way that they occurred at appropriate points during the interaction, mothers were in a position to provide maximum help to the language-learning child: labels were supplied at times when the mother could be sure that the child's attention was focussed on the relevant toy; language, that is, was tied to the non-verbal context as defined by the child's own behaviour. Once a child has acquired some degree of verbal competence this close association is no longer necessary, and there were indeed indications in Messer's data that among the oldest group studied the synchrony between speech and manipulation was no longer as strong as at younger ages.

Referential speech

In the adult reference is accomplished primarily by verbal means. The advantages of this method over non-verbal means are vast: reference need no longer be confined to the here-and-now but can encompass spatially and temporally distant objects and events; abstractions as well as concrete objects can thereby be introduced; and a much greater degree of referential precision is possible, making correct identification considerably easier.

In the child, during the early stages of language acquisition, a great deal of speech serves a referential function. The discovery that things have names seems to afford the child an enormous amount of pleasure, so that naming comes to be indulged in for its own sake. Yet he also learns that naming has a communicative function, for others use the same sounds to indicate certain things and a sharing of meaning thus becomes possible. He can indicate to others by verbal means his focus of interest, and equally he can in this way comprehend other people's interests. Referring thus involves (a) indication to some external object or event, (b) the use of a conventional signal, and (c) some communicative intent on the part of the speaker.

(1) Label learning

Early vocalizations in infancy tend to express subjective states and activities rather than indicate particular external objects. To be regarded as referential, a vocalization must be characterized by:
(1) differential use, i.e. it must indicate a specific object or event (or class thereof) and not be applied indiscriminately;
(2) consistent use, i.e. that label and no other should be applied to a particular

object (a requirement, however, that needs to be relaxed under certain circumstances, as when the child learns that his father is not only "Daddy" but also "Joe", "Doctor", and occasionally a rather less polite term).

Given such criteria, it appears that a large part of early word acquisition is concerned with the learning of labels for things and people. Nelson (1973), in a longitudinal study of language development during the second year, classified the first 50 words spoken by her 18 subjects according to grammatical category, and found that nominals (i.e. words used to refer to the "thing world") represented the majority by far. Thus 65% of these children's words served as labels, as opposed to only 13% for action words—the next highest category. Specific names did not, however, predominate; on the contrary, most labels were used to refer to all members of a category (e.g. ball, car, doggie, etc.). Yet there were considerable individual differences in the extent to which labels were used, and accordingly Nelson found it useful to distinguish two groups of children: the *referential* group, whose language was largely object-oriented, and the *expressive* group, where language was used more for self-oriented purposes. In the one case the child is learning a language that is designed to cope with the things in his environment; in the other he is acquiring a personal-social language where words are used primarily for the expression of feelings, needs and social interaction. This difference must not, however, be exaggerated: as becomes apparent from an examination of Nelson's figures, even in the expressive group nominals represent the majority among the first 50 words learned—53%, as opposed to 75% for the referential group. Nelson suggests that the difference may depend to some extent on the mothers and their own linguistic preferences, but for one thing the correlation found for mothers' and children's communicative style does not indicate the cause–effect direction, and for another object labelling was high for all of the mothers. Thus an analysis of maternal language showed 41% of all utterances to contain labels—a trend that may well reflect the mothers' awareness of the object-centred interest of their children to which it is a direct response.

The kinds of labels which children first acquire tell one something about the children themselves—though precisely what is still a matter of some dispute. According to Nelson (1973, 1974), referential words are initially *function-based*: the words the child first acquires designate things to handle, to eat, to put on and take off—in short, they relate to those features in the environment that the child can directly act on. For the most part, therefore, they apply to manipulative and movable objects. In contrast is Clark's (1973) *perception-based* account, which proposes that it is the perceptual attributes of things (size, shape, sound, texture, etc.) that give rise to early word meanings. Form, not use, is thus singled out as the basis for semantic learning. Evidence from recent studies (Gentner, 1978; Prawvat and Wildfong, 1980; Tomikawa and Dodd, 1980) that have experimentally contrasted perceptual with function attributes favour Clark's view on the whole, suggesting that the content of meanings in the earliest stages of language acquisition is more likely to consist of perceptual than functional information. However, the basic point remains: children learn to label the things around them in a highly selective fashion that has little relation to frequency of exposure to either the word or the object, but that reflects the way in which the child imposes structure on his environment. It is an active, personal process, not a mechanically passive one.

Label learning is also a long-drawn out process, and not merely because of the need to accumulate a vocabulary. Quite apart from quantitative changes in the sheer number of words known, the way in which the child uses labels also undergoes changes. Bates *et al.* (1979) believes that a three-stage sequence can be detected in referential development, leading from comprehension to non-referential usage of names to true naming. Thus initially children show comprehension of other people's labelling, e.g. "Where's Daddy?" elicits the correct orientation. Such comprehension is, however, limited to just a few words and is found only within certain set, highly specific routines. Subsequently the child himself begins to produce labels, but initially in a non-referential manner, e.g. the sound "mama" is used as a general request sound for any listener. Only later on will that same word be used specifically in relation to the "correct" individual.

There are three basic discoveries that the child must make with regard to label learning: first, that objects have names; secondly, that some objects but not others can be grouped under the same name; and third, that names can be used for communicative purposes. As to the first, it may well be that names are acquired before the child realizes that they have a naming function. As McShane (1979) has put it, "While the environment can supply the child with names for objects and a context appropriate to the learning of these names it cannot supply the concept of naming. This the child must construct out of his or her own experience in the environment." The realization that words are names for objects is, according to McShane, a sudden discovery which may well account for the dramatic increase in naming that is frequently observed around the middle of the second year. Having acquired the concept of naming the child now puts it to active use by seeking to acquire as many labels as possible.

This discovery is, however, only the first step. The child must now develop hypotheses as to which objects particular labels refer to. Even the names of specific people present problems, as many an embarrassed mother has found out on hearing her child address the postman as "daddy". There is no automatic pairing of labels and objects; it appears rather that the child puts to the test various hypotheses as to what sound goes with what experience. Clark (1973) has pointed out one strategy which she believes children commonly employ in this respect. For instance, after hearing the word *dog*, the child might set up the hypothesis that this sound refers to one particular salient feature of the object, such as four-leggedness. Subsequently, on hearing the word dog, he will look round for anything with four legs and thus come to apply it to horses, cows and cats as well. There is thus initial over-generalization in the use of labels; only with the addition of other features will the child be able to narrow down the meaning of the term to its correct referent, so that his strategies for use coincide with those employed by his social partners. Not everyone agrees with the details of this account (e.g. Bowerman, 1978; McShane, 1979), though over-generalization as an initial phase preceding the use of correctly differentiated names has been confirmed by Carter (1978) on the basis of a very detailed analysis of language development in one child.

The third discovery, that labels can have a communicative function, occurs in the course of social interaction and we shall return to it below. Not only does the child acquire the same sounds for particular objects that other people use but he also learns that they *are* the same. Verbal reference, like the rest of language, must become conventionalized if it is to serve communicative purposes. Idiosyncratic labelling (indulged in by most young children) may often be amusing, but it can also be frustrating if others fail to comprehend the child's meaning. The main function of reference is, after all, the communicative one, and the discovery that a *sharing* of meaning can be accomplished by means of a particular sound can provide a powerful impetus towards conventionalization. If the word "teddy", spoken by the child, can result in the mother bringing him the desired toy, or if his labelling of a picture during a joint book reading session results in the mother also looking at that picture, the realization that labels have an interpersonal significance is bound to follow. Whether labelling-for-others is always preceded by a labelling-for-self phase has not yet been established. As we have seen, pointing is initially used in a non-communicative way before it becomes a social gesture; in so far as labelling emerges at about the same age it would be surprising if these two types of communicative techniques did not develop along similar lines.

What is apparent is the child's active role in respect of all aspects of label learning. This is no mere automatic paired-associates learning; it is a process where the child himself (though with decisive help from his caretakers) determines what is acquired. For one thing, as Nelson (1973) showed, the child selects particular features of his environment as worthy of labels—features that fit in with his own interests and activities. For another, as Clark (1973) has pointed out, he constructs hypotheses as to the sort of objects that can be grouped under the identical label. And further-more, he actively refines these hypotheses in the light of his social experience which tells him what is acceptable and what is not. A mechanical learning process, based on other people providing verbal labels in conjunction with particular perceptual experiences, clearly is not sufficient. A complete explanation of label learning may not yet be available, but that social as well as cognitive factors are implicated in the acquisition process is now generally accepted.

(2) Labelling in dyadic settings

The ability to attach particular sounds to objects is clearly quite a sophisticated achievement that requires certain cognitive skills for it to emerge, but it is in the context of social interaction that the ability manifests itself. Yet in many descriptions of language learning the child's social partner is all but forgotten; Piagetian-derived accounts in particular pay little heed to the efforts made by adults continually to structure the child's experience in order to provide him with meaningful content, verbal and otherwise. To Piaget language was a tool for thinking, not for communication; he saw the child as an essentially lonely creature, surrounded by an inanimate environment with which he was progressively trying to come to terms, but without the help of any other human being. That help surely needs to be acknowledged.

Perhaps the most obvious part which the child's social partners play in his label learning is in providing content. Adults let him know which sounds are acceptable and which are not; they supply the appropriate sounds in the first place and subsequently respond to the child's own productions in a manner that will affect his further efforts.

Were this all that adults did a conventional learning account might suffice to explain the process. But it is not only a matter of *what* labels are introduced but *how* they are introduced, and it is this aspect which has implications for the child's motivation to acquire and use labels and, more-over, to see them as vehicles for the sharing of meaning.

Above all, adults supply labels to children in a carefully timed manner — not arbitrarily but by taking account of the child's own ongoing activity and orientation. We have already made this point in stressing the use to which episodes of joint attention are put by mothers: Collis (1977) for visual coorientation, Murphy (1978) for pointing, and Messer (1978) for manipulation have all shown that such episodes are seen by mothers as particularly suitable occasions for the introduction of speech, and especially of labels referring to the specific topics to which mother and child are jointly attending. The coordination of visual and vocal input is thereby ensured, and mothers generally convey by tone of voice and by gesture an air of excitement into their labelling that inevitably affects the child's motivation to attend to the coordinated input. A great deal of object naming occurs in early interactions: in Murphy and Messer's (1977) study of pointing, toy naming by mothers accounted for 46% of all maternal utterances in the 14-months and 42% in the 9-months group, despite the fact that there were only three toys available in an otherwise relatively bare room. In a richer, more stimulating environment the incidence of labelling would surely have been even greater.

Labels form such an important feature of early speech that it is not surprising to find mothers making special efforts to mark their occurrence when talking to young children. Speech recorded by Messer (1980, 1981) in a joint play session with children 11 to 24 months old involving a number of different toys had the following characteristics:

(1) It was highly repetitive, so that there was a tendency for utterances to refer to the same object that had been referred to in the previous utterance.

(2) A change in verbal reference was generally accompanied by a parallel change in manipulative activity.

(3) Intervals between utterances referring to different toys were about twice as long as utterances referring to the same toy.

(4) Labels were most likely to be introduced in the first utterance after a verbal or nonverbal change of topic, when the child would be made especially attentive.

(5) Labels were generally the loudest word of an utterance.

(6) Labels were also highly likely to be the last word of an utterance and therefore (according to a recency effect) most likely to be remembered.

Some of these characteristics were most marked in the mothers' speech to the youngest children; this group in particular received help in attending to semantically important words.

The mother's introduction of labels is clearly not random in respect of the child's concurrent activity. It is embedded in an orderly manner in the to-and-fro of the dyad's interaction. As Ninio and Bruner (1978) put it: "The most striking characteristic of labelling activity is that it takes place in a structured interactional sequence that has the texture of a dialogue." Ninio and Bruner base this assertion on a longitudinal study of one mother–child pair whom they observed repeatedly between the ages of 8 and 18 months in a picture-book reading situation. As Murphy (1978) has also found, pictures appear to be a preferred vehicle for vocabulary teaching; further-more, this situation also provides an excellent opportunity for observing the interactive sequences of which labelling is a part. These sequences, according to Ninio and Bruner, take the form of a highly ritualized dialogue that is marked by a number of regularities. One of the most salient of these is the turn taking pattern which was found at all ages studied for their particular mother–child pair. From the start of the observation period alternation was almost perfect, with only about 1% of utterances occurring simultaneously. As we have noted for other dialogues, this was largely due to the way in which the mother structured the dialogue: not only did she leave sufficient pauses for the infant to respond but she was also ready (initially at least) to accept any minimum participation by the infant as a turn. With increasing age the child's active participation also increased, and around 14 months vocalizations appeared which were recognizable approximations to lexical labels. Up till then the mother had accepted any vocalization as an attempt to label; from then on, however, she began increasingly to challenge the child to produce the correct sound. As Ninio and Bruner put it: "Looking at these phenomena from a broader point of view, it is possible to regard the mother as coaxing the child to substitute, first, a vocalization for a non-vocal signal and later a well-formed word or word approximation for a babbled vocalization, using appropriate turns in the labelling routine to make her demands."

Two further characteristics can be found in this mother's behaviour. For one thing, she was highly responsive to the child: in 79% of instances when the child turned to look at a picture the mother immediately labelled it; in the remaining cases she asked a "What's that?" question. The labels were inevitably stressed, often in an exaggerated manner. And for another, the mother set out to simplify the situation and reduce it to a highly predictable form. She did so largely by confining her utterances to four key types: attentional vocatives ("Look"); query ("What's that?"); label (It's an X"); and feedback (e.g. "Yes"). As the order in which these four kinds of utterance occurred was almost always constant, the mother was able to provide the child with an interaction of a standardized structure that must have made it very much easier for the child to fit in his own contributions.

One further feature of this study is worth mentioning, namely the extent to which the mother closely tailored the nature of her input to the child's own response characteristics. This is illustrated by the type of referents used by each partner: 88·9% of the mother's labels and 89·8% of the child's referred to common nouns of whole objects, the remainder being distributed among references to parts of objects, proper names and various miscellaneous referents. A clear correspondence is indicated: young children tend to single out whole objects for attention; their mothers appear to follow suit. In the words of Ninio and Bruner: "The comparison suggests why book-reading is such an effective means of assuring significative convergence between mother and child."

Joint book reading thus seems a particularly good situation in which language learning can proceed. It has a highly repetitive structure; it is easy for the mother to identify what the child is interested in; it evokes responses from the child; and it lends itself well to cooperative participation. The last point needs stressing: the mother does not play her tutorial role dogmatically, nor is the child's role confined to a passive listen-and-look pattern. On the contrary, the mother is continuously challenging the child to take part, and her effectiveness as a teacher can thus be assessed by herself and changes made in the light of the feedback which the child provides. Label learning is thus not an isolated achievement: it is just one part of what the child learns about participating in dialogues. Edwards (1978) has expressed the same conclusion:

". . . object-naming also has a social-relational and cognitive structure which underlies the nature of reference itself. Object-naming typically occurs in the context of what Brown (1956) called 'the original word game', in which child and caretaker (usually mother) supply each other with names for pointed-at objects and pictures, or point out things named by the other. Typically the 'game' is linguistically mediated by much more than mere object names; it is full of questions and answers, locative and deictic expressions like 'what's that?', 'there it is', 'that's a kangaroo', 'it's a box', 'it's over there', and so on. Moreover these expressions are integrated into a context of sequenced looks and gestures which are crucial to their function in the total communication setting" (Edwards, 1978, p.68).

The onus for integration, with respect to label learning as with all the other aspects of early interaction that we have talked about, lies very much with the mother. We can list three further aspects of label learning which highlight the mother's ability to adapt her own behaviour to that of the child's:

(1) The kind of things mothers label for their children correspond precisely to the children's own interests in their environment. Thus mothers' speech to children at the start of the second year contains labels that are mostly object words of proper names, rarely attributes or states or actions (Bruner, 1977).

(2) The use of onomatopoeic names (baa-lamb, moo-cow, etc.) is a widespread recognition that certain sounds are easier for young children. While some mothers fear that they will delay the use of "proper" speech, it may well be that the use of such interesting sounds will help the child with his discovery that things have names.

(3) Referential words can be relative to particular speakers (Clark, 1978); for instance, the words "I" and "you" shift whenever there is a speaker-switch. This can be confusing to the young child; mothers consequently use invariant labels (e.g. "Jimmy give the ball to Mummy", instead of "You give the ball to me").

These examples once again emphasize the sensitivity with which the adult adjusts her behaviour in order to provide the child with more manageable and more meaningful input. By no means is the mother an automatic dispenser of labels: labels are introduced into the dyadic interaction at appropriate moments and in appropriate ways. Language teaching is a social game, not a lesson.

(3) Relationship of verbal to nonverbal reference

Various suggestions have been made as to the way in which verbal referring is developmentally interrelated with nonverbal modes. In due course linguistic means come to dominate the individual's attention-guiding efforts, but as to their possible origins in gestural and vocal schemes data remain scarce.

According to Werner and Kaplan (1974), the earliest expressions of reference are to be found in pointing and some characteristic vocal utterances (such as *da* and *ta*). The gesture and the vocalizations are said by these writers to emerge together and then gradually to differentiate. Thus, "the motoric activity and vocalizations culminating in (denotative) reference are assumed to be, initially, aspects of action patterns by means of which the child interacts pragmatically with his surrounding milieus" (Werner and Kaplan, 1974).

Werner and Kaplan did not have the benefit of empirical data on which to base these assertions. Several subsequent writers, however, agree that an association between indicative gestures, such as pointing, and particular vocal utterances can be observed. Thus Carter (1978), in a longitudinal study of one child's communicative development during his second year, has described eight schemata used for communicating with others, and of these "Attention to Object" provides a large number of instances. It manifests itself in two ways, namely through pointing or holding out and through a characteristic sound which accompanies the gesture (basically *l*- or *d*-initial utterances, e.g. *la*, *daet*). The early association of gesture and vocalization is noted also by Bates *et al.* (1975): their subject Carlotta, whom they observed around the age of one, generally uttered a breathy "ha" while pointing to things. And Clark (1978) also refers to the conjunction of the utterance *da* with early pointing and considers this sound to be equivalent to the adult deictic term *that*.

According to Clark (1978) children move from reliance on deictic gestures to the use of deictic words in the following stage-like progression:

Stage 1: pointing without accompanying vocalizations;
Stage 2: pointing, combined with the sound "da" or "eh";
Stage 3: pointing accompanied by utterances such as "that shoe";

Stage 4: an utterance such as "that coat is mine", the gesture being
   optional.

Whether development takes place in quite so orderly a fashion remains to
be established. Even the invariable association of particular vocalizations
with pointing in one-year-olds has been questioned (Murphy, 1978). In
addition, it seems that nonverbal means do not simply drop out of the
child's repertoire, to be replaced by verbal means (Bates *et al.*, 1977); the
interrelationship of verbal and nonverbal devices is very much more
complex than one based on simple substitution—a conclusion that, as we
shall see, applies equally to mothers' communicative behaviour to young
children (Schaffer *et al.*, 1983). It may be true, as Clark suggests, that the
earliest referential words are always accompanied by pointing and intent
staring at the object, thus providing the other person with considerable
redundancy in cues offered. With increasing age there may well be some
reduction in such redundancy: looking may be used more to monitor the
other person's attention and apparent comprehension, and pointing may be
dispensed with altogether under many circumstances as the child learns of
the communicative function of verbal labels. But there are qualifications.
For one thing, the speaker's behaviour depends on the listener, and where
that listener fails to comprehend the amount of redundancy may need to be
increased (as happens in speech to foreigners). And for another, a lot also
depends on whether the speaker's vocabulary can do justice to the
complexity of the situation: if, for instance, a child has to indicate one
particular block out of several he can only dispense with gesture if he has
learned qualifying words such as "nearest", "biggest", or "blue". By late
childhood the individual has learned that drawing another person's
attention to an object can be accomplished by a number of functionally
equivalent means; however, which he uses and in what conjunction depends
on many additional factors defining each situation.

Conclusions

Topic sharing becomes an important issue from five months on when the
child's attention turns to the world of things. Under the impetus of newly
emerging manipulative abilities, aided also no doubt by increasing visual
skills, the child discovers the fascination of objects and his own power over
them. As yet, however, there are constraints on his attentional deployment:
initially he cannot easily switch from one focus to another, and he does not
therefore have the flexibility to incorporate objects into his social
exchanges. This is illustrated by phenomena such as pointing-for-self; the
child gets absorbed in one focus (such as an interesting object) *or* another

(such as a person) without yet being able to combine both into one sequence. This is a task for a later stage.

In the meantime it is up to adults to take responsibility for such combining. Parents generally act as though they know that the most effective way of maintaining personal contact with the child is by acknowledging his new interest in the world of things and by then ensuring that this is incorporated into social contexts. Topics become shared, that is, on the initiative of the adult. The relationship is thus still very much an asymmetrical one: for the major part of the first year children appear to lack the ability to home in on another person's focus of attention, and even when this ability does emerge it is often not exercised. For a large part of early childhood it is therefore left to the adult to follow the child's interests and so convert an individual situation into a dyadic one.

Various devices are used for topic sharing, in particular indicative gestures such as pointing, visual gaze, manipulation and referential speech. These are universal phenomena; there are no indications, for example, that pointing needs to be learned through training or imitation. They enter the child's repertoire at various ages; a considerable gap may also occur between being able to produce a particular device and the realization that it has communicative significance and can be used for interpersonal purposes. It seems likely that the child's developmental timetable in turn largely determines the devices that the parent selects for bringing about topic sharing: thus a progression can be hypothesized according to which the adult initially relies mainly on direct contact with objects through manipulation, proceeds subsequently to distal reference by means of indicative gestures, and eventually resorts to symbolic means, i.e. verbal labelling. Situational constraints to some extent obscure this scheme; moreover a large degree of redundancy is offered by parents in so far as several devices may be employed simultaneously. Nevertheless, the general tendency to rely primarily on one type rather than another according to the child's developmental status is one example of adult adaptation to child characteristics; another is the way in which the parent times her behaviour in relation to the child's ongoing activity. Her action is far from arbitrary but is based on a sensitive awareness of the child's focus of attention at any given moment of time; labelling of an object, for example, is synchronized with the child's interest in that object. Input from the parent thus tends to be provided in the context of the child's own activity and will consequently have greater impact.

In the past phenomena such as pointing and label acquisition have mostly been studied as manifestations of individual behaviour. For some purposes this may be justified, yet the significance of such phenomena is above all an interpersonal one and it is therefore essential to view them as they occur in interpersonal settings. Not only can one then describe how these behaviour patterns are used by partners in dyadic interchange, but one can also investigate the conditions under which they first emerge in the child's repertoire. The mechanical, paired-associate type of account of label learning is one example of the failure to study development in an interpersonal context; when one does so it becomes abundantly clear that the adult's role in this process is far from being just a reinforcer or a model or a passive bystander; it involves instead actively helping the child to discover a new dimension to his experience by incorporating verbalizations in a meaningful manner in the total communicative interchange.

5 From Pseudo-Dialogues To Dialogues

Of all psychological reorganizations that periodically take place in the course of development, that to be found around the age of 8 to 10 months is probably the most profound. It radically alters the quality of behaviour in many respects: the child becomes less reactive and more proactive; increasingly he operates in terms of events experienced in the past or anticipated in the future; he now becomes able to form permanent relationships with other people; he can separate means from ends and starts to formulate plans and intentions; he becomes able to appraise and evaluate his experiences instead of responding in a purely impulsive manner; and he begins to monitor his own activity and adjust it according to its perceived effects on the environment. In short, behaviour becomes vastly more flexible, more coordinated and more integrative, the change occurring in a relatively brief period and bringing with it profound implications for the child's social and cognitive functioning.

The development of relational abilities

The manifold changes to be found in infants' behaviour in the 8 to 10 months period have been commented on by various writers. Trevarthen and Hubley (1978), for example, refer to "a seemingly endless list of new achievements at about 9 months"; the instances they provide include such items as "invokes adult help in performing a task with an object", "performs functional play with toys", "imitates demonstrated actions on objects", "points to indicate object beyond reach", "plays peek-a-boo with another person", and "opens and closes a book, looking at mother after each move". Bretherton et al. (1981), having also produced a list of behaviour patterns that first emerge around that age, conclude that a "blossoming" of abilities takes place at about 9 months.

111

Listing and describing the various changes that constitute this onrush of new achievements is, of course, an important first step; explaining what takes place in the child's psychological organization at that time to account for these changes is a more difficult and controversial undertaking.

(1) Object–person integration

According to one proposal, a basic theme underlying many of the changes is the onset of the child's ability to combine acts towards people with acts towards objects. This is illustrated by Sugarman-Bell (1978), who believes that an infant's transactions with his environment progresses through the following three stages:

(1) *Simple single-orientation*. At this stage simple acts directed at objects (banging, waving, sucking etc.) or equally simple acts directed at people (looking, vocalizing, smiling, etc.) may be initiated. Behaviour clusters are limited to unitary, largely repetitive acts; there is as yet no combination of a variety of person or object schemes nor are person schemes combined with object schemes.

(2) *Complex single-orientation*. Different kinds of responses can now be combined, e.g. the child can look at the adult, vocalize to her and simultaneously tug at her clothing; *or* he may visually examine and shake and listen to a rattle all in one integrated pattern. But object-oriented and person-oriented acts remain separate; if, for instance, the adult gives the child a toy the child's attention is fixed solely on the toy, with no acknowledgment of the adult.

(3) *Coordinated person–object orientation*. The child is now able to insert person-directed acts into his play with objects, and use objects in order to relate to people. Bates *et al.* (1975), in putting forward a similar developmental progression, suggest that there are two kinds of combinations that become evident at this point: use of adults to obtain objects (referred to as "proto-imperatives") and use of objects to attract the attention of adults ("proto-declaratives"). An excerpt from the protocol of these authors' observations of one child, Carlotta, obtained when she was just over one year old, illustrates her newly found ability to combine object and social acts into a single imperative sequence:

"C. is sitting on her mother's lap, while M shows her the telephone and pretends to talk. M tries to press the receiver against C.'s ear and have her "speak", but C. pushes the receiver back and presses it against her mother's ear. This is repeated several times. When M refuses to speak into the receiver, C. bats her hand against M's knee, waits a moment longer, watches M's face, and then, uttering a sharp aspirated sound "ha", touches her mother's mouth." (Bates *et al.*, 1975, p.215.)

We can see quite clearly from this example how this child can relate to object and person at the same time; thus she pushes the receiver against the mother's ear, as though she is able to appreciate the connection between these two disparate objects, and yet only a few weeks earlier she would have attended *either* to the telephone *or* to the mother, not to both. Behaviour patterns such as showing or giving objects to another person provide good indications that the child is now able to coordinate schemata; the same applies to pointing, at least in its communicative form when the child not only points to the object but also, by looking back at the person, makes clear that he is gesturing *for her sake*.

There can be no doubt that children become increasingly able to co-ordinate multiple activities that they could perform only separately at earlier ages, and that combinations of person-directed actions and object-directed actions can be found from the end of the first year on. More controversial is the proposal that the combination is unique to objects on the one hand and persons on the other, for it arises from the view (already examined and dismissed) that the child comes into the world equipped with two quite separate systems to deal with things and with people respectively. It is these two systems that are now supposedly brought together. A much more likely view is that the growth of coordination applies to *any* set of actions directed at multiple stimuli and that it can just as well be observed *within* the social and *within* the object sphere. Let us consider the evidence.

(2) Inter-relating diverse events

Indications regarding the development of relational abilities come from diverse sources, including the following:

Developmental tests. According to the norms from several tests for infants (Bayley, Griffiths, P. Cattell), children first become able to combine different objects around the age of 8 or 9 months. It is then that items such as "strikes one object with another", "puts cube in cup", and "manipulates two objects at once", are added to the list of expected achievements. All these items refer, of course, to combinations within the object sphere.

Studies of play. More detailed examinations of children's play development come up with a similar picture. For instance, Fenson *et al.* (1976) observed infants playing with a tea set and found that the typical 7-month-old baby would play with only one thing at a time without combining that object with any other. "Simple relational acts", involving bringing two objects into contact with each other though not necessarily in an appropriate manner, were found in only 9% of 7-month-old infants; at the age of 9 months, however, it was observed in 92% of infants. There is thus a progression from simple play (with one object at a time) to relational play; this in turn will be succeeded during the second year by symbolic play.

Piagetian theory. According to Piaget, development in the earlier stages of the sensorimotor phase is largely concerned with the growing ability to coordinate initially separate schemata. Coordination becomes especially prominent towards the end of the first year with the separation of ends and means, when the child becomes capable of using one thing in the service of another (e.g. using a stick in order to obtain a toy out of reach, or removing a cover in order to retrieve a hidden object). This gives the infant's behaviour a more goal-directed quality: primitive intentions appear in that the child begins to act in anticipation of producing particular results. The child, that is, now purposively employs one action with a view to achieving something else.

Accounts of social development. The ability to relate one aspect to another within the social sphere has also been found to emerge towards the end of the first year. For example, when confronted simultaneously by the mother and a stranger infants around 7 or 8 months may repeatedly look from one to the other as though comparing the unfamiliar with the familiar (Schaffer, 1966). The same phenomenon has been used as evidence of "social referencing", namely the seeking of information from another person about an event that is beyond the child's own ability to assimilate (Campos and Sternberg, 1981): the child, that is, confronted by an unfamiliar person and unsure how to react, looks to the mother for her emotional response to this situation. Whatever the interpretation, the observation shows how the child is no longer absorbed in any one person at a time but can now inter-relate different individuals.

It becomes apparent that the trend to coordinate diverse features is seen in all aspects of behaviour and is not specific to linking social with inanimate stimuli. Initially the child is confined to attending to adult *or* to toy, mother *or* to stranger, one block *or* another; now he can relate several events—of whatever nature—to one another and thus produce more integrative response patterns.

Elsewhere (Schaffer, 1974) the new cognitive competence has been described as enabling the child to progress from the sequential to the simultaneous consideration of different events. Thus initially the infant is "stimulus-bound", i.e. absorbed in one particular feature of the environment with no concern for any other separated in time and space. As Piaget (1950) put it, his experience is like "a slow motion film, in which all the pictures are seen in succession but without fusion, and so without the continuous vision necessary for understanding the whole." Only later will the infant begin to consider different events simultaneously and jointly instead of sequentially and separately, thereby bringing about a marked increase in the temporal integration of his behaviour. The child's attention is then no longer pre-empted by any one event to the exclusion of all else; instead he becomes able to relate, compare, contrast, combine and associate diverse stimuli, be they objects or people, and include them in one integrated action pattern rather than as foci for separate activities. What is more, the new relational ability may involve an item that is not actually present but has to be retrieved from memory, as when a stranger is compared with the absent mother. The newly emergent ability to recall (Schaffer, 1974) is thus drawn upon as well.

The ability to integrate disparate events over time and space enormously widens the scope of the child's social behaviour. Thus he can now coordinate use of the parent as a safe base with exploration of other features of the environment. He can point out things to people; he can include another person in a game with toys; and he can look to the parent for approval when he has accomplished something in his object play. The character of his social interactions changes: he can send a message and simultaneously monitor the other person for the effect of that message; he can relate communications from his partner to external topics or to previous messages; and he can plan his interactive behaviour around particular goals that give direction to otherwise disparate responses.

All this means that the child has become a very different kind of social partner to the parent, and new adjustments need accordingly to be worked out to take these into account. In particular, as we shall see below, dialogues become more symmetrical with the child's growing ability reciprocally to participate in social interchange. How to establish dialogues on the basis of true reciprocity is thus the interactive issue that now comes to the fore. As the child increasingly becomes able to integrate his separate activities into more fluent streams of behaviour the parent's role changes accordingly. Take the simple act of handing a rattle to the child. Gray (1978) has described in detail how a mother goes about this task when the infant is still in his first half year, and in particular how she tries not to distract him with her own presence while focussing his attention on the toy. Verbalizations are suppressed or whispered, the mother's face is kept out of the immediate visual field, and it is not till the infant has successfully grasped the rattle that the mother attracts his attention to herself again. By thus sequencing the presentation of different stimuli the mother shows her respect for the infant's inability to deal with multiple stimulus sources. That same action a few months later will assume a very different form: maternal stimulation and object stimulation will be offered simultaneously; the act may well be embedded in a more complex routine such as a give-and-take game of which it forms only one component; and in such a game the child will be expected to understand the reciprocal nature of the participants' activities and to behave as though he knows the rules that govern the interchange as a whole.

Acquiring the concept of the dialogue

The asymmetry of roles played by adult and child that characterizes early interaction sequences means that we must think of these exchanges as "pseudo-dialogues", and thus it becomes important to investigate the means whereby the infant eventually acquires the concept of "true" dialogues. This is a continuous and long-drawn-out development, components of which emerge at various points throughout the early years. Two processes, however, are fundamental, namely the understanding of reciprocity and the capacity for intentionality. Both represent complex, many-faceted aspects of behaviour, and though their emergence is by no means an all-or-none affair both first become apparent somewhere towards the end of the first year.

(1) Reciprocity

One lesson that a child must learn on his way to full social participation is that other people are not just objects on which he can act but that they also function as *agents*, i.e. as independent sources of activity. The child, in other words, must *decentre* (in the Piagetian sense): he must realize that in a dialogue the other person is not merely the recipient of the child's activity but that he has a part of his own to play. Reciprocity refers to the knowledge that a dialogue needs to be sustained by *both* partners, that both are responsible for steering its course, and that in addition the roles they play are not only integrative but also inter-changeable.

One forum in which such learning can be observed is provided by adult–infant games — peekaboo, give-and-take, tickling and such like. Most mothers play these for the sake of the enormous amount of pleasure they obviously provide; in addition, however, they constitute a particular kind of interactive experience for the infant by virtue of the highly routinized format of each game — a format that can nevertheless also accommodate an element of unpredictability. Take the description provided by Snow *et al.* (1979) of the tickling game "Walking round the garden like a teddy bear": it contains a slowly performed initial phase during which the mother moves her finger in a circular fashion around the child's palm and chants the first line of the verse; this is followed by an even more slowly executed act of walking the fingers towards the child's underarm ("one step, two step"); and ends in a vigorous climax with the line "Tickly under there" while tickling the child under his arm. The structure of the game is very simple, for it is based on an invariable sequence of its few components, and frequent repetitions enable the child to anticipate each following step once the mother has begun the game. At the same time there is an element of unpredictability which mothers build into the timing of the final step, in that they vary the pause before the climax and thus heighten the child's excitement. It is this combination of routine and unpredictability that makes games so fascinating to young children.

Hay *et al.* (1979) list four features that characterize early games:

(1) Mutual involvement — a basic requirement, in that both partners must be performing in response to each other.

(2) Turn taking — a feature that is clearer in some games such as throwing and catching ball than in others.

(3) Repetition of the complex sequence of interaction, though sometimes with variation.

(4) Non-literality, i.e. the activities are not ends in themselves but serve as means for the game.

These criteria serve to draw attention to the essentially dyadic nature of games. Even in the tickling game described above the child is not just a passive recipient but plays his part in signalling when he is ready for the next phase. However, the extent of the child's participation varies with age: according to Gustafson *et al.* (1979) the proportion of mutual games occurring during normal activity at home in which the infant assumed an active role increased from 14% at 6 months to 93% at 12 months. Even more telling are longitudinal studies of the changes that occur in the way mother–infant couples play some particular game. Ratner and Bruner (1978) observed two such couples repeatedly between 5 and 9 months while playing games built around the appearance and disappearance of objects. Although the basic structure of the game remained constant throughout this period, the roles of the two participants changed, with the mother gradually handing over more and more responsibility to the child. This began with the child's attempt to bring about the appearances and disappearances himself; the mother, closely attuned to the child's efforts, furthered this attempt by skillfully altering her role to ensure the child's greater participation. The type of games mothers play, as well as the way in which they play them, clearly follow the child's increasing interactive capabilities.

The games that are most relevant to the development of reciprocity are those that involve a role relationship that is not only integrative but also interchangeable. Take Bruner's (1977) description of the development of give-and-take. Up to 7 or 8 months the infant's participation is entirely limited to "take". The game is a one-sided affair in which the mother offers the toy; it ends with the child merely dropping it. From about 10 months on the child begins to initiate the sequence by showing and even offering the object; he may also now hand it to the mother at her request. But although the child can be induced to take part in exchanges, he does so hesitantly, constantly checking between object and mother as though not sure of the procedure. By 12 months the game has become established as a "game". It is routinized, it can take diverse forms, possession time is decreased, the number of exchanges per game is increased, and the whole is played with great pleasure and enjoyment. The child, in short, has mastered the routine and learned the basic rule underlying the game, namely that the roles of giver and taker are reciprocal and reversible.

It may well be that games such as these, by virtue of their clearly articulated structure, simplicity and repetitiveness, foster turn taking and other inter-active skills. They are eminently suitable contexts in which the child can become aware that his behaviour is part of a wider unit defined by the behaviour of both participants, that the unit is based on rules and regularities concerning the coordination of both individuals' responses, and that he as much as his partner is responsible for maintaining it. To have mastered such sophisticated understanding of interactive role behaviour by the age of 12 months (on an action level at any rate) is no mean achievement.

(2) Intentionality

To the parent the behaviour of even the youngest baby has communicative force: a cry, a smile, a shift in posture, a gaze in a particular direction—each may provide the mother with some information as to the infant's state and condition and cause her to react in some appropriate way. Whether the infant's response should indeed by labelled "communicative" is a matter of definition, but there are those who consider the term appropriate only when the sender is behaving in a clearly intentional manner, and this hardly applies to the infant's behaviour in the early months of life. It is only towards the end of the first year that the first signs of intentionality become evident.

Not that it has proved easy to arrive at a consensus as to what these signs are—or not at any rate for psychologists, for in everyday life there appears to be generally little difficulty in recognizing this highly serviceable notion. The following criteria were suggested by Piaget (1954):

(1) The child has a goal in mind from the beginning and does not discover it accidentally.

(2) If an obstacle arises in the attainment of the goal some kind of indirect approach will be employed.

(3) The means used to overcome the obstacle are different from those used in the case of the goal.

Unfortunately such criteria do not yield the kind of unequivocal indices that would help one to identify instances of the relevant behaviour. The same applies to the list of features with which Bruner (1973) characterizes intention: anticipation of outcome, selection among appropriate means, sustained direction of behaviour, cessation of activity when the end state is achieved, and the substitution of alternative means for correction of deviation. To operationalize any of these would be no mean feat. No wonder most writers prefer loosely couched descriptions to anything more precise and measurable.

As Piaget has made clear, intentionality does not spring into existence suddenly at some specific point in the child's development; it has a history that one can trace back to the first months of life. There is, however, general agreement that it is not until sensorimotor stage 5, with the advent of means–ends differentiation, that behaviour begins to assume the kind of manner that we associate with intentionality. When secondary circular reactions first appear they are accidental acts not meant to produce interesting effects, and it is only as a result of repeated experiences of the contingency between act and effect that the infant learns to appreciate the consequences of his behaviour. Once the infant sees the connection he will wish to repeat the interesting event and use different means to accomplish the same end.

Piaget, as was his wont, provided a purely asocial account of intentional development. Applying the concept to social behaviour, we may distinguish between the infant in the early weeks of life who cries because he has a pain and the infant a year later who cries *for his mother* to deal with the pain. The former cries in a reactive fashion, with no thought for the consequences of his actions. The older child has had countless experiences informing him of the contingency between his behaviour and its effects, and as a result he becomes able to signal for his mother in a purposive fashion. Infants without such experience, such as the institutionally reared whose cries are not responded to contingently, eventually extinguish their communicative signals and retreat into apathy (Provence and Lipton, 1962). Their social experience has failed to provide them with the cognitive means that enable children under normal circumstances to graduate to intentionality.

As we have already seen, a great deal of the experience that a normally reared infant encounters tends to be of a highly repetitive and therefore predictable nature. In face-to-face situations in particular parents ensure that the infant has every opportunity of learning what comes next. The ability to anticipate is thus fostered. Proceeding from reactivity to anticipation is obviously an essential aspect of developing adaptive behaviour; it means that the child becomes able to transcend the here-and-now and plan his behaviour in the light of foreseen circumstances. Bowlby (1969), in his formulation of attachment theory, paid particular attention to this development. Initially, according to his proposal, the various fixed action patterns that are the constituents of attachment behaviour—smiling, crying, sucking and so forth—become activated by quite specific stimulus conditions; they then run their course in an almost mechanical fashion until terminated by further specific stimulus conditions. Thus the baby does not vary his cry according to whether the mother is far or near or whether she is coming or going; in short, his behaviour is not "goal-corrected". Bowlby uses the latter term, borrowed from control theory, in order to designate the kind of attachment behaviour appearing later on in infancy that is continually adjusted in the light of prevailing circumstances, that takes note of discrepancies between stimulus conditions and the child's goals, and that therefore is characterized by a flexibility and purposiveness that are absent from the earlier fixed action patterns.

The essential difference between the earlier and the later forms of behaviour to which Bowlby draws attention concerns the utilization of feedback information. In the younger infant the response, once triggered off, runs its course regardless of the effects it is producing. In the older child there is awareness that responses do have effects, there is a constant monitoring of such effects, and there is also the ability to change behaviour and substitute more suitable actions should the desired end not be forthcoming. Thus the emergence of goal-corrected behaviour may well coincide with the onset of means–ends differentiation as described by Piaget: both descriptions, Bowlby's and Piaget's, draw attention to the child's growing ability to plan his behaviour in the light of anticipated outcomes, i.e. to behave intentionally.

The role of feedback in the infant's interactional behaviour remains an enormously important area for further investigation. Its absence in the younger infant is seen strikingly in the joint attention episodes which we examined in the previous chapter. Compare the behaviour of mother and child during pointing: the mother is continually monitoring the child's responses to her attempts to direct his attention, so that she is constantly ready to adjust her behaviour in the light of the child's and employ alternative means if need be. The child's earliest forms of pointing, on the other hand, are non-communicative: they are directed at the object only and are not accompanied by any attempts simultaneously to observe the effect of the gesture on the other person. This is no doubt due to the cognitive constraints operating at this early age, i.e. the aforementioned difficulty the child has in attending to multiple stimuli and integrating them into one combined activity. As long as the child cannot consider the other person while acting upon some object he cannot engage in intentional communication with that person about the object. Only when attentional processes become more flexible can the child begin to consider several foci more or less simultaneously; only then will monitoring for feedback purposes become possible.

(3) Dialogue management

Once infants become capable of more reciprocal and more intentional inter-active behaviour the roles played respectively by adult and child change, assuming a more symmetrical form. Not that separating these roles is an easy task. An interaction may have all the characteristics of a "true" dialogue: a shared topic to which both participants attend, a regular sequence of turns, interchangeability of roles, and so forth. And yet (as we saw in the discussion of vocal turn taking) such characteristics may be brought about variously: in the more mature form by the two individuals assuming joint responsibility for the conduct of the interaction; in the less mature form by one partner as yet not "knowing" the rules but the interaction being guided and converted into a dialogue by the actions of the other partner. The recent emphasis on infants being "competent" and "active" may be a welcome reaction to the previous stress on helplessness and passivity; there is, however, a danger of going to the opposite extreme and ascribing abilities to the young child that he in fact does not possess, thereby avoiding the issue of how these first emerge and develop. Recognition must be given to the very differing levels of interactive competence at which parent and child initially operate; only as the child becomes more adept will the parent be able to remove the many props that she must first provide to maintain the interaction.

Take the phenomenon of imitation. As we previously saw, there are considerable doubts about the presence of this ability in the neonatal period; there is indeed little indication of it before the last quarter of the first year. But when the focus of the study adopted by the investigator is a dyadic one, where the behaviour of the adult is as closely scrutinized as the child's, it becomes apparent (as Papousek and Papousek, 1977 point out) that the first step in the development of imitation is taken by the *parent*: it is her readiness to imitate the infant — rather than vice versa — that is the more striking phenomenon. This is clearly seen in Pawlby's (1977) follow-up study of infants between 17 and 43 weeks of age — a study that did adopt a dyadic focus and that, moreover, examined naturally occurring imitation rather than experimentally set up episodes. The spontaneous imitative sequences that were observed were divided into those in which the mother was the imitator and those in which the infant played that part. As is apparent from Table 6, maternal imitations were more frequent than imitations by infants throughout the age range investigated; however, while there were no significant differences from one period to the next in mothers' imitative acts the infants steadily increased theirs. Thus, as Pawlby concludes, paradoxically the process by which the infant comes to imitate his mother is rooted in the initial readiness of the *mother* to imitate her child; from birth on mothers reflect back to their infants gestures and vocalizations which occur spontaneously in the baby's behaviour, selecting those which they can endow with some communicative significance. They usually do so by skillfully inserting their own copy of the infant's action into a sequence of his repeated responses so that a simulation of a deliberate act of imitation on the part of the infant is thereby created. That act is then greeted with delight by the mother — one of those "as if" reactions that may well make the infant in future more ready to perform the same behaviour under similar circumstances.

Table 6. *Mean number of maternal imitations and infant imitations at each of three age periods.*

	Age Period		
	17-24 wks.	26-33 wks.	35-42 wks.
Mother imitating infant	5·3	8·4	7·3
Infant imitating mother	1·0	1·9	2·5

(Adapted from Pawlby, 1977)

Thus the phenomenon of imitation, when studied in the context of dyadic interaction, provides a vivid illustration of the prepotent role which the adult must play at the earlier stages of development. In time the child too will become capable of imitation and other interactive skills and will exercise them as freely as the adult; dialogues then come to assume a more symmetrical form. This is seen clearly in a report by Holmberg (1980) which describes one of those studies, unfortunately only too rare, that trace the structure of interactive sequences over a relatively wide age range. Children between 12 and 42 months were observed in daycare centres and the nature of their encounters with adults was recorded. As shown in Table 7, the total number of positive social initiations that occurred over this period remained

Table 7. *Number of positive initiations (per 30 minutes) between daycare staff and children.*

	Age (in months)					
	12	18	24	30	36	42
Adult to child	11·2	10·1	9·5	9·0	5·5	8·8
Child to adult	1·7	3·2	4·4	6·3	5·0	4·7
Total	12·9	13·3	13·9	15·3	10·5	13·5

(Adapted from Holmberg, 1980)

relatively constant; the balance between adult-initiated and child-initiated encounters, however, changed markedly: at the younger ages adults took the main responsibility for maintaining the level of interaction, but with the children's growing competence to initiate exchanges themselves reduced their contribution in proportion, giving the child the opportunity to exercise the newly found skills.

The sophistication of children to engage in social interactions increases greatly in the course of the second and third years. Much of this increase is usually ascribed to the development of linguistic competence, and no doubt the capacity to participate in dialogues is vastly enhanced once communication at a verbal level becomes possible. But underlying any specific set of skills is the growth of a more general understanding by the child of himself in relation to other people — a kind of *meta-sociability*. Not only does the child learn that he is an agent and that others too are agents in their own right, but he also realizes that it is possible for these various independent individuals to come together and forge joint enterprises to their mutual satisfaction. Such meta-sociability is likely to grow slowly and to require powers of mental representation (the role of which we shall discuss later) for its full blossoming. Yet long before a child can verbally communicate his thoughts about himself in relation to others he is capable of demonstrating by action a deliberate desire to bring about enterprises of an essentially interpersonal nature. A study by Rheingold (1982) vividly illustrates how children as young as 18 months spontaneously engage in helping another person. Parents were asked to set about a number of ordinary domestic tasks (setting a table, folding laundry, putting things into a basket, etc.), and to do so without in any way encouraging their children to participate. Yet the children did participate — in 63% of the tasks at 18 months, increasing to 78% at 24 months and 89% at 30 months. Not only did they do so voluntarily and deliberately but with great alacrity, despite the various distractions of the environment which might have appealed to their more individually oriented interests. A number of specific social skills are required for such helping behaviour, in particular the ability to take up another person's action topic and to cooperate appropriately in carrying out the task. More fundamental, however, is the demonstration that children in their second year can take the initiative in deliberately bringing about an activity that is by definition an interpersonal one, and that they show thereby that, far from being essentially egocentric in nature, they actively seek to become part of interactive structures once they have the cognitive and motoric means enabling them to do so.

Peer interaction

The supportive role played by parents means that it is not always easy to assess the child's own skills in managing interactions. This is one reason for the renewed interest in peer interaction: here we can observe participants of equal psychological status who are unlikely to fill in for each other and who must consequently rely on their own resources. Unlike earlier studies, the interest lies primarily in discovering what infants and young children *can* do: those published several decades ago appeared under the shadow of the concept of egocentrism and seemed more concerned with what children *cannot* do. More recent work, taking a more positive approach, has emerged with a picture of rather greater capability in even very young children than had been painted previously.

(1) Developmental trends

As Mueller and Vandell (1979) point out in their review of this topic, various other-directed responses can already be found in peer interaction in the first year. These responses — smiling, vocalizing, offering toys, approaching and so on — appear in fairly predictable order at ages not very different from those found in behaviour with adults. However, the responses tend to be brief, passive and isolated — fleeting reactions to the peer as a stimulus object, rarely eliciting a contingent response from the partner.

It is not till the second year that there is a marked increase in the incidence of coordinated interactive sequences. Eckerman *et al.* (1975) observed previously unacquainted pairs of children at ages 11, 17 and 23 months. Only at the youngest age was there more solitary than social play; at later ages the infants were outgoing, interested in each other and far from encapsulated in their own shell. Moreover, the quality of their social behaviour tended to be largely positive: responses such as smiling and offering or showing toys outweighed by far negative behaviour such as struggling, striking and taking away toys. It is, however, the structural changes that are of most interest: the incidence of isolated responses directed at the peer (watching, contact, etc.) did not vary over age; what did change was the incidence of more complex sequences involving not only the peer but also toys. Thus marked increases occurred in the rate of object exchanges, in the frequency of imitation, in synchronous contact with the same toy and in direct involvement in the peer's play. This reflects the increasing importance of objects as mediators — identical to that already described for parent–infant interaction in relation to topic sharing. It also reflects the growing competence of infants to coordinate their behaviour with that of another person—even when that other person is not a supportive adult but an individual of the same developmental status.

The changes in the nature of interaction among peers that take place with age can be summarized in terms of three characteristics: length, contingency and complexity.

(1) *Length.* The one-way contacts found at earlier stages gradually give way to longer sequences that can be sustained over multiple turns (Mueller and Lucas, 1975; Ross and Goldman, 1976). At first child A may direct a response to child B, but the latter is unlikely to respond. At a later stage B does respond; A may then note his behaviour but does not take it up. Only towards the end of the second year do sequences of the form A-B-A-B-A-B become prevalent.

(2) *Contingency.* Interactions are, of course, not merely sequences of random responses: they are composed of *related* responses. There is evidence that the capacity to relate one's behaviour to another person's grows in conjunction with the lengthening of interactive chains (Mueller and Lucas, 1975); the child, that is, is not just triggered to respond by the other's behaviour but becomes able carefully to adjust the nature of his action to that of the partner.

(3) *Complexity.* Interactions not only include a range of *interpersonal* co-ordinations of varying degree of complexity; they also involve various kinds of coordination at an *intrapersonal* level: the child may, for instance, look and vocalize and offer a toy in one coordinated pattern. Mueller and Lucas (1975) have paid particular attention to the coordination of looking with other social acts: the fact that the child is gazing at the other member of the dyad while vocalizing or pushing him or manipulating the toy he is holding suggests that these responses are indeed "intended" for him. "Socially directed behaviours" (SDB) are thus defined by these authors by the co-occurrence of looking with some other action, and it is such SDBs that they regard as the building blocks of social interaction. In due course the SDBs of two or more children become interlinked, and then a whole series of increasingly complex coordinations appear as children learn the to-and-fro of social intercourse.

Mueller and Lucas (1975) have summarized the development of peer interaction in terms of a three-stage sequence:

(1) *Object-centred contacts.* During this stage children may cluster around an object of mutual interest but they are rarely able to act in a simultaneously coordinated fashion. Instead they show an "act–watch" pattern: each child in turn acts on the object; when the partner performs, he watches. Attending to the partner's behaviour while himself performing is still beyond the child's abilities—once again the operation of cognitive constraints becomes apparent. At this stage peer contacts are

consequently object-centred but not integrated with social interaction.

(2) *Contingency interchanges.* Children now actively seek and receive contingencies from one another. Child–child circular reactions appear, as when a child laughs at another's vocalization, thereby getting the latter to repeat the vocalization. The SDBs of both children thus become linked, forming increasingly longer contingent chains. This stage is said to mark the appearance of "true" social interaction.

(3) *Complementary interchanges.* Now children are not only able to exchange turns but also roles. The participants engage in different yet complementary activities: throwing and catching, offering and receiving, hide and seek. In each case two different activities are involved but each action derives its meaning from the reciprocal act. Coordination in time also now becomes important. The child must hold out his hand at the right moment to receive the toy. The earlier act–watch pattern is thus replaced by simultaneous and synchronous activity; a much more sophisticated form of interaction is now possible.

In general, much of the recent literature on peer interaction gives the impression that from a very early age on fairly sophisticated forms of social behaviour take place among same-age children. However, a useful warning note comes from a study by Bronson (1981), based on a longitudinal investigation of 40 children followed up from 12 to 24 months. Contacts between the children were classified into four types:

(1) *Single contacts,* when one child directed an act towards another child, who either ignored the approach or responded by no more than some single action.

(2) *Parallel play,* involving the concurrent engagement of the pair with objects from the same set of toys, interspersed with no more than occasional glances at the peer.

(3) *Contact bursts,* denoting the temporal contingency of the two children's actions (i.e. one following the other within 10 seconds), but containing no adult-detectable link in content.

(4) *Contact chains,* based on both temporal contiguity and adult-detectable mutuality, where the behaviour of one individual was clearly modified or sustained by the other's behaviour. Only this type was regarded by Bronson as indicating "true" social interaction.

The incidence of the various types of encounter as found at three age levels during the second year are given in Table 8. It is apparent that the most primitive type, single contacts, is the most frequent at all three age levels, though it does decline in the course of the second year from 73% to 58%. The category "contact chains", on the other hand, while showing an increase, remains relatively infrequent. In fact most of these chains were brief (the modal number of contacts within a chain was 2 at all ages), and most instances of more prolonged contact involved disputes over toys. As Bronson puts it, while instances of sustained social activities did occur on occasion "their markedly low incidence justifies description of sustained dyadic interaction in playgroups of unacquainted toddlers as a very low frequency event."

Table 8. *Proportion of four types of peer encounters during successive trimesters in the second year.*

	Trimester 1	Trimester 2	Trimester 3
	%	%	%
Single contacts	73	67	58
Parallel play	6	9	11
Contact bursts	15	14	17
Contact choices	6	10	13

(Adapted from Bronson, 1981)

This conclusion helps to put peer interaction into perspective and should ensure that we do not swing from one extreme to the other — from denying the existence of any social activity among children in the early years to making extravagant claims about their possession of a virtually mature set of interactive abilities. It is clear that an interest in other children does exist even in infancy; it is also apparent that this is only a beginning and that young children have some real difficulty as yet in translating that interest into joint, cooperative activity. To argue about the age when "true" interaction among peers emerges is to engage in a futile debate: much depends on the definition one assigns to this phenomenon and on the criteria one chooses to index it, and in this respect (as Bronson shows in a comparison of her own study with those of others) there is little consensus as yet among investigators. What is more, a great many factors are likely to affect the results obtained: the presence of the child's mother, the previous acquaintance of the children, the size of the group, the number and type of toys available, and even the size and shape of the room in which the session is held (see Smith and Connolly, 1980, for a review of some of these factors). Such influences tend to vary from study to study and, taken in conjunction with definitional differences, produce hardly surprising disagreements as to children's capabilities. More important than the search for age norms, however, are attempts to understand developmental sequences and processes, and it is in this respect that some of the findings mentioned above are more illuminating. But what they also seem to suggest is that much of the orderly, sustained nature of interactions with an adult owes, for the initial years at any rate, a great deal to the latter's supportive role. Remove that (as happens in peer interaction) and a picture emerges of rather greater fragility in the individual child's ability actively to cooperate with a partner.

(2) Peer interactions and adult interactions

Studies directly comparing child–child and child–adult interactions are rare. Indirect comparisons, based on different studies, seem to indicate a considerable gap between the mother–infant and the infant–infant systems in the age of onset of particular skills: for example, Bruner (1977) found reciprocity in give-and-take games played with mothers to emerge at the end of the first year; Mueller and Lucas (1975) do not expect to find it among infant peers till their third stage, i.e. about a year later. However, such comparisons are dangerous: they neglect crucial differences in methodology; they overlook different definitions of terms like reciprocity; and the familiarity variable is likely to exert its unchecked influence. The last point in particular needs stressing: familiarity, as defined by amount of previous acquaintance, has been found to exert a powerful influence on children's behaviour in studies of peer interaction (Mueller and Vandell, 1979); it is therefore likely that it is an important contaminating variable in any comparison of parent and peer as the child's social partner.

One way of avoiding this particular problem is by examining children's interactions in settings such as daycare centres, where peers and adult staff are likely to be familiar to a comparable degree. This was done in the afore-mentioned study by Holmberg (1980), in that children's exchanges with other children as well as those with adult caretakers were recorded. As we saw, the number of interactions between adults and children that were started by means of positive initiations remained constant over the whole of the 12 to 42 months age range, but only because at the earlier ages the adults took most of the responsibility for bringing this about. The same measure for peer interactions provided a very different result: at 12 months very few positive interactions were initiated, and not till 3 years did their frequency reach the level observed with adults. The same picture emerges from another measure, namely that of the complexity of interactions. The number of elaborated interchanges (i.e. those that included at least 4 act–react responses, 2 turns being contributed by each individual) remained relatively constant over age when the child was paired with an adult; amongst peers, however, far fewer such complex interchanges occurred initially, their number beginning to increase only at 30 months and climbing steadily there-after. It seems therefore that children in the first 2 or 3 years require an adult as partner if they are to experience frequent and rich interchanges; whatever the specific means that such an adult employs, it is thanks to her initiative that young children get involved in structured social interactions. Only subsequently do children become capable of sustaining the same level of interaction with an individual of their own age.

Whether the previous experience with adults brings about the skills required for subsequent peer interaction remains a moot point. On the basis of cross-lagged correlations Vandell (reported in Vandell and Mueller, 1980) concluded that mothers' behaviour to their children at 16 and at 19 months appeared to influence significantly their children's behaviour with peers at 22 months. Thus mothers who frequently offered toys to their toddlers had children who engaged a great deal in similar behaviour with peers; mothers who were often negative and seized toys from their children had sons who were subsequently more aggressive with their playmates. But such data do not provide unequivocal evidence of causal links; indeed the relationship between the two interactive systems is made to look even more complex by Vandell's finding that the direction of influence appears also to go in the opposite direction: for instance, children with characteristically longer interactions with peers at the earlier ages had significantly longer interactions with parents at the later age. Vandell's conclusion that skill at social interaction with peers affects the parent–child system needs to be treated with caution: neither priority in time nor correlation (even of the cross-lagged variety) provides conclusive grounds for cause-and-effect statements. And a further consideration to take into account is that interactions with parents and with peers may serve different purposes: as Lewis *et al.* (1975) have shown, peers elicit much more distal behaviour (especially looking), while parents elicit mainly proximal behaviour such as touching and proximity seeking; peers serve as playmates, whereas parents are used for comfort and reassurance. Any difference in the form of the interaction may therefore be a function of this difference in interaction content.

All one can definitely conclude at present is that there are differences in dyadic behaviour as a function of partner—hardly a startling conclusion but nevertheless one that needs to be documented. In this connection it is interesting to find that the dichotomy is not a simple one between adult and child partners. Ross and Goldman (1976) observed 18-month-old children interacting with a one-year-old or a two-year-old child, and found that the interaction was generally of a more complex form when the partner was older rather than younger. This finding raises doubts as to the wisdom of sharply dichotomizing interactive behaviour into two separate systems involving adults and children respectively. The situation is in fact similar to that which we previously discussed in relation to inanimate objects and social objects: there too we questioned the wisdom of thinking in terms of separate "systems" based on a sharp dichotomy of stimuli. Similarly in this case a gradation according to a variety of stimulus characteristics of the partner appears more appropriate: differential behaviour certainly occurs, but it is spread along a range according to the nature of the input provided by the specific partner rather than being sharply divided into separate classes.

Conclusions

A number of profound changes overtake children's behaviour in the 8 to 10 months period. Amongst these the development of relational abilities is a specially important theme; as a result the child becomes increasingly capable of interconnecting disparate events over time and space, as seen in particular in the way he begins to play his part in welding together an interactive sequence out of a series of individual responses.

From this age on interactions gradually become more symmetrical as the child acquires what we have called "the concept of the dialogue". Two processes can be singled out as heralding this development, namely the understanding of reciprocity and the capacity for intentionality. The former refers to the knowledge that a dialogue must be sustained by both partners and that their roles can be not only integrative but also interchangeable. The study of parent–infant games provides some especially clear illustrations of the growth of reciprocity, showing how the child's focus gradually widens from a concern with his own individual action occurring at a particular moment of time to an appreciation of the interactive unit as such, including the partner's behaviour and the anticipated outcome of the whole sequence—a kind of early decentring. As to intentionality, this has not proved an easy concept to operationalize, and yet its emergence gives a very distinctive flavour to the child's behaviour from the end of the first year on. Not only can the child now communicate messages to the partner with some specific end in mind, but he is also able continuously to adjust the nature of his communications in the light of feedback information from the other person. Again one sees here the ability to take into account several disparate events simultaneously and to integrate them into one coherent action pattern.

Such integrative ability needs to be regarded as the culmination of previously practiced separate activities. Initially the infant is absorbed in face-to-face encounters; he spends several months learning the characteristics of his caretakers and perfecting the art of fitting his behavioural flow to theirs. Then, as we have seen, he turns abruptly away to the world of things: his attention is absorbed by the newly acquired ability to act upon objects and several more months are spent in becoming competent in this sphere.

Eventually, towards the end of the first year, these separate accomplishments are put together; the emergence of relational abilities means that the constituents of an activity previously practiced separately become integrated into a higher-order skill, as a result of which the child can interact with other people via external topics.

Such a development parallels the account that has been given of the way in which sensorimotor skills are acquired (e.g. by Bruner, 1973, and by Connolly, 1973). According to the modular model of the acquisition process, units of action (so-called subroutines) are learned first and are practised to the point where they can occur with minimal conscious attention, leaving the child free to attend to those action units not yet mastered. The various components can then be juxtaposed into sequential, hierarchically organized coordinations, thus forming new, more complex higher-order patterns which may be applied to many different contexts. The acquisition of social interactive skills bears the same features: the various components are practised separately, starting with face-to-face routines; the turning away from people to things at 5 months occurs in order to free the child's attention to cope with the newly emerging ability to attend to objects; at the end of the first year the relative mastery of that ability makes possible its combination with previously acquired components; and thus, after practising the individual subroutines on their own, the child becomes capable of combining them into one higher-order, integrative skill to which in due course other components may also be added. There is accordingly an orderly sequential process of development whereby new achievements become integrated in time with earlier ones; accumulating social skills is thus not a haphazard affair but one which follows a definite developmental timetable.

Once the child's new relational capacities emerge at the end of the first year he becomes a much more "social" partner. Yet for quite some time to come the adult must still assume the major share of responsibility for the maintenance of interaction. This becomes apparent when one examines exchanges among peers during the first 2 years or so: though they occur in some form from a very early age on there are indications that they lag behind in richness and sophistication when compared with adult–child interactions. The fragility of the child's social skills at that period and the supportive role that the adult accordingly needs to play are thus highlighted.

6   Into Conversation

Around the middle of the second year a further major change in the child's psychological organization is to be found, with profound implications for social behaviour. It involves the development of the capacity for symbolic representation: the child, as Piaget (1950) so carefully documented, has now reached the point where he is no longer functioning entirely on the level of overt actions performed on concrete objects; instead, these actions and objects can be represented internally in symbolic form. Among various consequences one is prominent: language, as a meaningful and shared system of representing reality, can now be used for communicative purposes, so that henceforth social exchanges increasingly assume the form of conversations. The interaction between parent and child thus moves to a new level, where the child's verbal abilities are a major determinant of the kinds of mutual adjustment the partners need to work out.

Symbolic representation

The progression from sensorimotor functioning to the use of symbols is one of the major transitions in cognitive development to which Piaget (1950) drew attention. From about the middle of the second year on there are various indications of representational processes that one may see in the child's behaviour; they show that the child has come to realize that one thing may "stand for" another, and that an absent object or an action not yet carried out may be evoked by symbolic means. Amongst the manifestations which Piaget lists of this new capacity is the onset of symbolic play, the ability mentally to reconstruct invisible displacements of an object, deferred imitation, and the use of language. Take the first of these, play: as Fenson *et al.* (1976) have shown, between 13 and 20 months a sharp rise occurs in the incidence of symbolic play activities; children during this period realize that a piece of wood may be thought of as a boat, that a doll may be a baby or a mother or a father, and that one can talk on a toy telephone pretending to be speaking to someone else. In each case the use of symbolic processes is indicated, where the child represents one thing for another. The child's world thus becomes less literal; what is more, it becomes less tied to the here-and-now as events belonging to past or future can be represented and used to guide action.

(1) Language as symbol use

Of most immediate concern to us are the implications for the onset of verbal means of interpersonal communication. The precise relationship between language and cognitive development is still an unsettled issue; in particular, the dependence of language on preceding sensorimotor events remains a matter of controversy unilluminated by any constructive proposals as to how it may be resolved. According to Vygotsky (1962), "thought and speech have different roots"; according to Piaget, on the other hand, sensorimotor development provides the essential precursors to language usage, and not until the capacity for representational thought emerges will the child realize that a word can be used as a symbol to designate an object or event in the environment. The fact that children begin to use words many months before the capacity for symbolic representation emerges in the middle of the second year is explained by Piaget as a shift in the way in which words are used. Early words, that is those that appear within the sensorimotor period from 10 or 12 months on, are of a different order: they are "semi-signs" (or verbal schemata, as Piaget also referred to them), in that they are idiosyncratic and highly variable in meaning, being purely personal to the child and regarded by him as an attribute of the object or event to which they refer (Ingram, 1978). The child, in other words, cannot as yet appreciate that one can distinguish between a sign and its referent, nor does he realize that signs can be shared and therefore serve as means for communication. Just as social gestures like pointing go through an initial non-communicative phase so, according to this account, are words first used without the intention of transmitting information to others.

With the onset of representational thought this situation changes, for now symbols become differentiated from their referents and the child is now able to use the former in order to indicate the latter to other people. Language, as a socially shared symbolic system, thenceforth becomes the primary vehicle for communication. Reference to past events, linguistic play, multi-word utterances and the use of questions are among the main indications used by Piaget for the transition. It is therefore not so much the onset of speech, i.e. the appearance of the first recognizable words, that is of significance; it is rather the discovery that words have a symbolic function the meaning of which may be shared with others. Using a verbal label in the absence of the object to which it refers, or its spontaneous use in a new context, are indications that the child realizes that symbols can be substituted for their referents for certain purposes. Using words in order to influence the behaviour of another person (e.g. "I want . . ." or "Look at . . .") means that the communicative purpose of verbal behaviour is now appreciated. Halliday's (1975) distinction between the *mathetic* function of language, whereby the individual comments on the world, and the later appearing *informative* function, used for communicating with others about the world, provides a similar account of the child's linguistic progression. It may be paradoxical that such essentially communicative devices as indicative gestures and words first appear in a non-communicative form, but perhaps the child needs to practise them on his own before he tackles the more difficult task of simultaneously attending to the other person, integrating word (or gesture) with object referred to and with the social partner. And it may also be that the spurt in language usage after the plateau between 13 and 18 months to which Nelson (1979) drew attention is due to the child's realization of the social function of words and the consequent motivation experienced to employ them in order to communicate with and influence other people.

Continuity and change

With the onset of language the child's interactive behaviour becomes vastly enriched. Of all forms of interaction a conversation is the most sophisticated: it can transmit information in a very economical fashion, it allows highly subtle shades of meaning to be communicated, and it enables the participants to transcend the here-and-now and interact via abstract as well as concrete topics. It will take the child many years to develop the manifold skills that characterize the mature conversationalist, and it is not intended here to provide a full account of this development. A lot of research has been carried out on this topic in recent years (for summaries see deVilliers and deVilliers, 1978; and Howe, 1981); our concern is more with the child's initial entry into linguistically based interactions.

What is a conversation? Its essence lies, of course, in verbal exchange between people, and as such it is distinguished by a number of features. Some of these refer to *formal* aspects; thus a conversation involves a turn sequence containing a minimum of two exchanges (A → B, B → A); the sequencing is carried out according to precise rules of exchange; and while the roles of the interlocutors need not be identical they must be complementary. Other features refer to *content* aspects: in particular, the participants must refer to a common topic and they need to be intelligible to one another. These are features that can also be found in preverbal interactions; there too rules of sequencing and a common frame of reference are distinguishing characteristics. The main obvious difference lies in the vehicle of expression: words rather than actions now carry the message. Thus the skills which the child must acquire to make him into an effective conversationalist are by no means specific to the usage of words: knowing whether to respond, when to respond and how to respond to the partner are general interactive skills that would have to develop even in the absence of language. But just what the relationship is between the pre-verbal and the verbal phase of interacting with others turns out to be an extraordinarily complex question. Are early pre-verbal interactions in some sense equivalent to later verbally based interactions? Is experience gained during the earlier phase necessary in order to graduate to the later phase? Are early interactions functionally related to later ones? Change—primarily in mode of expression—there obviously is, but is there continuity as well?

(1) Continuity

The theme of continuity in psychological development has preoccupied many writers in recent times, with particular reference to two issues, namely the stability of individual characteristics during the course of development and the extent to which early experience leaves irreversible effects. However, the problem with which we are faced here is whether the ability to communicate verbally arises *de novo* with the onset of speech, or whether it is founded on interpersonal experiences during the earlier period.

Arguments about this relationship tend to be based on any one of the following considerations:

(1) *Formal continuity.* To qualify as an interaction we require certain formal characteristics such as mutual attention, topic sharing, temporal regulation of the participants' responses, and so forth. On their basis we group together otherwise diverse phenomena and apply to them a common label ("interaction", "dialogue", etc.). To do so is, of course, often very useful; however, the sharing of formal characteristics need not imply common underlying processes. We have seen this in the phenomenon of turn-taking: in the vocal interactions of early infancy it may be every bit as precise as in later conversations; the mechanisms of bringing it about, however, are quite different. The same applies to Trevarthen's (1977) "pre-speech" syndrome: overt similarity of infants' expressive movements and those made by adults during speech cannot on its own guarantee identity of

processes. It is true that such overt similarities may provide useful starting points for hypothesis formation and empirical enquiry; without further evidence, however, this kind of proposition is based on analogy alone.

(2) *Functional continuity.* Encounters between individuals fulfil certain functions: becoming acquainted, exchanging information, having fun together, comforting each other, and so on. These functions are independent of the modes whereby they are expressed—one can draw someone's attention to a particular object by pointing, by a head movement, with a glance or by some verbal remark. Messages can thus be conveyed in a variety of forms, the choice depending more on such factors as social convention or various situational constraints than on the purpose of the communication.

The transition from preverbal to verbal interaction could thus be seen as involving a change in mode but not necessarily in function. There is certainly no doubt that children are capable of expressing a number of social meanings well before the onset of conventional speech. Halliday (1975), from intensive study of one child, produced the following list:

Instrumental:	"I want"
Regulatory:	"Do as I tell you"
Interactional:	"Me and you"
Personal:	"Here I come"
Heuristic:	"Tell me why"
Imaginative:	"Let's pretend"
Informative:	"I've got something to tell you"

Each of these functions may initially be expressed by non-conventional means, such as vocalizations of a highly idiosyncratic nature that are nevertheless systematically applied to particular circumstances. Similarly Carter (1978) believes (though on the basis of a rather different list that includes such functions as "requests object", "attention to object", "dislike", and so on) that it is possible to find for each function a combination of gestures, prelinguistic vocalizations and words that regularly co-occur and thus constitute communicative schemes. During the preverbal period each scheme is allegedly expressed by a specific gesture–sound combination; subsequently this is replaced by words, used either on their own or still in conjunction with sensorimotor acts.

There is little doubt that functional continuity exists and that words do come to serve the same purposes that have already been expressed by other means during the preverbal period. Yet, just as with formal continuity, functional continuity on its own is no proof of any aetiological link. The different systems may have evolved separately to express particular purposes; the fact that both an earlier and a later appearing system deal with the same purpose need not imply that developmentally one is a prerequisite for the other. Again analogy should not be confused with homology.

(3) *Process continuity.* The strongest claims for continuity are those that postulate identical processes operating at both levels. Irrespective of any formal or functional similarity, the case rests on the claim that the same mental operations are brought into play and that preverbal and verbal interactions are based on similar mechanisms. The further assertion may also be made that the practice that the child obtains preverbally with interaction formats accounts for the relative ease with which language comes to be used for the same purpose.

One such plea for process continuity comes from Bruner (1977). Language, according to Bruner, derives both its semantic structure and its pragmatic functions from the nature of social interaction. Reference, for example, has its origins in the joint attention routines that mother and child develop in the early months. Verbal communication is thus rooted in achieving cooperation in action preverbally—the very structure of language reflects the requirements of joint action in carrying out tasks. A formal similarity exists between communications carried out preverbally and those executed later on by verbal means; however, Bruner goes further than merely pointing out such likenesses, for he puts forward a definite aetiological link:

"... what the child learns about communication before language helps him crack the linguistic code ... Specifically, mother and child develop a variety of procedures for operating jointly and in support for each other. At first, these joint actions are very direct, specially geared to assistance and comfort. In time, the two of them develop conventions and requirements about carrying joint tasks. The structure of those tasks ... may shape the structures of initial grammar by the nature of the jointly held concepts it imposes. The evolution of grammar may then only be a reflection of the changing requirements of joint action between members of the evolving hominid species. It would not be surprising, then, if the ontogenetic development of joint action between mother and child contributed to the mastery of grammar, to the cracking of its code. If this is so, and I am taking it as a working hypothesis that it is, then one would have to understand the child's acquisition of the rules of joint action before one could understand the nature of grammatical acquisition—and I shall indeed be arguing that the mastery of procedures for joint action provides the precursors for the child's grasp of initial grammatical forms." (Bruner, 1977, p.274)

Thus the child's entry into language is said to be preconditioned by his involvement in joint enterprises at a preverbal level, the connection being the common processes which are developed and practiced initially in the course of interactive experience during infancy and which then provide the foundation on which verbal communication takes place.

The problem lies in ever being able to verify such a hypothesis. The belief that passage through one stage is essential to equip the individual with certain structures necessary for performance at the next stage underlies many developmental theories. However, that stage A precedes stage B is in itself no proof that it is required as a prelude to the latter. While in theory there are several methods that could be employed to investigate this association, in practice each one has severe disadvantages. One such method is the *deprivation technique*, i.e. depriving the individual of A in order to see whether B still occurs. For ethical reasons this is rarely feasible with human subjects; it is in any case not a pure test as it usually introduces other confounding factors implicated in the deprivation experience. The same applies to a second method, namely the *training technique*. In this case, instead of taking away A one adds to it in order to determine whether B also increases subsequently. This need not entail any ethical objections; once again, however, one is likely to alter more than just the particular function investigated. The third method, the *correlational technique*, examines whether individuals naturally high (or low) on A will also be high (or low) on B; this too is not wholly convincing as it only measures the relative status of individuals and is thus unable to make statements about the aetiological factors at work producing whatever similarities one may observe.

There are thus problems with all the recognized methods of making statements about continuity. Even the suggestion by Bretherton and Bates (1979), that one should break down the transition from A to B into many smaller steps, does not yield proof of aetiological links, even though it can generate intuitively more convincing material. But in the absence of any foolproof method one ought at least to make a clear distinction between analogy and homology and not dress up arguments based on the former as though they involve the latter. Developmental continuity, in the sense discussed here, is still largely a matter of faith, not fact. Describing transitions is not the same as explaining them.

(2) Change

The onset of language does not mean a simple changeover from nonverbal to verbal means of communication, with one system merely replacing the other. Many language studies, by concentrating on the individual's verbal utterances, may give such an impression; in fact even after linguistic modes of communication have become well established between child and parent both partners continue to rely heavily on nonverbal means.

As far as the child is concerned, far from nonverbal devices dropping out of his repertoire once he has reached linguistic proficiency their number may actually increase with age, becoming more sophisticated and precise with growing diversity. As Jancovic *et al.* (1975) have put it, previous discussions of this topic have mostly been based on the assumption that nonverbal communicative behaviours are (a) *nothing but* early precursors to later verbal forms, (b) *nothing but* primitive substitutes for more complex verbal forms, and that they are therfore (c) trivial in comparison to verbal behaviour, (d) unlikely to occur with much frequency except in special, inarticulate populations such as young children or mental patients, and (e) likely to occur only under special circumstances in which preferred verbal forms of communication are not possible. These investigators examined the use of hand and arm movements for communicative purposes in the age range 4 to 18 years and found that such movements *increased* with age, especially those serving more complex functions such as semantic modification. A simple substitution model is clearly inadequate to explain the relationship between verbal and nonverbal means; the latter are not merely primitive precursors to the former but themselves develop and diversify during childhood. Unfortunately the two communicative modes have mostly been studied in isolation from one another, and far more work is thus required on the nature of their relationship and its change over age.

When we look at the way in which parents communicate to children similar conclusions emerge. Here again only a little work has been done on the relationship between verbal and nonverbal communicative modes, but this too gives no support to a substitution model. In a study of mothers' techniques for conveying task directives to children aged 10 and 18 months (i.e. at a preverbal and an early verbal level respectively), Schaffer *et al.* (1983) found a greater reliance on verbal means at the older age (as given by an utterance rate of 20·11 per minute, compared with 14·43 at the younger age), but no corresponding decrease in nonverbal devices (the rates per minute being virtually identical, i.e. 20·21 at 10 months and 21·19 at 18 months). Thus a cross-over effect, whereby usage of one communicative system declines as usage of the other increases, was not found for this age range: the greater competence of the older children to comprehend the mothers' verbal utterances did not involve a counterbalancing decrease in the mothers' nonverbal activity. On the contrary, at both ages mothers rarely observed nonverbal ''silence'' while speaking: 84% of utterances in the younger and 86% in the older group were accompanied by some kind of nonverbal behaviour relevant to the task in hand. It is also noteworthy that the form which these verbal–nonverbal combinations took gives little support to the idea that children learn to crack the linguistic code through association with nonverbal messages sent by the adult simultaneously and containing the same information (Macnamara, 1972). At 10 months there was little functional equivalence in the two kinds of signals sent; verbal and nonverbal behaviour co-occurred but the association was not of a parallel kind that would enable the child to acquire the meaning of utterance on the basis of accompanying nonverbal actions. At 18 months regularly occurring verbal–nonverbal associations were found, yet the patterning provided no unequivocal evidence of functional equivalence in the meaning conveyed: a mother's directive to carry out some action might, for example, be accompanied by pointing to the locality where that action was to be performed, thus giving supplementary information but not thereby making it possible to decode the verbal by means of the nonverbal signal.

The change to language-based patterns of communication is clearly not one that involves going from action accompanied by silence to speech isolated from all other behaviour. After all, even during the preverbal stage adults use speech to infants (even to neonates, as documented by Rheingold and Adams, 1980). It is true that there are some cultural variations in this respect: among the Luo of East Africa, for instance, Blount (1973) found little inclination to talk to infants below the age of 9 months or so. When requested by the investigator to elicit cooing or babbling Luo adults became ill-at-ease, their attempts were brief and sparing and generally ended in embarrassed laughter, with explanations that the child was too young to understand and unable to respond. Yet even here Blount noted that on occasion mothers did talk, and that they addressed remarks like "Why are you crying?" or "Hello" even to their newborn babies. Certainly among Western adults it would seem unnatural to relate to a baby without talking; routines like bathing or dressing are often occasions for considerable speech input, while in more playful situations there is generally an almost continuous stream of language directed at the infant. Children may initially be unable to make use of this mode of communication, yet parents do so from the beginning—curiously perhaps, although one may well speculate whether the massive input of speech to which the child is subjected day in, day out from birth on has implications for the subsequent acquisition of language.

Language acquisition and social interaction

Just how children become capable of language remains a matter for conjecture. Under the influence of earlier nativistic approaches language was treated as a beneath-the-skin system, explicable wholly in terms of the psychological organization of the individual. Even its acquisition was considered in isolation from the social environment, partly because of the assumption that the speech heard by the child is too disorganized and confusing to serve as a basis for learning, and partly because there seem to be no obvious indications of "teaching" on the part of the child's care-takers. Innate factors were thus considered as all-important in the acquisition process, and few attempts were made systematically to investigate possible relationships between language development and the behaviour of the child's social partners.

It is only more recently, following growing disillusionment with extreme nativistic positions and increasing interest in semantic and pragmatic rather than syntactic aspects of language, that speech has come to be viewed as essentially a communicative function, with the consequent need to study it in interactive settings. The child's partners, it is now believed, do have some sort of role to play in helping it to achieve competence in the use of language, and to describe that role and assess its part in language develop-ment has become one of the main topics of research in this area.

(1) Reinforcement and imitation

One view of the adult's role in language development is that derived from learning theory. It is that the same mechanisms account for such development as for all other forms of learning, and that consequently the adult's function is primarily to act as a dispenser of reinforcement and as a model to be imitated. Children, that is, are rewarded for progressively approximating the speech sounds and constructions that make up the language of their community; at the same time mere exposure to the language as used by other members of that community will result in its acquisition.

There is no question that both these processes, reinforcement and imitation, do play some part; there is, however, every reason to doubt that this is a substantial part, sufficient to explain the essential facts of language acquisition. The following points must be considered:

(a) Language learning children rarely get corrected by their parents for making syntactic errors; correction is nearly always based on the truth value of what is said (Brown and Hanlon, 1970). Expressions such as "He a girl" and "They sings" are accepted without disapproval if they express facts with which the parent essentially agrees; factual inaccuracies, on the other hand, however well formed syntactically, are at once corrected. Yet children progress in their mastery of grammar, apparently uninfluenced by their parents' pattern of reinforcement.

(b) Modelling "correct" language appears to have limited influence on children. In an experimental study Cazden (1965) divided children into two groups: one who simply conversed daily for three months with an adult, the other who for a similar period heard all their utterances completed and placed into proper grammatical form by the experimenter. At the end of the period the first group showed considerable advancement on a variety of linguistic measures over the second group: correction and provision of adult-approved versions of language had had comparatively little effect.

(c) The frequency with which parents use particular linguistic constructions has little to do with the ease with which children learn them. For instance, Brown (1973) noted that certain morphemes occur with varying frequency in the speech of different parents; however, the order of acquisition by children of these same morphemes showed little relationship to the parents' usage. Some minimal frequency is obviously required to enable children to learn speech characteristics; the almost invariant order of morpheme acquisition among children generally suggests, however, that factors other than modelling by parents are responsible. Also relevant is an observation by Van der Geest (1977), namely that mothers start using certain semantic categories in their speech to children with any degree of frequency only *after* the children have begun to use these categories themselves.

(d) Children differ in the extent to which they imitate adult speech, yet these differences do not predict language development. Among six children studied intensively by L. Bloom *et al.* (1974), two rarely imitated and yet learned to speak as well as the others. Moreover, none of the children imitated linguistic structures that were completely absent from their spontaneous speech.

(e) Finally, it has often been observed that children construct sentences quite unlike any their parents would use. They create novel combinations like "Allgone pudding" and use grammatic forms such as "wented" or "eated" that could not possibly depend on imitation or selective reinforcement. Instead, these examples illustrate a very different feature of language development, namely the way in which children actively seek to make inferences about language use and, quite independent of reward, attempt to construct rule systems to govern their expressions.

It is this last consideration which represents the most cogent argument against any view based on reinforcement and imitation. These latter mechanisms are basically associated with the notion of a passive child, who responds in a more or less mechanical fashion to environmental stimulation. Yet whatever the precise role of input in language acquisition may be, the notion of a passive child cannot be sustained in the light of evidence that children are highly creative in the way they use the language they hear in order to construct their own messages. The use of forms like "wented" and "eated" is one example of the child's attempts actively to make sense of the speech to which he is exposed—even when the illogicalities of English defeat his own commendable logic. The child, that is, brings his own strategies to bear on language heard by him in order to decipher the code and become a language user himself; he certainly does not just passively absorb language. Hence also the sudden, across-the-board nature of new acquisitions: Bellugi-Klima (1969), for instance, found that auxilliaries like "can" and "will" may be completely absent at one age and yet, just a few weeks later, appear in all their common forms and within a wide variety of structures. To quote Bellugi-Klima: "In terms of learning theory based on frequency of occurrence, transition probabilities, reinforcement contingencies, etc., there is absolutely no reason to expect the appearance of grammatically based processes across the board and at one period in the child's speech."

It seems therefore that the role of caretakers in the child's language acquisition cannot adequately be explained in terms of concepts drawn from associationist theories of learning. Reinforcement and imitation may play some limited part, but they are essentially one-way conceptions of adult influence on children and so do not do justice to the reciprocity that exists between an active child and a sensitive caretaker. *Learning* (probably the single most abused term in psychology) is in any case too closely linked to various experimental and theoretical paradigms to do justice to facts derived from outside these paradigms. It is for this reason that the more neutral term *acquisition* has been adopted; as Miller (1978) points out, this at least leaves open the possibility that something different from conventional learning processes is at work in child language, something that may be internally programmed as well as externally guided.

(2) The facilitating role of parents

The claim that parents "teach" their children to speak depends largely on the way one defines that term. For instance, the assertion advanced by Moerk (1983), that mothers actively and intensively teach language in the home, rests on his description of an array of specific techniques with a *potential* tuitional function that mothers use in their everyday interactions with their children. Included in this list are such devices as labelling pictures, giving verbal commentary on the child's or the mother's own ongoing activity, expanding the child's utterances and imitating in agreement. All these offer linguistic information or serve a corrective function. They provide an opportunity for the child to learn to associate his experience with language; that acquisition of language is indeed affected by such input has, however, not been demonstrated.

Teaching need not, of course, be understood as a crudely didactic activity; indeed there are indications that highly directive teaching may actually interfere with language development. Nelson (1973) classified mothers according to the extent to which they accepted or rejected their children's speech productions. Rejecting mothers, i.e. those who took an active part in directing their children's speech by imposing their own views and concepts, had children with the slowest developmental rates; by their intrusiveness they prevented the child from effectively formulating and naming his own concepts. An accepting, non-directive pattern, on the other hand, helped successfully to launch the child into language acquisition by virtue of the mother's willingness to listen, watch and interpret the child's behaviour. Paradoxically, the more tolerant the mother was of her child's "wrong" words the more rapid the process of vocabulary building; in this way progress towards a matching of the adult's and the child's language worlds could more easily be achieved than in instances of high intrusiveness and rejection.

The ability of the adult to tune in to the child emerges as a basic requirement. This is also seen in Moerk's (1975) observation that the mean length of utterance (MLU) of mothers' speech to children in the age range 2 to 5 years closely matched the children's own MLU, but in such a way that the mothers' MLU always slightly exceeded the child's. However, the value of the maternal MLU invariably lay below the maximum point of the child's MLU range—as though the mother was attempting to incite the child to advance to higher linguistic levels by confronting him with more complex speech though remaining well within the range of his competence.

Parental "teaching" of language appears to involve the adoption of a facilitating role, played out in the context of cooperative enterprises in which the adult's behaviour is determined largely by awareness of the child's interests and abilities. A useful indication of the extent to which such cooperation is established is provided by the *relevance* of the parent's remarks to the meaning intentions of the child. To illustrate: Cross (1978) formed two groups of children according to their rate of language development, a "normally developing" and an "accelerated" group. Comparison of mothers' speech to the children of these two groups yielded just one significant difference: the mothers of the accelerated group made greater use of utterances that were semantically related to the child's preceding utterance. By thus following up on topics introduced by the child and linking their remarks to his, these women ensured that the child was properly motivated to attend to their speech—with possible consequences for language development, though these are conjectural. In another correlational study Newport *et al.* (1977), while noting no consistent relationship of the child's language development to such measures of maternal speech as the complexity or length of utterance or the amount of repetition, did find that an extensive use of feedback in response to the child's own utterances was related to language growth. And Wells (1979), examining the various contexts in which conversations occur between mothers and children, found a significant relationship between language development at 2½ years and the proportion of speech occurring within *joint enterprise* contexts (i.e. shared activities such as doing housework together, play with adult participation, looking at books or just talking together). The more rapid development of first-born children which Wells found was similarly ascribed to the greater opportunity that mothers of only children have for engaging in talk in the context of shared activities.

Adults differ in their preferred styles of conducting conversations with young children (Wood *et al.*, 1980; Howe, 1981), and these differences lead to varying opportunities for children to participate linguistically in the interaction. Not only has this implications for the amount of information provided to the child as to the nature of spoken language, but, as Howe points out, there are also associated variations in the extent to which children are *motivated* to contribute by verbal means. Where there is a direct connection between the parent's remarks and the child's, and where therefore the meaning content of the exchange is mutually agreed and a topic is shared, a conversation can be jointly constructed. It may well be (even if we cannot prove it as yet) that such experiences aid language development. As Snow (1979) has put it: "If one were asked right now to advise an anxious mother how to teach her child to talk, the best answer would be 'Watch what he's doing, listen to what he's saying, and then respond'."

(3) Adult speech adjustments to children

The sensitive adaptation of adults' behaviour to children that we have commented on repeatedly is also found in the speech used to address children. Such speech differs markedly in a number of ways from that used among adults, hence the term "motherese" to designate it as a distinct code.

Over 100 features have been identified whereby motherese can be characterized. They refer to syntactic, semantic, pragmatic and phonological aspects, some of which are listed in Table 9. Several of these have already been referred to in previous chapters, for they characterize adult behaviour during the child's preverbal as well as the verbal period. Most of these features are said to be universal across all languages; in sum, they make speech to children simpler, briefer, more complete, more repetitive and more attention worthy in comparison with speech to adults. In theory at least, motherese represents an input well-suited as a teaching device.

This is particularly so because a fine tuning of motherese according to the age (or more precise, the linguistic stage) of the child has been repeatedly demonstrated. Snow (1972), in one of the first reports on this topic, compared the speech of mothers to 2-year-old children with that to 10-year-old children on three measures of grammatical complexity and found significant increases with child age for all three. Fraser and Roberts (1975), using somewhat different measures and more narrow age spacing among their groups (1½, 2½, 4 and 6 years old), also found significant differences in the mothers' speech ordered according to the children's age. And Phillips (1973), investigating age groups even younger and still more narrowly spaced (i.e. 8, 18 and 28 months of age), also obtained confirmation that various aspects of mothers' speech change according to the age of the addressee. While no differences occurred between 8 and 18 months (a point to which we shall return), a significant difference was found between 18 and 28 months, indicating the increasing complexity and the wider range of vocabulary used in talking to the older children. An even greater increase was found when the mothers' speech to an adult (also present during the recording sessions) was analysed and compared with that to the children.

Table 9. *Some features of "motherese": adaptation of adults' speech to children in comparison with speech to other adults.*

Phonological characteristics	*Semantic characteristics*
Higher pitch	Limited range of vocabulary
Exaggerated and more varied inton-	"Baby talk" words
ation	Reference to here-and-now
Lengthened vowels	More words with concrete referents
Clear enunciation	
Slower speech	*Pragmatic characteristics*
Longer pauses	
	More directives
Syntactic characteristics	More questions
	More deictic utterances
Shorter utterance length	More attention devices
Sentences well-formed	Repetitions of child's utterances
Fewer subordinate clauses	
Fewer embeddings	
Fewer verbs	

These are but some of the many studies which have documented the nature of adult speech to young children and the way it changes with age. Not all features of maternal speech show the same degree of adjustment. Ellis and Wells (1980) included 34 speech variables in their study of adult–child conversations in the preschool period, but found that only a small proportion showed adjustment to the child's level of linguistic development. Some features of speech are less easily influenced than others: Schaffer and Crook (1979), for example, found an association between child's age and the length of maternal utterance in the case of action directives but not in the case of attention directives. The latter tend to be of a rather stereotyped nature, consisting of brief, conventional expressions that remain constant across a wide range of circumstances. Nevertheless, there is a general pattern that encompasses many different measures, including syntactic, semantic, pragmatic and discourse features. Bellinger (1980) investigated 12 such variables for maternal speech to children in the age range 1 to 5 years, and found striking consistency across mothers in the general patterning of language. He noted, however, that the change over age was not a regular one: the rate at which the mothers' speech (as given by one composite index) changed was greatest when the children were between 1 year 8 months and 2 years 3 months old and least between 2 years and 3 months and 5 years. This closely mirrors changes in the child's growing linguistic competence: here too the period around the end of the second year shows the greatest rate of advance. The mothers, we assume, were sensitive to the child's linguistic competence at that particular time and adapted their input accordingly.

There are a number of indications to suggest that mothers adapt their speech to children on the basis of feedback provided by the children. One piece of evidence is that previously referred to: the mothers of 8-month-old infants in Phillips' (1973) study did not differ from the mothers of 18-month-old children on any of the measures examined and indeed showed a slightly greater level of complexity on several. An 8-month-old, being unable to comprehend speech, is not yet able to give the mother feedback information as to the meaningfulness of her verbal communications; the 18-month-old, on the other hand, can provide such indications and is thereby able to help the mother find the appropriate level. Presumably the same explanation lies behind the finding that adults use *more* complex language when speaking to severely retarded individuals than to mildly retarded ones (Siegel, 1963; Siegel and Harkins, 1963): the former are less able to provide clear signals as to whether they comprehend what is being said than the latter. And similarly, when Snow (1972) asked mothers to speak to an imaginary child of a specified age she found that the features of motherese were not as marked as they were to a physically present child. Just what cues (verbal or nonverbal) provide the necessary feedback is, however, as yet unsettled.

It seems reasonable to conclude that sensitivity to the child's behaviour in communicative situations is the essential precondition for speech modification. It is, however, also important to note that this appears to be by no means the prerogative of mothers and that the term "motherese" is in this respect a misleading one. For one thing, Snow (1972) found childless women to modify their speech in almost the same fasion as mothers; for another, fathers use the same speech style as mothers (Berko Gleason, 1973); and finally even 4-year-old children modify the manner of their talk according to the age of the addressee (Shatz and Gelman, 1973). We are thus concerned with a general phenomenon, referring to the sensitivity of one person for another. The phenomenon is not even limited to spoken language: according to Cicourel and Boese (1972) deaf parents adjust their manual signing to their deaf children in comparable ways. On the other hand one must also draw attention to the findings by Ellis and Wells (1980) that substantial individual differences exist in the parents' fine-tuning to children; as they put it: ". . . in the population as a whole the level of adult speech adjustment relating to communicative intent may constitute a continuum with, at one pole, a group of adults highly sensitized to the communicative needs of their children and, at the other, a group of adults who monitor their speech only in coarse syntactic terms."

Why do people tend to adjust their way of speaking to young children? The most likely explanation is that motherese helps to bring about effective communication with the child. This is accomplished partly by the use of attention attracting features (e.g. high and varied pitch, exaggerated stress), partly by reducing the cognitive load on the child (e.g. by grammatically simple expressions, frequent repetition, reference to the here-and-now), and partly by adopting techniques that make it easy for the child to respond (e.g. a high proportion of interrogatives, a pattern of short utterances and long pauses). As Snow (1977) concluded, mothers seem to adopt a conversational model: their primary aim is to involve the child in some form of interchange in which the child is capable of participating. They therefore work hard at making the interchange both interesting and meaningful to the child.

What is much more problematic is the effect this way of talking has on the language acquisition process itself. This is mainly a methodological problem: motherese would appear to be ideally suited as a teaching device, yet to demonstrate that children are indeed able to profit from it is far from easy. A number of studies (e.g. Cross, 1977; Ellis and Wells, 1980) have shown that relationships between certain aspects of maternal speech input and the child's language acquisition rate do exist, but these suffer from the usual inability of correlational work to demonstrate cause and effect. In an attempt to circumvent this difficulty Furrow *et al.* (1979) adopted a cross-lag correlational approach and found that several characteristics of mothers' speech sampled when the children were 1 year 6 months old significantly predicted language development nine months later. They consequently concluded that the child's linguistic environment "must be considered a significant contributor to all aspects of the language learning process", that "motherese is an effective teaching language", and that one can safely conclude that "not only CAN input make a difference but that it DOES". Unfortunately such confidence cannot be sustained in the light of recent criticisms of cross-lagged techniques (e.g. Rogosa, 1980), which indicate that this may not be as effective a method of separating cause and effect as had been hoped. As yet the evidence for a determining influence of motherese on language acquisition is no more than suggestive; it remains a matter of (quite understandable) faith that a naturally occurring, quite unconsciously adopted and widespread pattern of relating to young children does indeed have a developmental effect.

(4) Parents as conversational partners

As in nonverbal interactions so in verbal conversations: there is an initial asymmetry in the roles played by adult and child. The child's ineptitude forces the parent to take the major responsibility for keeping the conversation going; only with the child's gradual acquisition of interactive skills will she relinquish her role in managing both sides of the dialogue.

Let us list some of the things parents do to maintain a conversation with a young child:

(1) Parents frequently allow the child to set the topic of the conversation, confining their role to providing comment on that topic (Shugar, 1978). This is particularly noticeable at the one-word stage, when the child labels an object of interest and the parent then elaborates on that object. The child may then produce another label, thus shifting topic, and once again the parent will provide comment. Continuity is thereby maintained, thanks to the adult's willingness to follow the child's interests.

(2) When the parent does introduce a topic she tends to adapt it closely to the child's orientation and activities, thus ensuring the likelihood of his response. In a follow-up study of two children between 3 and 18 months Snow (1977) found striking changes in the content of the mothers' remarks. At the earlier ages they talked mainly about the child himself (being tired, hungry or bored, what he was looking at, etc.); at later ages, when the children were taking an interest in their environment and able increasingly to act upon it, the mothers concentrated on the objects and events in that environment. This adaptation is found at all ages; once again its function is primarily a dialogic one.

(3) Adult speech is full of questions addressed to the child—or, to be more precise, full of utterances ending in rising intonation, for syntactically these may not always be in the interrogative form. Sachs *et al.* (1972) found as many as 50% of utterances to be of this type when adults read stories to young children; similarly Broen (1972), recording the spontaneous talk of mothers during free play with their 2-year-olds, noted the inordinately high percentage of "questions". Sometimes these utterances are requests for information; at other times tag questions are put at the end of statements; and at still other times an "eh?" or "hm?" is coupled to the utterance and

converts it into an apparent question. Many of these appear already in speech addressed to young infants, where there is no expectation of an answer. Instead, the function of such questions is to involve the child in the conversation by challenging him to respond—not necessarily verbally but in some way to indicate that he is interested and is attending to his partner (Snow, 1977). At its most basic, rising intonation appears to have an attention-getting function in its own right. This was shown by Ryan (1976) in a study of 1-year-old children and their mothers during play. It was found, first of all, that nearly half (43%) of maternal utterances ended in rising intonation (though syntactically nearly as many of these were declaratives as interrogatives); secondly, that mothers were more likely to use rising intonation when the child was attending to a different toy to the one the mother was manipulating; and finally, that the child was more likely to look at or reach for the mother's toy after a rising than a non-rising utterance. It seems that mothers use this prosodic device in order to attract the child's attention; the fact that they succeed shows that, at the age of 1 year at any rate, children are sensitive to its use. In time, as children get more competent, mothers will no longer be content with such minimal nonverbal responses; as Snow (1977) makes clear, the same question can be used for different purposes at different ages: as an attention-getting device with infants and as a way of enabling an older child to contribute to a complex, high-level discussion.

(4) Parents time their contribution to the conversation in such a way that they leave plenty of space for the child's reply. As found by Schaffer *et al.* (1977), the vocal interchanges of 1- and 2-year-old children with their mothers were marked by the great watchfulness of the mothers, enabling them to time their own contributions so as to give the child every opportunity to play his part in the interchange. Thus the mothers kept their utterances short, frequently paused to see if the child was ready to join in, and in this way showed that they were constantly ready to concede the floor to the child.

(5) In some instances parents may go even further, in that they fill in for the child when he fails to respond, supplying the answer for him. Take the following "conversation" reported by Snow (1977):

Mother: "Oh, you are a funny one, aren't you, hmm?"
"Aren't you a funny little one?"
"Yes."

Here the mother takes both parts, the child's as well as her own. She wants to avoid a purely one-sided conversation, but can only do so by taking the child's turn for him. Thus she makes up for the inadequacies of the child as a conversational partner and can preserve the illusion that an interchange has occurred. One can also speculate that she thereby models for the child what his answer ought to have been.

Adults differ, of course, in the extent to which they are willing to shoulder such responsibilities. In a seven-months follow-up of three children from 18 months onward Lieven (1978) noted a number of such differences: for instance, the proportion of child utterances to which the three mothers responded were 76%, 51%, and 29% respectively. The proportion of child utterances to which the mothers provided extensions were 44%, 24% and 18%, the rank order being identical for both measures. There are, in addition, differences in the type of dialogue sustained by mothers, as given by the extent to which they initiate exchanges with requests for information or provide extended replies to the child's questions—differences which Howe (1981) suggests might well have implications for the child's ability to acquire language.

Development of children's conversational skills

Listening to mothers and children gives one the strong impression that bona fide conversations begin in the second half of the second year (Howe, 1981). At 18 months most children already have a string of one-word utterances that they can use to bring about some desired effect in interpersonal situations. Verbal interchanges thus occur, but at this early stage much still depends on the adult's willingness to maintain the conversation. The child has learned that he is expected to respond when spoken to, but his response is rarely related to the previous topic: it is as though the adult's remark is seen as an invitation to say whatever is in his mind already (Shatz, 1978a). He cannot as yet preserve continuity of theme. Nor has he mastered some of the more basic social conventions on which discourse is based, as seen for example by his interruptions of other people's conversations or by his introduction of new topics before old ones are exhausted (Snow, 1977).

In the period of 2 to 4 years, however, some very considerable advance in conversational skills occur. The child's responses become more relevant to and more contingent on his partner's preceding remarks; he learns to maintain conversations, first by simply imitating the adult's utterances and subsequently by providing new information; he comprehends questions not merely as requests for attention but as demands for some form of verbal reply; and he quickly increases the range of interpersonal purposes for which he employs his messages to others. Conversations thus become lengthier, more explicit and more cohesive, and the respective roles of adult and child gradually change towards a greater degree of symmetry.

(1) Nature of conversational skills

The following are among the principal skills a child must acquire in order to become effective at verbal communication:

(a) He must learn to initiate the interaction, attracting the other person's attention as a first step by, for instance, the use of his name or by some nonverbal signal.

(b) He needs to make himself audible and not take it for granted that being able to hear himself means audibility to the other person.

(c) He must devise ways of maintaining his partner's interest and be able to sustain the exchange over successive turns.

(d) His own turns in the conversation need to be appropriately timed in relation to those of his partner. This requires sensitivity to the various signals people use to indicate floor-holding or floor-yielding; he must also learn to use these signals himself in an effective manner.

(e) He must develop the ability not only to initiate topics himself but also to follow up those raised by his partner, responding to them contingently and appropriately.

(f) He must adapt the form and content of speech to the comprehension skills of his partner.

(g) He also needs to take into account the other person's perspective in relation to the topic referred to, realizing (for example) that his own framework of past experience is not necessarily shared by others.

(h) He has to show sensitivity to the physical and social context of the interaction: what can be discussed at home with a family member may not form an appropriate topic in a public place with a stranger.

(i) He must learn to integrate his verbal with his nonverbal behaviour, producing unambiguous messages with a certain degree of redundancy.

(j) a great many specifically linguistic skills need to be acquired for effective communication in conversational contexts. To give just one example from many: the child needs to learn the relativity of words like "yours" and "mine" or of "here" and "there" if they are to be used appropriately in interactive situations.

(k) Most basically, the child has to learn how to perform speech acts, i.e. how to accomplish different goals by means of language: attracting attention, making a request, giving information, seeking comfort, etc. Language is a tool for satisfying individual purposes in interpersonal contexts; the rules for expressing these purposes by linguistic means, laid down by social convention, have to be acquired in the course of childhood.

These are just some of the constituents of conversational ability. To acquire them all is a long-drawn-out affair, perhaps never completed in some individuals. To trace the development of each requires a considerable research effort that has only just begun.

(2) Peer conversations

Once again it is interaction among peers that throws particularly illuminating light on the child's emerging abilities. Can young children, without the support of a more senior partner, engage in and maintain a conversation among each other? Recordings made by Keenan (1974) of her own two children are of particular interest, for the children were twins (aged 2 years 9 months at the time) and thus at about the same level of linguistic and communicative competence. The recordings were made while the children were still in bed in the early morning hours and so took place without the medium of toys or of other sustaining concrete objects.

That "proper" conversations occurred between these two children cannot be doubted. Take the following example (quoted by Clark and Clark, 1976):

Toby: (alarm clock rings) "Oh oh oh, bell"
David: "Bell"
Toby: "Bell. It's mommy's"
David: (mumbles indistinctly)
Toby: "Was mommy's alarm clock. Was mommy's alarm clock"
David: "Alarm clock"
Toby: "Yea. Goes ding dong, ding dong"

There is a definite coherence to this exchange, derived in part from its turn taking character and in part from the common theme to which all the individual contributions refer. On the one hand the children alternate their remarks in an orderly fashion, each waiting for the other to finish before starting his own utterance. And on the other hand the children clearly listen to the content of each other's remarks, imitating or expanding the previous utterance and thus preserving continuity by repeatedly addressing the same topic. These features typified many of the exchanges that Keenan recorded. The children attended to the form of each other's utterances; they were able to take up the topic introduced by the other twin; they acknowledged each other's assertions; and they even adapted the loudness of their comments in an appropriate manner. It is true that topics were often quickly exhausted, yet the very fact that they could be sustained over a number of turns shows that the coordination problem that faces any pair of interlocutors was already being solved by this particular pair.

The way in which conversational partners bring about temporal coordination throws further light on the growth of children's interactive skills. Lieberman and Garvey (1977) investigated how dyads composed of previously unacquainted 3½-year-old children time their conversational exchanges, and found a mean value of 2·01 sec. for inter-speaker switching pauses in the initial exchange of conversational episodes and of 1·2 sec. for all remaining exchanges. These values are rather greater than those reported for adults, where Jaffe and Feldstein (1970) found an average of 0·66 sec. for speaker-switch pauses. It may well be, however, that the playroom situation in which the children were observed by Lieberman and Garvey makes comparison with adults difficult: children absorbed in toys are not likely to produce the same smoothly coordinated verbal interchange that adults produce when attending only to each other. It may well be therefore that 3½-year-olds are capable of even more impressive temporal coordination.

A further study of dyadic conversations among preschoolers, conducted by Garvey and Berninger (1981), gives additional support to the conclusion that children in the preschool age range have already acquired a sense of the variable yet patterned rhythm that typifies dialogue. In the first place, the duration of speaker-switch pauses was found to decrease with age, from 1·1 sec. around 3 years to 0·8 sec. around 5 years. In addition, simultaneous speech occurred rarely; even the youngest children could manage their dialogue so as to avoid overlapping utterances. When these did occur they were terminated quickly, generally by the child whose turn had begun earlier; the normal alternating mode was usually immediately resumed and the clashes did not seriously impair the interaction. Finally, Garvey and Berninger investigated those instances when a child failed to elicit a response from his partner (after asking a question, for example, or following a request for repetition). They found that in such instances a second attempt to elicit the response was generally undertaken within a relatively restricted period, i.e. about two seconds. This period somewhat exceeds the length of most speaker-switch pauses, suggesting that the speaker waits for his partner's turn before eventually prompting him. It seems that these children had a norm in mind as to the time limits within which they could expect to receive a reply; only when that limit was exceeded did they take further action.

Let us note one further test of the child's conversational skill, namely his ability to adjust his speech to the level of his partner's understanding. According to Shatz and Gelman (1973) such adaptation can already be found among preschool-age children: four-year-olds, paired in turn with an adult, a peer, and a two-year-old, adopted a speech style that differed systematically with the developmental status of the partner. With two-year-olds, for instance, the children used shorter sentences, few complex constructions and more attention-getting devices than they did with older partners. Similar Sachs and Devin (1976) found that the speech of 4- to

5-year-old children to babies differed on a variety of measures from their speech to peers and to adults. The ability to make such modifications is further testimony to the young child's rapidly developing interactive competence.

Altogether there is little about the preschool child's verbal interactions which justify labelling them as "egocentric". According to the view widely attributed to Piaget (1926), children throughout the preschool period are so firmly embedded in their own viewpoint that they cannot take into account another person's needs and requirements. As a result their speech, right up to the age of five or six, is said to take the form of monologues: children, that is, talk *alongside* of one another but not *with* another. To use language as a communicative device requires its adaptation to the listener, and of this the egocentric child is said to be incapable. There are in fact reasons to doubt whether Piaget ever meant to establish quite so firm a developmental dichotomy between egocentric speech and sociocentric speech as is generally said; however this may be, it was widely believed until quite recently that young children are cognitively incapable of engaging in dialogue. Yet closer examination provides a rather different picture. Garvey and Hogan (1973), in their study of dyads of children aged 3½ to 5 years, found that even among the younger children there was an abundance of social speech, i.e. of utterances that were mutually responsive and adapted to the speech of the partner. Private (or egocentric) speech did occur but at nothing like the frequency that a Piagetian perspective would lead one to expect. At a still younger age, Keenan's (1974) twins produced only 6·6% of utterances that were not unequivocally addressed or adapted to the other child. The precise proportion of communicative as opposed to egocentric speech found in various samples is to some extent a matter of the definitions which different writers attach to these terms; what cannot be doubted is that from an early age on children do seem capable of socially adapted speech, using it to achieve and maintain contact with others. Compared with mature individuals their communicative competence is still severely limited in many respects, yet the evidence suggests that from at least the third year on children are able not only to string together their own utterances but also to link these in a reasonably cohesive manner with the preceding utterance of the other person. Conversation thus becomes possible.

Meta-sociability

The representational abilities that emerge in the second year and help to launch the child into language use continue to exert their influence on social development in other ways. In particular, they make it possible for the child in due course to become capable of reflecting upon his own behaviour in social situations as well as that of other people, of consciously monitoring the way in which he and his partners forge joint enterprises and, on the basis of these reflections, of deliberately changing the nature of his contribution to the exchange. As a summary label for these achievements the term "meta-sociability" will be used. We have already referred to this concept as designating an awareness by the child of himself in relation to other people (see p.123); it is thus analogous to the term "meta-cognition" which Flavell (1979) uses to describe an individual's ability to be aware of and reflect upon his own and others' cognitive processes. In the same way an individual's interpersonal behaviour will, in the course of development, become an object of contemplation, to be reflected upon, analysed and evaluated. To do so the individual must be able to represent to himself the behaviour and attributes not only of other people but also of himself, as well as be able to construe the relationships that exist between himself and these others.

The term "social cognition" has been used mainly to designate the individual's awareness of other people. In her review of developmental aspects of social cognition Shantz (1975) describes it as referring to "a child's intuitive or logical representation of others, that is how he characterizes others and makes references about their covert, inner psychological experiences." This seems unduly restrictive; as Brooks-Gunn and Lewis (1978) point out, three aspects need to be jointly taken into account: (1) knowledge of others, (2) knowledge of self, (3) knowledge of relationships between self and others. Studies of social cognition have confined themselves largely to the first of these; the term meta-sociability draws attention to the fact that the other two aspects must also be considered, and that in particular a degree of self-awareness is essential to the individual's cognizance of his social world.

The ability to conceive of a coherent self involves knowledge of one's psychological states and actions and their association in one unitary entity. Such a conception would hardly be possible without relating the self to non-self aspects of the environment, especially other people; its development is therefore likely to be dependent upon a history of social interaction, in the course of which it becomes progressively refined and modified.

Lewis and Brooks-Gun (1979) have traced that development through the first 2 years of life; their account emphasizes the fact that the notion of self does not refer to a single, unitary entity but that it is composed of a number of ingredients which become apparent at different ages. At 5 months the child already shows a primitive sense of agency in performing actions upon objects; by 8 months the initial attainment of object permanence solidifies the self–other distinction; and after 12 months self-recognition becomes apparent. But it is not till the middle of the second year that one sees evidence of self-awareness; for example, it is not till after 18 months, as Kagan (1981) has shown, that self-descriptive utterances appear in children's speech, increasing dramatically in incidence thereafter. By means of representational functions the child is then able to stand apart from himself and use that self-awareness to guide his own behaviour.

Just how children construe themselves and others in the 2 to 5 year period is a topic about which not a great deal is known. This is largely because of methodological difficulties: meta-abilities are generally assessed on the basis of the child's verbalizations (indeed are often equated with verbalizable knowledge, Flavell, 1979), and during the preschool range children's utterances are still too limited to provide much insight into their conceptions. Yet there is no reason to think that at this period children are not already learning to understand about such matters as relationships, especially those involving themselves, about other people's states and intentions, and hence about the appropriate ways of behaviour that they themselves should adopt in interacting with these people. Interpersonal behaviour, that is, becomes a much more self-conscious, planned and thought about affair than it was previously, even if initially children proceed more on the basis of vague intuitions than of precisely articulated verbal plans.

A considerable body of literature is now available with regard to children beyond the preschool period which attests to the increasingly sophisticated understanding of other people and their psychological characteristics. Empathy, the ability to see another person's point of view, has indeed been ascribed to children as young as 3 years (Borke, 1971), though its more mature, self-consciously articulated forms do not appear for some years thereafter (Chandler and Greenspan, 1972). Meta-communication, that is the ability to take a verbal message as a cognitive object and analyse it (Flavell, 1977), appears later still; by its means the child can deliberately monitor the effects his messages have upon a partner and alter them by taking account of that individual's characteristics as a listener (Glucksberg *et al.*, 1975; Robinson, 1981). There are diverse other aspects to such more mature expressions of meta-sociability; we shall not spend time discussing them for they have been reviewed elsewhere (Shantz, 1975). All such skills have their roots in the child's capacity for symbolic representation which allows him to reflect upon the social situation of which he is a part and which enables him to build up a fund of knowledge about such situations. But let us emphasize that such knowledge does not merely exist in a vacuum; it is used by the individual as a guide to behaviour, thereby ensuring that under the appropriate circumstances certain desirable outcomes can be attained. How such a link between knowledge and action is forged in the course of development is something about which a lot more needs to be found out.

Conclusions

With the onset of representational abilities in the second year the child's social behaviour undergoes a number of drastic changes. Above all, his interactions with others increasingly take the form of conversations; language now becomes the prime vehicle for communication. As a result, the child's world becomes less literal and less tied to the here-and-now, and mutual adjustment of parent and child accordingly moves to a new level at which interactions assume a more symbolic and a less physical form.

Little is known as yet about the mechanisms which make possible the transition from preverbal to verbal communication. Whether experience of the former is a necessary condition for the latter, providing the child with interactive formats that are subsequently applied to the use of language, remains conjectural; in common with other arguments about the continuity of preverbal and verbal communicative behaviour it is based on analogy, there being no obvious methodology whereby one can unequivocally demonstrate such a relationship. All that can definitely be maintained is that the verbal system does not simply replace the nonverbal system in the course of development; in children nonverbal behaviour increases in incidence and sophistication with age, while in parents speech to children continues to be embedded in an action context well beyond the point of language acquisition. Multi-modal messages are thus the norm, and to concentrate solely on verbal behaviour (as so many child language studies tend to do) is therefore misleading.

The relationship between language and social interaction is a reciprocal one. On the one hand, language comes increasingly to influence the child's interactions with others; on the other, it is in the context of social interaction that language first develops. Just how it does so, and the precise role in the acquisition process that the child's partners play, is still uncertain. Reinforcement and imitation appear to be of little significance; explanations based on such mechanisms neglect the highly active and constructive manner whereby the child creates language. It seems much more likely that the parent's role is of a more indirect and subtle nature, played out in the context of joint enterprises in which she can tune in to the child's ongoing interests, uncritically accept his contributions and make her own contributions relevant to whatever topics have captured the child's attention.

Verbal interactions require many skills over and above a knowledge of words, and these are initially slow in appearing in the child's repertoire. Parents compensate for these deficiencies by employing a variety of devices to maintain conversations with their young children; yet, as studies of peer interactions show, from the third year on children themselves can begin to assume responsibility for sustaining verbal interactions. Conversations then become lengthier, more cohesive and more meaningful, and consequently also more satisfying as a means of interaction.

One further consequence of the capacity for symbolic representation is to be found in the development of meta-social skills, i.e. the individual's ability to reflect upon his own and other people's interpersonal behaviour. This involves both self-awareness and an understanding of others' psychological states and intentions, and though some components of this ability appear as early as the second year many others are not manifested till well after the preschool period. The child is thereby enabled to stand apart and evaluate his own contribution to interpersonal enterprises, and also to conceive of relationships between people as entities that one may reflect upon as objects in their own right. Action in interpersonal settings will be increasingly guided by such understanding, and interactive behaviour will thus assume a much more self-conscious, planned form than previously.

7 Socialization through Interaction

Socialization refers to the developmental changes that are brought about as a consequence of interacting with other people. Yet strangely these two aspects, socialization and social interaction, have rarely been considered in conjuction; sometimes the terms are treated as though synonymous, but more often they are discussed separately with no attempt to emphasize their interrelationship. As we shall see, such separation is largely a function of the way in which aspects of socialization have been studied, i.e. as end products remote from the processes that gave rise to them originally. The point we wish to stress here is that the two topics need to be brought together: socialization processes occur in the context of social interaction and can only be understood if viewed in this light.

The study of socialization

Socialization is an umbrella concept that refers to a wide range of topics frequently bound together in only the most tenuous manner. This is reflected in the considerable diversity of definitions given to the term: LeVine (1969), for example, distinguishes three principal views of the process, which treat socialization respectively as enculturation, as the acquisition of impulse control and as role training. The three views are said to correspond roughly to the orientation of cultural anthropology, psychology and sociology respectively. Writers differ, moreover, in the extent to which they stress the "moulding" role of the adult or, alternately, the "learning" task of the child; only rarely is the process thought of as an interactional one. Zigler and Child (1973) provide us with one such exception, when they refer to socialization as "the whole process by which an individual develops, *through transactions with other people*, his specific patterns of socially relevant behaviors and experience" (italics added). Attention is thereby drawn to the essentially *interactive* nature of socialization, which inevitably involves two (or more) participants each of whom is already equipped with his own set of predispositions, aims, intentions and predilections; any interaction between them must therefore involve a negotiation process, as a result of which progressive modification in the behaviour of *both* partners takes place—that of the adult as well as the child's. It is, however, the change in the child that is most dramatic and to which most attention is consequently paid.

Developmental change as a result of interacting with other people is found in virtually every aspect of a child's behaviour. With regard to some functions the part played by others is limited even though its effects are far from negligible: given a minimally supportive environment a child will almost inevitably come to sit, stand, crawl and walk within a specifiable age range. His caretakers need to provide an overall level of stimulation, adequate opportunities for practice of skills, and the motivation that follows their expressions of delight at the child's attempts and achievements; in short, they must furnish a facilitating context in which inherent tendencies unfold, though they do not provide content for these tendencies. Where content is provided, on the other hand, the role of the caretaker assumes a more obvious significance: acquiring skills such as spoon feeding or doing up buttons, learning to communicate according to a particular code, developing a specific set of rights and wrongs—such functions are more obviously dependent on some sort of input from adults and have therefore attracted most attention from students of socialization. The great diversity of these functions is some indication of the extent of the problem confronting anyone intending to construct a theory of socialization, and particularly so as there is at present no guarantee that the same set of theoretical principles may be equally applicable to all aspects of development, so that, say, the acquisition of sex roles and the development of language are explicable in terms of identical mechanisms. The basic question asked in each case maybe the same, i.e. in what way does social interaction affect developmental change; there is no assurance, however, that the answers will always be identical.

(1) Three models

Historically, a number of models of the socialization process have influenced our thinking about child rearing, each based on a particular concept of the nature of children and hence also of the role the parent plays in their development. Of the three principal models put forward so far, two need only brief mention: they are of historical interest only in that their inadequacies are now widely recognized. The third remains widely prevalent and deserves rather more discussion.

(a) *Laissez-faire model* The greater the role one ascribes to inherent forces in the child's nature as determinants of development the less weight will be attached to parental influences. Preformationism is the most extreme expression of a belief in inherent forces; its essence is the idea that all basic aspects of an individual's personality are laid down at birth and merely unfold in the course of subsequent development. It follows that the child's caretakers have but a limited part to play: as Rousseau, one of the most articulate proponents of this view, asserted, the only proper role of the environment is to avoid all interference with the processes of self-regulation and spontaneous maturation. The task of parents is thus to provide a maximally permissive atmosphere and thereby allow the child to grow as his nature dictates. Rousseau's advice to parents not to attempt to teach their children and not in any way to impose restrictions or coercive goals was subsequently carried further into the educational field by Pestalozzi and Froebel: even in schools, they believed, the laissez-faire policy should be adopted by providing unstructured environments in which children could give free expression to their spontaneous interests and activities. And more recently Arnold Gesell similarly urged children's caretakers to adopt a primarily passive role: adults, he feared, would only interfere with the orderly development of inherent capacities if they asserted themselves more vigorously in the child's development.

Arguments about permissiveness still continue, but few would now advocate the extreme passivity that proponents of the laissez-faire view urged upon parents. Were we to take this view seriously it would virtually kill off all socialization research; the role of parents as bystanders makes an unexciting study topic.

(b) *Clay moulding model* At the other extreme we have a conception of socialization as a clay moulding process: the child, that is, arrives in the world as a formless lump of clay and society, as represented by mothers, fathers, teachers and other such figures, proceeds to mould him into whatever shape it desires. The end product is then wholly explicable in terms of the external forces which the child has encountered in the course of its impressionable years, and all attempts to understand how socialization comes about must therefore concentrate on the behaviour of the adults with whom the child is in contact. It is their schedules of rewards and punishment, their ways of habit training and the examples which they set that provide an explanation of the final product. Instead of holding a concept of the child as preformed, the child is seen as a purely passive, reactive organism; instead of viewing parents as mere bystanders their role is regarded as a wholly determinative one. Human beings arrive in the world infinitely malleable, and the child's caretakers have consequently total responsibility in shaping development.

Historically this view is usually associated with John Locke, yet the blank slate (*tabula rasa*) to which he likened the newborn child's mind was used by him in a very specific sense only, namely as an argument against the prevailing belief in innate ideas. Children, Locke asserted, have to be provided with mental content; their minds are blank only in the sense that ideas can be derived from experience alone, and experience must be provided by caretakers. Locke did not, however, doubt the presence of mental structures and predispositions; indeed in his discourse on education he stressed the need for parents to restrain the child's "natural impulses" and to control his "appetites". Nor, for that matter, did he deny the existence of innate differences in intelligence and temperament.

A much more extreme expression of the clay moulding model emerged this century in the writings of J. B. Watson (1928). As he put it: "The behaviourist finds that the human being at birth is a very lowly piece of unformed protoplasm, ready to be shaped by any family in whose care it is first placed." Watson's belief in the power of adults to change children's behaviour became the starting point for much of the research in the past few decades that examined child rearing practices from a behaviourist point of view (Bijou and Baer, 1962), with its emphasis on training and learning, its faith in the shaping influences of reward and punishment, and its assumption that in reinforcement and association we find the mechanisms to explain the course of child development. Socialization, as Bijou (1970) put it, is simply the product of the individual's reinforcement history.

It has become increasingly evident in recent years that there are many difficulties with such a view. Above all, the concept of the child as a passive recipient of other people's stimulation has had to be abandoned in the face of mounting evidence that children from birth on are capable of themselves exerting influences on their caretakers (Bell, 1968). Even the neonate, far from being a "piece of unformed protoplasm", already has a psychological structure by virtue of which he can behave in an organized, selective and spontaneous manner. In addition, difficulties have arisen with respect to the concept of reinforcement as the principal mechanism to account for developmental change. For one thing, biological constraints are operative in determining what is learned (Hinde and Stevenson-Hinde, 1973): organismic factors may limit or predispose an individual to form particular associations; the linking of *any* reinforcer with *any* response does not produce learning. Furthermore, the laboratory-based demonstration that the frequency of a response is directly related to its consequences in a universally predictable manner has run into difficulties when studied under real-life conditions. Patterson (1979), for example, found no clear relationship between children's aggressive behaviour and parental reactions: in some instances punishment *increased* the incidence of aggression, though not invariably so; in other cases non-reinforcement, or positive reinforcement of competing prosocial behaviour, failed to make any impact. Add to that evidence that the process of language acquisition cannot be explained by selective rewards administered by adults, and one has to conclude that the concept of reinforcement is of limited value to the developmental psychologist.

Asymmetry in the power balance between adults and children is, of course, not in question: by definition socialization is an adult-initiated process, the end-point of which is to transform the child into something regarded as desirable by his caretakers. But the manner of bringing this about, its timing and sequence, and the eventual result achieved depend as much on the nature of the child as on that of the adult. Developmental change of any kind cannot be explained in terms of environmental input alone.

(c) *The conflict model* By far the most pervasive view is that which sees socialization in terms of confrontation. Children, it is agreed, are not passive; from the beginning they have wishes and desires of their own which impel them to behave in certain ways. The trouble is that these ways are antithetical to those of society; they bring the child into conflict with his caretakers, whose task is then to compel him to give up his natural preferences and adopt unnatural modes of behaviour regarded as desirable by society.

This view has a long historical tradition behind it. It is based on the doctrine of original sin: the idea that man is conceived and born in sin and that childhood is the crucial period for curbing and eradicating the innate evil in his nature. As Thomas Hobbs, writing in the 17th century, saw it, children come into the world as little savages whose constant aim is to attain power over others, irrespective of the cost. Uncurbed, their natural depravity would be a threat to the whole social order, and the primary purpose of child rearing is therefore to take the base and negative nature with which the child is endowed and, by virtue of the parent's greater power, to force him into gradually adopting the role of good citizen.

"Breaking the will of children" thus becomes the central theme in socialization. As Mrs. Wesley, mother of the founder of Methodism, wrote in the 18th century:

"I insist upon conquering the wills of children betimes; because this is the only foundation for a religious education . . . Heaven or hell depends on this alone. So that the parent who studies to subdue self-will in his children works together with God in the saving of a soul: the parent who indulges it does the devil's work . . . Whatever pains it cost, conquer their stubbornness; break the will, if you would not damn the child." (Quoted in Newson and Newson, 1974)

Such a view can be found in the writings of many philosophers and preachers of that time (Shorter, 1976), convinced that obedience and submission to authority were the essential virtues of children and that they could only be attained by harsh, corrective measures. Socialization was thus seen as a difficult, conflict-full enterprise, in which parents were charged with the task of bringing recalcitrant children to heel. The harsh treatment of children in former times (de Mauser, 1976), and the a-sentimental view of their nature that prevailed for so many centuries, stemmed to a large extent from the conviction that this was the only way to spare the child from eternal damnation.

Parents are no longer thus motivated, yet the conflict model of socialization remains prevalent in psychological writings. To a considerable degree this is due to the influence of Freud: he more than any other modern writer propagated the idea of natural man as basically anti-social, as a creature whose instinctual drives are of a selfish, destructive nature and thus incompatible with the conditions of societal living. The "conflict between civilization and sexuality" was, to Freud's mind, the central theme in social adjustment; he saw a need for "culture to call up every possible reinforcement in order to erect barriers against the aggressive instincts of men" (Freud, 1963). The psychoanalytic view of young children is accordingly that of little savages:

"They certainly are not socially adapted . . . Feelings of shame, disgust or pity seem to be wholly absent; the toddlers are intent only on doing what gives them the greatest pleasure for the moment. And this pleasure is mostly gained by activities which, if present in the adult, would be classified as criminal, insane or perverse." (Friedlander, 1947, p.13).

Instinct renunciation, according to Freud, occurs only because of "dread of an aggression by external authority" (i.e. the child's parents) which in due course is replaced by an internal authority (i.e. conscience).

Freud's conception of socialization is thus also of a conflict model, addressed to the problem of how the child learns to restrain his inborn anti-social impulses. Various control mechanisms are required, operating both within and outside the child, that make it possible for him to fit into society, though only at the cost of his original nature. Development is thus a painful process, for it requires the resolution of the basic antagonism between the child and his social group. And the picture that emerges of the parent–child relationship is a thoroughly negative one: on the one hand parents are characterized predominantly in terms of prohibitions, commands, threats and exhortations; on the other hand children are painted as aggressive, selfish, fearful and guilt-ridden.

Current versions of the conflict model are, however, by no means solely associated with psychoanalytic thinking. They can also be found in the writings of theorists as diverse as Piaget and Eysenck. In Piaget's work the concept of *egocentrism* expresses (in analogous fashion to psychoanalytic theorizing) the self-seeking aspects of human nature that are said to constitute so all-pervasive a characteristic in the early stages of childhood, and here too conflict (though primarily between the different viewpoints of peers) is evoked as the mechanism for graduating to a more socialized stage. And Eysenck (1977), in discussing the origins of crime, also expresses the view that man is basically anti-social in nature: given his psychological hedonism, criminal behaviour is the straightforward expression of man's inherent constitution ("the most natural thing in the world", as Eysenck refers to it), and what requires explanation is law-abiding behaviour rather than delinquency. Conformity with sets of man-made laws can only come about by the child's parents, teachers and other authority figures enforcing unnatural standards of behaviour onto the child.

Much of the recent work on moral development is derived from a similar conception of what transpires between parent and child. A good example is found in Hoffman's (1977) description of the way in which parents bring about the child's conformity to the moral requirements of society:

"Moral internalization implies the motivation to weigh one's desires against the moral requirements of the situation without regard to external sanctions. The central conflict in the moral encounter, then, is between the person's egoistic needs and the moral standards applicable in a given situation. It seems reasonable to assume that the key socialization experiences must therefore include the child's early encounters with analogous conflict, that between his desires and the prevailing moral standards, which are at first, of course, external to him. These standards are embedded in many of the physical and verbal messages from the parent regarding how the child should and should not act, that is in the parent's discipline techniques. The discipline encounter, then, has much in common with many later moral encounters. In each there is conflict and the individual is compelled to work out a balance between behaving in accord with his desires, on the one hand, and subordinating his desires and acting in line with moral standards, on the other. The moral requirements are external in the discipline encounter and, with proper socialization, they eventually become internalized in the moral encounter. The child's experiences in the discipline encounter—the type of discipline to which he is repeatedly exposed and which determines the options available to him—must therefore weigh heavily in determining the extent to which he acquires internal resources for controlling egoistic impulses and behaving morally." (Hoffman, 1977, p.86–87)

The discipline encounter, according to this formulation, is seen as the primary context within which socialization occurs. The encounter is based on a clash of wills: parent and child have different aims, and the task of the parent is to ensure that, by virtue of being more powerful, her wishes are imposed on the unwilling and resentful child. The conflict element in the relationship is thus given prominence and is seen as providing the motive power for the child's socialization.

(2) Methodological considerations

A number of features distinguish the empirical work on which much past theorizing about socialization processes is based. Four in particular deserve mention:

(1) *The use of "indirect" methodologies.* Until quite recently the actual manner in which parents went about their socializing task was rarely systematically observed and recorded. Thus the way in which a mother steers her baby's feeding habits to more socially approved levels, or the means whereby a toddler's aggressive episodes are contained, have only recently come to be investigated *in situ*. Instead, the bulk of information has been obtained indirectly, i.e. from reports usually supplied by the parents themselves — a source now regarded with caution on account of the distortions so frequently found in self-reports.

(2) *Concern with products, not processes.* Socialization research has on the whole interested itself far more in the final outcome of child rearing than in the detailed examination of how these outcomes are brought about. Moral internalization, impulse control, sex role behaviour — these are the sort of phenomena that have been investigated as end products, with questions about their origins being answered only by the use of indirect methodologies. An exception is the body of research (stemming largely from social learning theory) which has applied a laboratory approach to the study of adult effects on children's behaviour and which has attempted by experimental means to analyse the way in which such effects are brought about. Unfortunately, the applicability of this approach to the understanding of real-life phenomena has not been demonstrated; as Walters and Grusec (1977) showed, laboratory studies of punishment (to give just one example) have yielded results often directly at variance with those stemming from reports about child rearing in everyday situations. The relevance of such results is therefore doubtful.

(3) *Time gap between antecedent and consequent conditions.* Not only were investigators primarily interested in the end-product of development, but they were also for the most part convinced that this product could be largely explained by the child's early experiences. As a result, a research methodology evolved which attempted to find relationships between antecedent and consequent conditions that were often separated by considerable gaps of time. Concurrent events, that is the immediate impact of parent

on child, tended to be neglected in the eagerness of investigators to jump straight to final, presumably permanent outcomes. The assumption that a child's early experiences necessarily furnish the crucial formative events for personality development has now been seriously challenged (e.g. by Clarke and Clarke, 1976); a much more precise analysis of what transpires between parent and child, together with consideration of intervening events, is called for before long-term consequences can be ascribed to earlier events.

(4) *The summary nature of variables.* The final source of difficulty in understanding socialization processes concerns the choice of variables to designate parental and child characteristics. These have only too frequently involved all-encompassing descriptive labels that, on closer inspection, have turned out to be too global in nature to yield the unambiguous antecedent-consequent relationships originally hoped for. Much of the literature on parental attitudes suffers from this shortcoming, making predictive statements about child behaviour hazardous (Becker and Krug, 1965). Similarly with variables used to describe child effects: as Sears *et al.* (1966) found to their cost, such aspects as dependence, aggression and conscience development cannot be regarded as the unitary traits they are so commonly believed to be. Empirical research has frequently been unable to uphold the assumption that terms used in everyday speech to describe behaviour necessarily refer to "real" entities. Much more minute analyses are required to yield the variables that will usefully describe socializing effects.

The use of indirect means of obtaining data, the preoccupation with long-term consequences, the temporal separation of assumed cause and effect, and the global constructs commonly employed—all these have meant an overloading of the concept of socialization with inferences as to what in fact transpires between parent and child that could account for the latter's development change. The belief, formerly so widespread, in the uni-directional nature of the parent–child relationship is just one consequence of the failure to study socialization in the context of social interaction. Such a study involves an approach that is both more modest and more ambitious than previous efforts: more modest, in that it is less concerned with long-term, permanent effects or with wide-ranging personality functioning; more ambitious, in that it aims to produce much more precise and detailed statements about the role which the various interacting conditions involved in specific situations are likely to play.

Parental control techniques

Past efforts to understand the socialization process were determined to a large extent by sets of assumptions about what transpires between parent and child. We have summarized these assumptions in terms of the various models of socialization that previously prevailed. Each model is associated with a particular concept of the child to be socialized: the laissez-faire model sees the child as *preformed*; the clay moulding model as *passive*; the conflict model as *egoistic*. Each model directs the research worker to different aspects of the parent–child relationship: respectively to those features of child behaviour that develop with apparently minimal parental intervention; to the shaping and training practices of parents; and to conflict situations and the techniques used to resolve them. Yet any account of socialization must be in accord with what is known about the everyday pattern of interaction between parent and child, and in this respect the material presented in previous chapters leaves all three models open to criticism. Two points in particular need to be taken into account:

(1) Both parent and child play an active part in determining the nature and course of interaction — so much so that it is often difficult to sort out the contribution of either partner alone. A view of the child as *participant* is thus a more appropriate one.

(2) Mutual adaptation, not conflict, is the basic theme that runs through the course of parent–child interaction. Conflicts occur, of course, but there is no indication that they constitute the key socialization episodes in a child's life.

A model of socialization based on parent–child *mutuality* is thus indicated. Such a model (as Stayton *et al.*, 1971, have also cogently argued) acknowledges the fact that the infant, far from starting off as an anti-social being that must be coerced into sociability, begins life preadapted for social interaction. Far from seeing the parent–child relationship as a never-ending battle investigators have come to be impressed by the "fit" of the two individuals' sets of behaviour patterns. And far from being merely at the mercy of adult whim the child is recognized as an active participant in all social encounters. What is more, a picture has emerged of parents taking great care to fit their behaviour to the child's, sensitively taking account of his particular state and condition at the time, adjusting their behaviour accordingly, and all along ensuring that their stimulus input is properly adapted to the child's abilities meaningfully to absorb it.

It must be acknowledged, however, that this picture has emerged almost entirely from one particular kind of study, namely one which places adult and child in situations that are largely unstructured and unconstrained: face-to-face situations, for example, in which the parent is merely told to amuse the child, or free play situations where the participants can do as they wish with whatever material is available. The goal of the interactants in such a context is the interaction itself; their aim is simply to enjoy each other's company and have fun together. Studies based on such situations maximize the possibility that the infant will take the initiative and the parent will confine herself to following his lead, fitting in with his particular requirements of tempo, mood and topic. But what of those situations where parents do have to take the initiative, where they do have purposes and goals and needs of their own which they wish to convey to the child and with which the child has to comply? Thus, when the parent has a particular end-result in mind which she wishes to communicate to the child, is the picture of mutuality no longer applicable and does the interaction then become a uni-directional one and conflict-laden? Parents after all do require from their children conformity to demands that, from the child's point of view, may seem arbitrary and incomprehensible: eating with a spoon, using a potty, clearing away toys, going to bed at a particular time—these and many other examples are events where one might well wonder whether a different view of the interaction is not required. Indeed much of the socialization literature has fostered just such a view, according to which powerful adults act (often forcefully and dogmatically) on helpless children and obtain conformity by virtue of their superior power. Mutuality is then an end-result to which children are driven through socialization pressures rather than (as we would argue) being a prerequisite without which the adult could not produce any effects at all. The need to examine those social inter-action situations in which parents exert a measure of control over their children's behaviour and attempt to obtain compliance to their demands is thus apparent.

(1) The nature of control techniques

The study of control techniques seeks to describe the way in which adult requests, concerned with everyday task demands, are communicated to children and how they impinge on the children's ongoing behaviour. The emphasis is thus on immediate and not on long-term consequences; on the initial step in the socialization process and not on its end result; on how adults convey an aim in their mind in such a way that the child comes to comply with it, rather than with the eventual internalization of the values expressed by these requests.

The term "control techniques", as used here, is not to be understood in purely negative fashion, denoting force, restraint, inhibition and punishment. Rather, control techniques refers to all those behaviours employed by one person to change the ongoing course of another's activity. Their function is to channel behaviour in certain directions, inhibiting some tendencies but enhancing others. They are all those communications from one individual to another that are designed to "impel, inhibit, direct, guide, shape or otherwise influence the recipient's behaviour" (Flavell, 1977). Although they can be found in the interaction of any two or more individuals, their significance is particularly marked in the encounters of parent and child and especially so in the early years. Their content need not by any means involve the largely distasteful things which so much of the socialization literature has concentrated on; they are to be found in any situation where the adult wishes to communicate a purpose in such a way that the child comes to share this purpose.

The nature of control techniques and the way in which they were applied in one particular setting is illustrated in a study by Schaffer and Crook (1979; 1980). The subjects were two groups of mothers, one with 15-month-old and the other with 24-month-old children. The mother–child dyads were observed in a semi-structured play situation. In order to ensure that the mothers took an active part in the situation they were instructed to make certain that the child played with all the toys available rather than spend the whole session with just one or two toys, and actively to intervene in order to direct the child's play accordingly. The sessions were held in a laboratory playroom and were recorded by video-cameras from behind a one-way screen.

The large number of controls that were found in the transcripts of maternal speech attests to the fact that these mothers did indeed interpret their task as a directive one. Nearly half of all verbal utterances in both age groups had a control function, in that they were attempts in some way to influence and change the course of the child's behaviour at the time. This means that such controls impinged on the children at an average rate of one every 9 seconds. Had these been of the authoritarian, forceful nature so commonly suggested as the norm by the socialization literature the children would have been quite overwhelmed. Impressionistically, this clearly did not happen: in every case the mother appeared to accomplish her task in an atmosphere of harmony.

There are several reasons for this outcome. One is that the controls used by the mothers were often of an indirect and subtle nature. For instance, very few prohibitives (i.e. controls concerned directly with preventing or terminating behaviour) were found; when the mothers wanted to put a stop to a particular activity they relied more on distraction than on direct negative command. Furthermore, almost half of all controls were expressed in a grammatical form other than the imperative, i.e. as ''indirect directives'' rather than as ''direct directives''. As writers on speech act theory (e.g. Searle, 1969) have stressed, the act indicated by a sentence is separable from the precise linguistic form used: a request expressed in the interrogative form (''Would you bring the teddy over here'') may have the same illocutionary force as an order expressed in the imperative (''Bring the teddy over here''). It appears that even speech to children who are only just beginning to comprehend language often takes this indirect and (in a sense) less clear form. However, trying to get children to do things by asking them questions instead of issuing commands does have one important consequence, in that it serves to reduce the emotional intensity of the interaction that would otherwise be created by showering the child with a succession of explicit orders.

A further and particularly significant reason why these children were apparently not overwhelmed by the barrage of controls related to the way in which the mothers timed their interventions. Controls rarely descended in bolt-out-of-the-blue fashion; for the most part they were carefully timed by the mother to ensure that the child's attention was appropriately focussed on a toy before some action on that toy was requested. This is seen in Fig. 7, which illustrates the children's visual and tactile contact with the toy at the point when the mother is about to request some action to be performed on that toy. In the case of the older group, over half of these maternal controls occurred when the child was already looking at and in some sort of physical contact with the relevant toy. In 68·4% of instances children were in physical contact with the toy, and in 75·5% of instances the child was at

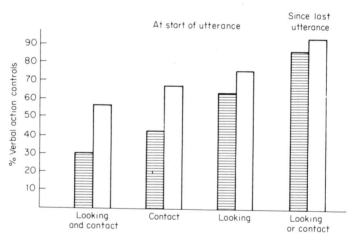

Fig. 7. *Distribution of all maternal verbal action controls according to child's orientation toward toy referred to (hatched bars = 15-month group; blank bars = 24-month group). (Schaffer and Crook, 1979).*

least already looking at it at the time. If we base the figures on a wider time scale by considering the period since the mother's last utterance, we find that on 90% of occasions the children had either just looked at or touched the toy that the mother was now referring to. The pattern is similar for the younger group, though the percentages are lower, particularly on the measures referring to contact — a reflection presumably of the less active manipulatory activity found at this age. Even here, however, it is apparent that the mothers generally timed their action controls to occur at optimal moments, that is when the child was already appropriately oriented to the respective toy.

Monitoring the child's attentional focus, and ensuring that he was oriented to a toy before asking him to act on that toy, was thus a regular feature of these mothers' behaviour. They would bring this about either by waiting till the child's attention went spontaneously to the toy, or by employing some attention directing device (of a verbal nature such as "Look", or of a nonverbal kind such as waving or tapping the object). Mothers thus often employed sequential strategies, whereby attention-directing devices were used as a preliminary to action controls. Establishing a mutual focus of attention was consequently seen as a necessary first step; mothers rarely leapt in with an action control without previously ascertaining that the child was appropriately oriented. It seems highly probable that the adoption of such a sequential strategy was yet a further and especially important contribution to the over-all harmony that prevailed in these sessions.

In addition, the mothers carefully adjusted the nature of the controls used by them to the child's age. For instance, nonverbal devices were more frequently used with younger than with older children. In particular, mothers of younger children put more effort into making toys more accessible and more easily manipulable, thus compensating for the more limited motor abilities of these children. They were more likely, for example, to prompt the child to act by holding out a stick for rings to be put on, thus initiating an activity that an older child might have undertaken on his own; or they would move toys within the child's range or actually present them to him, in this way altering the physical distance between child and toy. A more active role was thus played by these mothers in maintaining the momentum of their children's play.

The findings of the Schaffer and Crook study have recently been confirmed and extended by McLaughlin (1983). A free-play rather than a directed play session was investigated, the setting of the study was the home rather than the laboratory, and fathers as well as mothers were observed. In addition a wider age range was examined, in that children aged 1½, 2½, and 3½ years were included.

Even under the free-play conditions studied here, a large proportion of parental verbal utterances were found to have a control function. This applied mostly to the youngest group, where 30% of utterances were so classified. Here too only a tiny number (5% of all control utterances) took a prohibitive form, and most controls (66% of the mothers' and 58% of the fathers') were expressed indirectly in question or statement form. Nonverbal concomitants of verbal controls were frequent and especially so in association with attention controls, where they were found in 90% and 87% respectively of the mothers' and fathers' utterances. They were also more likely to be used with younger than with older children. On the whole mothers and fathers behaved remarkably alike: fathers expressed themselves in the direct command mood somewhat more frequently and more often demanded action as opposed to attention from the children, but such differences were greatly outweighed by the similarities between the parents. Again, it appears, adults were able to direct their children's behaviour by subtle and harmonious means.

The over-all picture that emerges from these observations is very different from the conflict situation that is usually conjured up as the proto-typical setting in which the child's socialization is accomplished. Conflicts, of course, do occur; of that there can be no doubt. But when we examine in detail how parents attempt to change their children's behaviour a clash of wills need not always and inevitably be involved. There are many circumstances, occurring repeatedly in everyday life, where behavioural change is accomplished smoothly and easily. For this purpose parents have at their disposal a wide variety of techniques whereby they can convey a purpose to the child with which they want him to comply, and these include subtle and indirect means as well as the more forceful methods that have so far captured the attention of investigators.

Such control attempts appear to be a regular and constant feature of parent–child interaction, by no means necessarily dependent on any specific instructional set given to the parents. Power and Parke (1982) observed naturally occurring parent–child interactions in home and laboratory settings, and found that the vast majority could be classified as attempts to influence the child in some way, either by facilitating, elaborating or controlling the child's social and exploratory behaviour or by setting boundaries through managerial interactions. This applied equally to both parents and to both settings. Socialization attempts, it should be concluded, are not a class of caretaker behaviour patterns that are confined to certain situations (toilet training, feeding, discipline encounters and the like), nor do they constitute a distinctive cluster of responses that are set apart from other kinds of communicative interactions. Rather, they represent a constant theme in parent–child encounters of all kinds—a theme which expresses the adult's vision of the child's developmental progression and which is designed to help the child along that progression. Socialization attempts may be a more prominent feature of certain kinds of situation in which parents have a very specific aim in mind with which the child is expected to conform; however, they occur in even the most playful and relaxed encounters and are thus part of the very act of interpersonal communication between parent and child.

(2) Communicating controls

Compared with earlier attempts to understand the socialization process (Goslin, 1969), the level of descriptive analysis employed in the above studies is based not on global variables but on the same kind of molecular approach that has generally been used in recent years to examine the nature of early social interaction. Applying this approach means analysing in detail the manner whereby parents communicate messages of directive intent to children, whether by verbal or by nonverbal means. Getting children to do things is dependent on successful communication; the nature of that communication and its effects need describing.

For older children the verbal content of a message contains the main communicative burden. Not so at earlier ages; there is evidence that children in the second and third years, though already responsive to other people's verbalizations, are not influenced by the precise nature of the verbal message. Wetstone and Friedlander (1973) gave 2 to 3-year-old children commands with which they were expected to comply, expressing these either in normal form ("Show the clown to Mommy") or in scrambled sentences (e.g. "Mommy clown to the show"). The majority of children responded as readily to the latter as to the former; word order appeared to carry as yet no communicative significance; instead, the children seemed to rely on whatever familiar words they heard and also on the nonverbal context in which the commands were presented. The importance of the latter is shown well in a study by Kramer (1977), in which children 21 to 34 months old were given situationally anomalous commands such as "Throw me the chair" or "Sit on the telephone". As Kramer put it, "It is difficult to convey the nonchalence with which children would sit in the chair in response to 'Throw me the chair'." In other words, at this early stage of linguistic development children interpret utterances probabilistically, using context and a few familiar words as cues. The fact that children as young as 18 months have been found to respond as readily to their mothers' question-directives as to requests expressed as imperatives (Shatz, 1978b; Schaffer and Crook, 1980) is presumably due to the same tendency; rather than indicating a very sophisticated level of understanding, namely that the syntactic form of the parent's utterance need not be a clue to the purpose she is expressing, it shows again these children's selection of well-known referent words and their responding to them in a way that is appropriate in that context.

The younger the child the more important the nonverbal context is likely to be. According to L. Bloom (1973), the gradual move away from contextually bound cues is "the major task for the child in the course of language development". Yet there has been little research into the communicative significance of parental gestures and other child-directed actions that accompany speech; studies of maternal language seem commonly to assume that the only part of the mother that is moving is her mouth. Yet everyday observation suggests that adults talking to young children tend to be extremely busy, whether with gestures or with actions on objects being attended to, and it seems likely that the function of such behaviour is to clarify, underline or elaborate in some way the meaning that the adult is attempting to convey linguistically to the child.

In order to throw some light on the association between verbal and non-verbal components of adult directives to children, Schaffer *et al.* (1983) asked the mothers of 10- and 18-month-old children to get the child to carry out a number of simple tasks. The sessions were videotaped, and it was thus possible to analyse in detail how the mothers set about conveying particular requests. As already mentioned, an increase occurred over age in the mothers' reliance on verbal means of conveying the message, yet no corresponding decrease was found in the use of nonverbal means. At both ages mothers resorted to a great deal of nonverbal activity with a clearly communicative intent; what is more, the same kinds of nonverbal actions were observed at both ages. Many of these involved the particular toy on which the child was expected to perform a specified action: some served to highlight that toy, making it more interesting and attention-worthy by, for instance, rhythmically bouncing it in front of the child or by playing peek-a-boo with it; others were used to show off the attributes of the toy, and still others served to make it more accessible. Thus by a variety of nonverbal means the mothers attempted to convey to the child that the toy was something of interest and then, having captured his attention, create possibilities for action and finally lead him into the particular act required. Much of the mothers' nonverbal behaviour was designed to make it as easy as possible for the child to comply with the request that had been verbally conveyed to him: things that had to be combined were put in close juxtaposition; materials were handed to the child in appropriate order; physical support was provided when difficulties of coordination were frustrating the child's attempts; and all distractions were removed in order to concentrate the child's attention on the task in hand. The physical situation was thus manipulated by the mothers in such a way that the child's behaviour could eventually be channelled in a manner appropriate to the demands of the task. Whatever speech occurred was embedded in all these other, nonverbal activities. There was little evidence of parallel encoding: simultaneous verbal and nonverbal actions frequently conveyed different rather than identical messages, and for children to have unravelled the meaning of the mother's linguistic utterances on the basis of her accompanying other actions was thus rarely possible. What the mothers' nonverbal behaviour did instead was to provide a setting for their speech: while talking about the relevant object their actions ensured that the child's attention was captured by it in the first place, that his interest did not then stray to other things, that he came into direct physical contact with the toy, and that his behaviour was appropriate to the task he was meant to carry out. Given the uncertainties of verbal communications to such young children, nonverbal behaviour served above all to arrange the physical setting in such a way that it would have been difficult for the child not to have carried out the request.

(3) Compliance

Whether a child has complied with a request or not may at first sight seem an obvious decision, yet further consideration shows that there are two definitional problems to which attention needs to be given. They are respectively concerned with the time period following the adult's control within which one expects compliance to occur, and the degree of match required between the adult's request and the child's responses.

As to the first, most investigators have taken some more or less arbitrary figure which varies widely from one study to the next, in some being as low as 5 seconds and in others as high as 30 seconds following the control. Rarely is any reason given for the particular choice made. A different approach was adopted by Schaffer and Crook (1980): rather than impose a specific time limit the period considered was that between the mother's control utterance and her following utterance. In this way it was left to the mother to judge the appropriate interval within which a response was accepted. When faced by non-compliance, parents, of course, often continue to press the point, repeating their requests (though possibly in different form) and eventually succeeding to a greater extent than an examination of parental controls treated as single units would lead one to conclude. The *eventual* success rate may thus be another criterion; again the point is less whether the criterion is "right" or "wrong" as that it needs to be clearly stipulated in reports.

With regard to the second definitional problem, i.e. the match required between request and response, there is again considerable variation among different studies. In some, touching the relevant object is taken as the sole criterion, even though the specific act requested by the adult has not been carried out. In others, more exacting criteria such as the comprehension of both the noun object and the specific verb used in the directive are employed. In many the match is left unspecified, presumably on the assumption that it is obvious whether a child has complied or not. Rather than treat compliance as a unitary entity, however, it is helpful to distinguish between the three kinds of compliance to an action request that represent different degrees of match (Schaffer and Crook, 1980):

(1) *Orientation compliance*, referring to the success of directing the child's visual attention to the respective object.

(2) *Contact compliance*, involving the establishment of physical contact with that object.

(3) *Task compliance*, that is whether the child carries out the precise act specified by the adult.

Thus credit can be given to a child for at least looking at the object or touching it, even though he has not wholly complied with the request. The three kinds represent successive approximations, with orientation compliance being the easiest and task compliance the most difficult to obtain.

There are no doubt many factors that determine whether compliance is obtained under any given set of conditions. Amongst those that have received some attention are the following:

Type of adult control. Verbal requests in the direct imperative mood appear to be no more effective than indirectly phrased forms. Indeed Lytton (1980) found the highest rate of compliance among 2½-year-old children to occur to "suggestions" (usually put in question form), with "command-prohibitions" being rather less successful. There was some tendency for the parents in that study to use these two types of control for different purposes; for example, commands were most likely to be given when the parent's aim was to stop a nuisance behaviour like shouting or whining, whereas suggestions occurred much more frequently in play situations. This makes it difficult to compare the over-all success rate of the different types of control; nevertheless, it seems that more forceful controls are no more effective than subtle ones. This conclusion is reinforced by Lytton's further finding that if some negative action (e.g. a slap) was added to the control, far from enhancing its effectiveness it tended to detract from its effect. On the other hand positive action (e.g. a smile or an expression of affection) added to the likelihood of the child complying. According to McLaughlin's (1983) findings in the previously described study, nonverbal concomitants in general greatly enhanced the likelihood of compliance to verbal controls. There are also indications from this study, however, that the syntactical form of the verbal control varied in its effectiveness with age: at 3½ years of age children's compliance rate to indirect requests was higher than to direct requests (76% and 54% respectively); a similar but less marked trend was found at 2½ years (64% and 50%); at 1½ years, on the other hand, the trend was reversed, the respective figures being 45% and 52%. And one further point regarding type of control used: both McLaughlin and Schaffer and Crook found attention controls to be considerably more successful in eliciting compliance than were action controls—a finding which may, of course, be due to the previously mentioned greater likelihood of demands for attention being accompanied by some form of nonverbal behaviour.

Child involvement state. The extent to which the child is already involved with the object on which the adult wants him to act is an important consideration. We have already stressed the efforts parents generally make in ensuring that their controls do not descend in bolt-out-of-the-blue fashion, in that they time their demands to coincide with the child's orientation to the relevant object. In comparing those instances when the request for an action was administered by mothers without due consideration of the child's involvement in the relevant object with those that were timed appropriately, Schaffer and Crook (1980) found a significantly higher incidence of compliance to the latter. The bolt-out-of-the-blue approach, in other words, was much less successful than one based on sensitive monitoring of the child's ongoing behaviour. Thus the imposition of controls by an adult on a child is not to be regarded as a unilateral process; it is dyadic in nature, in that both the behaviour of the adult and the outcome (compliance or non-compliance) are a function of the child's state as well as of the adult's disposition. By taking this state into account the parent can avoid the clash-of-wills whereby compliance is supposedly extracted from an invariably reluctant child.

Relational factors. Any given control episode does not, of course, occur in isolation but takes place against the background of a particular kind of relationship that has developed between that adult and that child. There are several indications that the quality of that relationship influences the likelihood of the child's compliance. In two studies (Matas *et al.*, 1978, and Londerville and Main, 1981) the child's attachment to the mother was assessed in the Ainsworth Strange Situation; both claim that securely attached children have a higher compliance rate to maternal demands than non-securely attached children. Stayton *et al.* (1971), investigating infants 9 to 12 months old, found compliance rate to be strongly related to a variety of maternal qualities that promote mother–child harmony, with particular reference to the mother's sensitivity, her acceptance and her cooperativeness vis à vis the child, but not to the frequency of her commands or of her forcible interventions. And Lytton (1980), also concerned with parental characteristics that relate to compliance, found the most important positive predictors to be the amount of the mother's play with the child, her consistency of rule enforcement, her encouragement of mature behaviour, and the extent to which she used such psychological rewards as praise and approval. The most marked negative predictor, on the other hand, was the amount of physical punishment by the mother.

There is one general conclusion to which these various results point: compliance is obtained most effectively in *conflict-free* situations. The use by parents of non-forceful techniques, their application at moments of time sensitively chosen to take into account the child's current state, a generally harmonious relationship to serve as background—these produce a combination of factors most conducive to children acceding to their parents' wishes. An atmosphere of harmony, it seems, is more likely to lead to compliance than one in which force prevails. Whether a high rate of compliance is necessarily a "good" thing or not is, of course, another matter; during the post-infancy period in particular a growing sense of autonomy, generally regarded as desirable, may well manifest itself in some degree of self-will and hence of non-compliance. But the capacity for compliance to adult demands must be present; not only is its development the first step in the socialization process but it is also essential for the survival of a still immature and dependent being. The conditions under which compliance is manifested must thus be determined, and according to the findings summarized above these conditions indicate this tendency to develop most easily on the basis of a cooperative rather than a conflictful relationship.

Such a conclusion was also reached by Stayton *et al.* (1971), who summarized their findings as showing that "a disposition toward obedience emerges in a responsive, accommodating social environment without extensive training, discipline, or other massive attempts to shape the infant's course of development." That socialization cannot be reduced to "training" is surely right; much more dubious is the proposal by these authors that there is an "initial unspecified disposition toward compliance" which forms the basis of the child's socialization. Like the "conformer genes" suggested by Wilson (1975) for the same purpose, there is a danger that a *deus ex machina* type of explanation is advanced which in fact impedes rather than facilitates analysis of the conditions giving rise to compliance by simply reducing these to "natural" causes. There is no more direct evidence for such an "initial disposition" than there is for the existence of conformer genes.

A more profitable line of enquiry is to consider the development of cognitive competencies on the basis of which a child is enabled not merely to understand but also to accede to another person's requests. Thus it can be argued that some degree of self-awareness is an essential prerequisite, that it is not till there is differentiation between self and non-self that a child can truly be said to be capable of compliance with another's wishes. Compliance implies choice—making a decision as to whether to do as the other person demands or to adopt some alternate course. The ability to say

"No" indicates self-assertion; it means rejection of a course of action suggested by the adult in favour of one generated by the child himself. Such differentiation requires cognitive operations of a relatively sophisticated nature which may not come into being till the second year of life. It is then, as we have seen, that unequivocal signs of self-awareness emerge; it is then also, according to Kagan (1981), that children display for the first time a preoccupation with adult standards and an awareness of their own ability or lack of ability to meet these standards. As a result the child can now evaluate his actions in relation to another's wishes and comply or not comply accordingly.

This does not mean that parents make no efforts to control their children's behaviour before such developments, nor that compliance-like behaviour cannot be seen in children at earlier stages. It suggests rather that control–compliance sequences are of a different order at those earlier stages, and that phenomena occurring then need to be examined and compared with later ones.

(4) "Control"–"compliance" in early infancy

It is sometimes asserted that the issue of control does not arise until the second year of life as it is then that the child becomes increasingly mobile and in need of supervision and restraints, and that the earlier period is one of nurturance and indulgence during which the parent's role is confined to that of comforter. As Hoffman (1977) put it, at the end of infancy "the parent's role shifts dramatically from primarily that of caretaker to that of socialization agent. His actions change from being facilitative and nurturant to disciplinary."

This is much too sharp a dichotomy. Socialization pressures are brought to bear on the child from the moment he is born, and though the increasing motoric competence of the toddler does seem to elicit rather more assertive behaviour on the part of parents the infant is by no means immune from direction, regulation and restriction. As Rheingold and Adams (1980) found, even speech to newborns is full of control statements. There is, however, one crucial difference compared with controls found later on: the parent has as yet no expectations that the child will comply; the techniques she adopts differ accordingly.

This is illustrated in a study by Hepburn and Schaffer (1983) of mothers' interactions with their 5-month-old infants during a bathing session. The sessions were observed at home and videotaped. Even at this early age there were many occurrences of maternal control behaviour; in every one of the 18 mothers observed one found various such instances, designed apparently to change the infant's behaviour. Some took the form of purely verbal requests, others were of a nonverbal nature, and many combined verbal and nonverbal elements, but all seemed intended to convey some message, indicating an action that the mother wanted the infant to execute or terminate. However, closer inspection, based not just on the mother's behaviour but on the interaction as such, showed that a considerable proportion of these demands were far from genuine; they were delivered at such a time and in such a way as to suggest that the mother in fact had no expectation of the child's compliance. There were three types of such "pseudo-controls":

(1) Control-like utterances used when the child was already carrying out the act: e.g. the child is trying to pick up a toy; mother says: "Pick it up".

(2) Control-like utterances used by the mother when she herself was already carrying out the act: e.g. mother says "Sit up" while she puts the child in a sitting position.

(3) Control-like utterances used by the mother to prescribe an action that was quite inappropriate to a five-month-old child's competence level and known by the mother to be so: e.g. mother says: "Get into your bath."

Such pseudo-controls comprised 9·7% of all maternal utterances; "genuine" controls accounted for 8·5% of utterances. Yet the distinction between these two types was by no means an absolute one, for the latter frequently represented instances where mothers were clearly inserting a control into the stream of the child's behaviour at a point where they knew from past experience that the child was about to act in a particular way anyway. The control thus anticipated the child's action rather than brought it about — something that is particularly easy in the context of a structured routine such as bathing, where certain set sequences of behaviour tend to occur with predictable regularity. This is reminiscent of the previously described finding by Pawlby (1977) with respect to imitation: here too mothers tended to insert a model action just before the infant was about to perform the very same response, thus providing a somewhat misleading picture of the infant's capability to imitate.

Under the circumstances it is not surprising to find compliance rates in these infants that at first sight seem extraordinarily high for so young a being. The over-all rate was 45·6%; in Table 10 that rate is broken down according to a number of different types of maternal controls. That non-verbal controls (e.g. the mother tapping the side of the bath in order to elicit the child's attention, or offering him a toy so that he may take it) elicit a much greater degree of compliance than purely verbal controls is hardly surprising, though it is also interesting to note that the addition of verbal utterances to nonverbal controls seemed to detract from the effectiveness of the latter rather than add to it. What does need emphasizing is that the apparent compliance of these young infants was in fact very much due, in part, to the prevalence of "pseudo-controls" as described above, in part to the mothers' ability to anticipate behaviour due to occur anyway, and in part also to the embeddedness of controls in the general interactive context of a familiar routine.

Table 10. *Infants' compliance rates according to type of maternal control.*

	Attention control	Action control
Verbal control	35%	25%
Nonverbal control	77%	88%
Verbal plus nonverbal control	66%	59%
Verbal control plus unrelated nonverbal behaviour	49%	25%
Nonverbal control plus unrelated verbal behaviour	55%	60%

(From Hepburn and Schaffer, 1983)

Thus examining the mother's behaviour alone may suggest that she is treating the young infant as though he were already an independent actor capable of complying; studying it in relation to the child's concurrent behaviour indicates no such thing. Knowing his limitations the mother fills in for him; she may request a particular action ("lift your legs") or prohibit something undesirable ("don't put that in your mouth"), but it is the mother herself who then lifts the child's legs or removes the forbidden object from his mouth. Or she may make requests which in fact turn out to be comments, for the child is already engaged in that activity; alternately, from past experience the mother knows he is about to engage in that activity and thus anticipates it with her remark. It is perhaps surprising that adults indulge in such apparently unrealistic requests, yet (as we saw in the case of questions put to babies) this reflects a general tendency on the part of parents to involve their young children in interactive formats long before the child can properly participate in them. There are advantages for both partners in such an apparent lack of realism: for the child it provides him with plenty of experience of that format so that, in the instance of control–compliance sequences, he becomes acquainted with the association of word and action and hence with the demand characteristics of other people's requests, enabling him more easily to learn in due course to respond on his own behalf; for the parent it makes it easier to judge when the child becomes capable of acting independently and when she is able to hand over responsibility to him.

(5) The transition to self-control

The ultimate function of parental control is not that the *parent* should be the regulator of the child's behaviour but that the *child* should assume that role. As Vygotsky (1962) in particular has pointed out, the transition from other-control to self-control is one of the most important developments of childhood, yet we are still extraordinarily ignorant about its nature and the conditions under which it takes place. What work exists has concerned itself with two specific aspects: the role of language as a regulative device, as found in particular in the work of Luria (see Zivin, 1979); and the development of impulse control and inhibitory mechanisms (Mischel and Patterson, 1979; Schaffer, 1974). Yet for one thing, the self-regulation of behaviour involves processes not necessarily of a verbal nature, just as other-control can be accomplished by numerous nonverbal means; and for another it is concerned with initiatory and facilitatory aspects as well as inhibitory ones. The transfer of control from others to self is a gradual process that may be observed throughout childhood (Kopp, 1982); it is dependent on the development of various cognitive prerequisites such as the capacity to be aware of, reflect upon and monitor one's own behaviour. And no doubt it is also dependent on the particular control strategies that parents adopt, fostering the development of self-control in varying degree.

Empirical investigations of the beginnings of self-control are few — probably because it is by no means easy to obtain unequivocal evidence of this phenomenon in very young children. According to Stayton *et al.* (1971), internalized controls (defined as self-arrest or self-inhibition) are already evident in the 9 to 12 months period; however, as a total observation time of 16 hours yielded examples for only 20% of their sample, i.e. for just 5 babies, self-control in the sense adopted by these investigators appears to be a somewhat rare phenomenon at this age. An essential definitional requirement is, of course, that the child should assume control over his behaviour independently of other people's directives — preferably in their absence, so that it is clear that he is responding to his internalized dictates and not to cues provided by others. Thus Lytton (1980) included any rudimentary manifestation of self-restraint as seen, for example, when a child started to climb on furniture with his shoes on but then *spontaneously* took them off before proceeding. A similar measure was adopted by Londerville and Main (1981); as these authors rightly point out, however, this necessarily underestimates the prevalence of self-control, in that a child with flawless internalized controls would be given no credit according to this definition. All these studies concentrated exclusively on instances of self-inhibition, i.e. on the *prevention* of behaviour — partly no doubt because it is easier to detect but partly also presumably because of the prevailing assumption that impulse control is the principal phenomenon with which socialization studies should be concerned. The notion of self-control is, however, equally applicable in its positive sense, i.e. with respect to the *initiation* of behaviour, and if full justice is to be done to the development of self-control then this aspect too must be investigated.

The relationship between compliance to the controls of others and self-control remains obscure. Neither Stayton *et al.* nor Londerville and Main found any significant association between the frequency of compliance and of internalized controls; in view of the limited number of instances observed and the restricted definition adopted this need not be taken as conclusive. In any case, the relationship between frequencies provides one with little indication of the developmental processes involved in the transition from one to the other; for the present we can only assume that compliance to others is a necessary forerunner to being able to control one's own behaviour. The nature of the transition is a gap in our knowledge that requires to be filled most urgently; it should lead us directly to an understanding of the way in which social demands and standards are internalized and thus to learning about the conditions under which the development of conscience has its beginnings.

To summarize, a three-stage developmental sequence can be used to describe the nature of control-compliance patterns:

(1) In the earliest stages of development parents provide controls, yet with no real expectation that the child will comply. Either the parent herself carries out the action on behalf of the child, or she skillfully inserts her control so as to give the illusion of the child complying.

(2) In due course the child does become able to carry out the actions demanded by the parent, and true compliance can now be observed.

(3) Eventually, controls are internalized and the child is no longer dependent on constant parental regulation of his behaviour; he has progressed from other-control to self-control.

This sequence is almost certainly an over-simplification: thus the stages are by no means disparate but are likely to overlap to a considerable extent, in that their age specification will vary according to such factors as the kind of response demanded from the child, the identity of the adult, the familiarity of the routine, and so forth. Nevertheless, the sequence provides a useful framework at this stage of our knowledge for viewing the operation of early socialization processes.

Developmental consequences

The multiplicity of encounters with other people that the child experiences every day of his life must inevitably channel his behaviour in certain directions.

The precise nature of these consequences for his development, cognitive and social, have for long been a matter of intense speculation, yet our knowledge of this basic issue remains almost embarrassingly sparse. That social interactions leave behind them enduring effects, and that the child's developing personality is markedly shaped by the specific form which these encounters take, are propositions which provoke almost universal agreement. There are, however, some formidable methodological problems to overcome in any effort empirically to support these beliefs; in the meantime we have only isolated hints as to the nature of the relationship between interactive experience and developmental outcome.

(1) Cognitive aspects

The idea that cognitive functions develop in a vacuum and that an individual's experience has no impact on his intellectual growth has been abandoned long ago (Hunt, 1961). For one thing, studies of children brought up under conditions of extreme environmental deprivation have shown the potent and sometimes disastrous effects that lack of stimulation may have on development. And for another, the impact of Piagetian theory has transformed our thinking about intellectual growth by drawing attention to its epigenetic nature, seeing it as a progressive modification of the child's mental structures through his encounters with the environment, thus in turn modifying the child's ability to act on that environment.

However, as we have already commented, Piaget's account was almost entirely a-social in nature. To him infants were lonely creatures, surrounded by a multitude of inanimate objects but never apparently interacting with other people. Take his description of object concept development: Piaget concentrates entirely on the infant–object relationship, taking no note of the multitude of ways whereby the child's social partners contribute the experiences that enable the child gradually to acquire notions about the permanence of absent objects. Observe, for instance, the hiding games that mothers play with young infants—how they teasingly cover the toy again and again for a second or two at a time, how they make it disappear very slowly to ensure the child's attention is properly focussed on the hiding place, or how they leave it half exposed to tempt him to recover it. Or take the peek-a-boo games mothers play with their infants (Bruner and Sherwood, 1976), when hiding becomes even more personalized but again carried out in a manner carefully adapted to the child's present capacities yet at the same time challenging him to further achievements. Thus in the period preceding object permanence the child has been involved in a series of many experiences, set up and flexibly managed by other people, that would appear to be highly relevant to the acquisition process. Add to that the fact that the most salient object in the child's environment, the parent, is herself involved in almost continuous departure–reappearance sequences throughout each day of the child's life, and one can appreciate that in this aspect of cognitive development, as in others, the social context cannot be neglected. As both Mead (1934) and Vygotsky (1962) have stressed, intellectual development takes place through the child's interactions with salient others; indeed according to Vygotsky each cognitive function (concept formation, logical memory, voluntary action, speech and so forth) appears in the first place as a social phenomenon, i.e. in the interaction between people, before it can become interiorized as an individual attribute.

Attempts to spell out the relationship between social experience and the growth of cognitive ability initially adopted a largely global approach, with social class on the one hand and I.Q. on the other as the favourite concepts for which a relationship was sought. But with such umbrella terms the nature of the relationship and the way in which it is brought about is not easily elucidated; a more precise analysis is therefore required in which specific aspects of the child's recurrent interactive experiences are observed and related to particular aspects of his cognitive development.

Unfortunately the various studies that have addressed themselves to this issue present, *in toto*, a far from clear picture. It is true that most find some positive association between aspects of parental behaviour and children's cognitive development, though the correlations are often unimpressively low and account for only a small part of the variance. Several methodological difficulties help to account for this state of affairs. For one thing, there is a great diversity in the choice of indices for assessing both social experience and cognitive functioning, making comparisons among studies a most difficult undertaking; secondly, while social interaction measures are becoming more specific there remains a preference for such global cognitive indices as DQ or IQ scores; and thirdly, the ages at which the two sets of measures are taken vary considerably from one study to the next, with the interval between them ranging from zero to a gap of several years. Add to that differences in the type of sample investigated (in terms such as social class, maternal or child pathology, the influence of other socializing agents, etc.), and one is indeed confronted by a situation where it is difficult to arrive at general conclusions.

The various ways in which interactive experience has been operationalized by different investigators of its cognitive consequences show up well this difficulty. One approach is to select a very large number of measures: Yarrow *et al.* (1975), for instance, obtained 38 different indices from mothers observed at home with their 5–6 months old infants and, relating them to a similar large number of infant variables, produced a plethora of correlations that are far from easy to comprehend. Another approach involves the use of composite scores, where a variety of specific measures are combined according to either *a priori* or empirical considerations. Thus Bakeman and Brown (1980) combined all 42 maternal communicative acts coded from observations of early feeding sessions in order to assess merely whether the mother was active or quiescent—a procedure which tends to lump together functionally very different behaviours and which may well account for the fact that these authors failed to find any predictive relationships between these early measures and later scores on developmental and intelligence tests.

A much more appealing alternative is to be highly selective in the choice of indices and to base that choice on some explicit conceptual scheme regarding the nature of parental influence. A good example is provided by Belsky *et al.* (1980). In a study of mothers and their children at ages 9 to 18 months maternal effects were operationalized in terms of efforts made to focus the child's attention on objects and events within the environment, whether by verbal or nonverbal means. As we have repeatedly seen, attention focussing techniques have major significance in early interactions, and to select measures accordingly makes good sense, especially as Belsky *et al.* also clearly hypothesized a link with child behaviour, namely that infants as a result of exposure to such techniques should gain control over their own attention, learn to stimulate themselves and hence become competent at self-directed exploration. Evidence of positive associations between these particular aspects of maternal and child behaviours were indeed found in this study, providing one with clearly interpretable results.

There are certain other aspects of parental behaviour which can be equally well singled out on the basis of some articulated rationale, and of these particular attention deserves to be paid to the dimension of *sensitive responsiveness*. Again our account of interactive development has highlighted the important role of this variable; however, it is also necessary to refer to doubts as to its unitary nature. Three different aspects are generally subsumed under this term, namely (i) the promptness, (ii) the consistency, and (iii) the appropriateness of the adult's behaviour in response to some child initiative. There is no good evidence at present that the three components express the same behaviour tendency and that they necessarily covary; tighter definition is clearly required. In the meantime, Martin *et al.* (1981) have most usefully drawn attention to the need to include measures not only of responsiveness to the child's bids for adult attention but also of non-responsiveness to the child's non-bidding. The latter refers to the parent's tendency not to intrude when the child is engaged in some course of action of his own; it is thus also an indication of sensitivity though one rarely taken into account. Both responsiveness and non-responsiveness, as assessed from direct observation when the children were 9 months old, were found by Martin *et al.* to predict willingness to explore at 18 months, but (confusingly) in opposite directions for the two sexes: positively in boys and negatively in girls.

The conclusion that the sensitive responsiveness of parents is in some way related to their children's developmental progress receives support from several studies. Nelson (1973), for example, found an association between a mother's language "teaching" style and her child's linguistic development: mothers who showed an accepting attitude to their children's language productions had children making much greater progresss in vocabulary acquisition than the children of mothers who were highly directive and arbitrarily imposed their own concepts on the child's speech. A similar kind of relationship emerges from a study by Rubenstein and Howes (1979) of the experiences encountered by 18-month-old children at home and in daycare centres: in both settings restrictive control on the part of the caregiver was associated with low developmental levels of child play. For instance, a negative relationship was found between the frequency with which adults directed the use of objects and the children's competence at play; however, the latter was positively related to an adult activity categorized as "facilitation of use of objects". Facilitation referred to help provided by the adult to a child actively engaged in an activity chosen by himself; directing, on the other hand, usually took the form of "Why don't you play with your car?" and thus involved a didactic imposition of an activity on the child rather than taking as the starting point the child's already ongoing activity. And a similar trend is seen in the observational study of preschool children and their mothers at home conducted by White and Watts (1973). A great many encounters that take place between mother and child can, according to these authors, be characterized as "core teaching situations", in that it is in their context that the adult has the opportunity of influencing and directing the child's behaviour in a way that can contribute towards his development. Such an episode may take no more than 20 or 40 seconds, but dozens of such would occur in the course of each day. In the sample as a whole "low-keyed facilitative techniques", such as suggesting, encouraging, supplying materials and so on, took up a considerable part of the total observation time (between 13 and 19%) in preference to patently didactic measures. However, children developing a relatively high degree of competence generally had mothers who tended to demonstrate and explain things at the *child's* instigation rather than their own; these women also usually provided help, guidance and enthusiasm oriented around the child's interests and at times determined by the child himself. Children of lower developmental competence, on the other hand, tended to experience rather more didactic handling from their mothers, whose respect for the child's own interests was thus relatively limited and discouraging.

Considering the complexity of the relationship between early social interaction and cognitive development, including the many facets of both antecedent and consequent conditions that can be chosen for study; considering also that not all studies have produced positive associations and that the relationships found are sometimes low; and finally bearing in mind that some of the investigations deal with such special groups as high-risk children (Ramey *et al.*, 1979) and preterm infants (Beckwith *et al.*, 1976), one must conclude that the relationship is still not firmly demonstrated and precisely documented. Even if an association can be demonstrated it remains necessary to show that an aetiological sequence is involved. Attempts to do so have used cross-lagged correlations (Ruddy and Bornstein, 1982), but more convincing are experimental demonstrations such as that by Belsky *et al.* (1980). In a follow-up to their above mentioned observational study these writers experimentally increased mothers' attentive behaviour by commenting on it periodically in the course of the observation sessions, thus making mothers more aware of what they were doing and more inclined to repeat such actions. In consequence the infants' exploratory behaviour was increased in certain respects in comparison with an untreated control group, though for some reason the effect was a delayed one which showed up two months later yet not immediately after the experimental treatment. Such experimental approaches do indeed furnish the necessary evidence that adult practices influence the course of cognitive growth, and moreover can provide welcome insight into the precise way in which this effect may be brought about.

(2) Social aspects

The idea that the nature of the child's interactional experiences influences the course of his social development seems, on *a priori* grounds, eminently plausible. In particular, interpersonal relationships can be expected to arise from a history of specific interactions, and the quality of the relationships ought thus to be a function of the nature of those interactions. Yet the research that has examined this issue is even more sparse than that dealing with the effects on cognitive development. There are too few studies to provide a proper overview, and in addition methodological problems once again obscure the findings that have been obtained.

The most notable effort that has been made to deal with this issue stems from the work of Ainsworth and her colleagues on the nature and development of individual differences in attachment formation (Ainsworth *et al.*, 1978). Ainsworth's conception of attachment, closely modelled on Bowlby's ethological theory, is especially concerned with the qualitative differences that emerge in this behavioural system towards the end of the first year and that express themselves in the security of the child's relationship to the mother. Thus securely attached infants are confident of their mother's availability and are able to use her as a base from which to explore their environment; insecure infants, on the other hand, tend to be anxious regarding the mother's whereabouts and show little confidence in their reactions to the world.

To highlight such differences Ainsworth devised the "Strange Situation", a standardized laboratory procedure in which infants are introduced to a variety of events designed to put the child under stress and thus evoke an intensification of attachment behaviour. These events, which take place in an unfamiliar playroom, include being introduced to a strange adult, being left by the mother with the stranger and being left entirely alone, and are built into a series of seven three-minute episodes presented in fixed sequence. From her observations of 1-year-old children in the Strange Situation Ainsworth has concluded that three main groups can be distinguished, the criterion being primarily their behaviour towards the mother on reunion following two brief separation episodes:

Group A infants are conspicuous by their avoidance of the mother following reunion; they are judged to be insecurely attached.

Group B infants actively seek contact with the mother after the separation episode and show little or no avoidant behaviour; they are thus said to show secure attachments.

Group C infants are ambivalent, in that they seek contact with the mother on reunion but mingle this with resistant behaviour towards her; they too are thus regarded as insecurely attached.

Of particular relevance to us are attempts to link the emergence of these relationship patterns to the nature of the mother's interactions with the child in earlier months. Thus, according to Ainsworth, it is the mother's sensitive responsiveness to her child across a wide range of interactive situations that gives rise to secure attachments; maternal insensitivity, on the other hand, is associated with the formation of insecure relationships. A study by Blehar *et al.* (1977) describes this link. It is based on a longitudinal investigation of 19 infants followed up during the first year of life, 10 of whom were classified as "secure" (Group B), while the remaining 9 were described as "anxious" (a combination of Groups A and C). When comparing the nature of the early interactive experiences of these two samples between the ages of 6 and 15 weeks it was found that the mothers of the securely attached infants were more often contingent in their pacing, more encouraging of further interactions and more playful and lively with the child, and that the interactions more frequently continued for longer than the initial S-R sequence. The mothers of the anxiously attached children, on the other hand, were found often to initiate face-to-face interaction with a silent, impassive face and frequently failed to respond to the babies' attempts to initiate interaction. They also tended to adopt an abrupt and routine manner with their infants, and interactions generally were rather brief. It would appear therefore that the quality of attachment found at the age of 1 year is associated with differences in maternal behaviour that are evident in the first few weeks of life. The child's social relationships, it is concluded, grow out of and are shaped by his earlier interactive experiences.

The following points need to be considered in evaluating this conclusion:

(1) The exclusive reliance on the Strange Situation as the measure of the attachment relationship is questionable. This technique has rightly attracted much attention, for its advantages include not only a focus on individual differences in children's behaviour but also an effort to express these differences in terms of *patterns* rather than by means of single responses. The technique, however, brings with it considerable methodological problems (for a detailed statement of some of these see Lamb *et al.*, 1984); for our purposes the following are particularly relevant:

(a) The situation is a highly artificial one, being made up of a continuous succession of departures and arrivals of the mother and the stranger at pre-determined points that are arbitrarily imposed onto the interaction. Such a procedure has little ecological validity and thus presents problems in any attempt to generalize the findings so obtained.

(b) The mothers are instructed to adopt a highly constrained form of behaviour within the various episodes; thus they are expected to remain passive, not to introduce the child to the toys, not to initiate any interaction with him and not to give warnings of impending departures. The intention is to keep the situation as constant as possible across children by controlling the adults' behaviour, in the belief that standardization of stimulus conditions will highlight the individual differences of the children's behaviour. Were such control effective, questions of ecological validity would again need to be raised; in fact one must doubt whether mothers do standardize their behaviour as much as is assumed: though no systematic descriptions of *mothers'* behaviour in the Strange Situation have ever been supplied it is probable that the differences among children are, to some unknown extent, a function of the mothers' behaviour at the time. The situation is thus an interactive one yet is treated in individual terms, in that the child's behaviour is assessed in isolation without reference to the specific nuances observable in the adult's ongoing behaviour. Main and Weston's (1981) finding, that the infants may fall into different classificatory groups when assessed in the Strange Situation with the father as compared with the mother, could well reflect the influence of such *current* behaviour on the part of the adult.

(c) Not only is the Strange Situation artificial and constrained, it is also extremely brief when used for diagnostic purposes. Classification into the Ainsworth categories is in fact primarily dependent on the type of behaviour displayed in the reunion episodes: responses at these points are said to provide the principal cues to the child's status, despite the fact that the relevant behaviour may appear for no more than a few seconds. It has been claimed that the classification system that is derived from the Strange Situation has predictive value of a high order (Matas *et al.*, 1978; Waters, 1978); in view of the extraordinarily narrow data base, such claims are astonishing, even unique among efforts to derive predictions from one age point to another. They are thus in urgent need of further investigation.

(2) The proposal that it is the child's *early* interactive experiences that account for the nature of his subsequent social relationships is a much too simplistic explanation, in that it neglects the influence of intervening and concurrent events. A relationship between early experience and later outcome can generally be demonstrated only when there is continuity in the child's environmental circumstances (Clarke and Clarke, 1976); under such conditions earlier experiences are constantly repeated and their effects maintained. A secure attachment is thus not to be explained on the grounds of sensitive mothering received in the first few weeks of life (as Blehar *et al.*, 1977, do), but by the sensitive mothering still being received subsequently at the time the child's attachment is assessed. This is confirmed by the finding that discontinuities of experience are associated with changes in the Strange Situation classification (Vaughn *et al.*, 1979): where samples of families characterized by instability of living arrangements are investigated, no consistent relationships between early interactional characteristics and subsequent attachment classification are likely to emerge.

(3) Attempts to demonstrate an association between interactive experience and relationship formation generally keep the child's social encounters with particular individuals in watertight compartments, as though the child's developing relationship with (say) the mother were influenced only by experiences with the mother and not at all by his experiences with other caretakers. Yet children are generally exposed to a multiplicity of social experiences involving different partners; these various sets of experiences are likely to interact in complex ways and influence the relationship formed with any one person. Thus one can expect that a child's attachment to the mother will vary according to the nature of the interaction with the father: sensitive mothering, for example, will not inevitably produce secure attachment irrespective of the nature of the father–child relationship. It is therefore unfortunate that investigators have generally confined themselves to just one relationship at a time without taking into consideration the multiple-person world in which the child lives

and hence the possibility of mutual influence among relationships.

Given these various considerations it is necessary to conclude that there is as yet little persuasive evidence that the child's specific interactive experiences have predictable consequences for his interpersonal relationships. To provide convincing evidence it is necessary to perfect better means of assessment of relationship formation; it is also necessary to abandon critical period modes of thought and instead take into consideration intervening and concurrent experiences; equally one has to do justice to the complexity of the child's social world and regard his interpersonal behaviour as the product of interacting with a diversity of individuals. That social relationships are formed as a result of a history of specific social encounters is, of course, highly plausible; to understand the nature of this development and learn what aspects of experience with other people are crucial in leading to particular consequences is a task yet to be undertaken.

Conclusions

That developmental changes take place in children's behaviour as a result of interacting with other people can hardly be doubted. How these changes are brought about, on the other hand, is a matter about which we are still largely ignorant.

One reason for this ignorance is that past attempts to understand socialization have failed to examine this process in the context of social interaction; the precise manner whereby parents try to communicate to their children particular goals and steer them in certain directions has mostly been neglected in favour of more global approaches based on the end-products of this process. Divorcing socialization from the study of social interaction in this way has led to various misconceptions, the most prominent of which are the unilateral view of parental action on children and the emphasis on conflict situations. As to the former, the study of parental control techniques shows clearly that the demands a parent makes on a child are every bit as much a function of the child's state and behaviour at the time as of the parent's requirements; socialization, that is, cannot be understood merely by looking at the parent but must be considered as an interactional activity. And as to the latter, conflicts between parent and child do, of course, occur, but to concentrate on them exclusively is to overlook the basis of mutuality on which the interaction of parent and child takes place. As the data on compliance suggest, parents are more likely to get their children to carry out desired actions if they integrate their demands with the child's ongoing behaviour rather than arbitrarily impose their own ideas on an unprepared child.

Studying the immediate impact of parent on child is an essential first step in the investigation of socialization processes. There is admittedly no guarantee that the same conditions that lead to short-term compliance are also those responsible for long-term changes; the former must nevertheless be established initially if investigation of the latter is not to be conducted in an atmosphere of unreality. It enables one to understand what in fact transpires between parent and child that could help to account for developmental change, and especially so if the same highly detailed level of enquiry is adopted that is generally used for unravelling parent–child interaction. Not that one should underestimate the ambitiousness of such enquiry; as a review of findings concerning both cognitive and social changes in children's behaviour shows, we still know extraordinarily little about how such changes result from interacting with other people. And even less is known of what is surely one of the most central themes of childhood, namely the transition from other-control to self-control, that is how the child gradually frees himself from the immediate regulation of his behaviour by caretakers and assumes responsibility himself as an independent agent. But what is becoming apparent is that parents start to exert socialization pressures on children from the early weeks of life on — not, as is sometimes suggested, only from the post-infancy period on. These early pressures differ in various ways from later ones, not least with respect to the parent's expectations of the child's ability to comply. They are nevertheless the beginnings of the long drawn-out process whereby the parent gradually comes to hand over to the child responsibility for behavioural control once the requisite cognitive and motor abilities have emerged.

8   Polyadic Interactions

Our concern so far has been almost wholly with those situations where interactions occur on a one-to-one basis. Yet in real life "pure" dyadic interactions are relatively rare, for what transpires between any two individuals tends also to be influenced by the wider social systems of which the couple are a part. To study dyads is thus to study an abstraction. Not that such abstraction is unjustified (indeed some degree is unavoidable in any investigation): the simplifying nature of the dyadic approach has had much to recommend it, for as a result of adopting it we have learned a great deal about the nature and development of interpersonal meshing. But for the sake of a fuller account the focus must be widened and cognizance taken of the fact that adult and child generally interact in settings where other events occur that may well influence the nature of the interaction.

In one respect above all dyadic studies, and particularly those taking place in specially set up situations such as the laboratory, give a misleading impression. They present a picture of parent and child totally absorbed in each other, engaging in prolonged and unbroken periods of interaction of great intensity—a picture that is then taken as characteristic of the daily lives of young children. Yet reality is generally different. By means of a combination of interview and observational techniques Douglas *et al.* (1968) plotted in very great detail the experiences of young children as they occurred over a typical seven-day period in the family setting. Their interactions with other people were categorized as *play* or *basic care*, each of these being further subdivided into *concentrated* interaction (where adult and child give each other their full attention and share in some mutual activity), *continuous* interaction (in which the child is under constant supervision but without any more direct contact taking place), and *available* (referring to those situations where the adult is available without delay when required, though not actually present). The findings for the seven-day period, averaged out in terms of daily amounts of contact with *all* individuals each child encountered, are given in Table 11. It is apparent that the total time spent in concentrated play—the activity on which most of the literature has focussed—was confined to about three quarters of an hour per day. A similar picture is presented by White *et al.* (1977, 1979), again derived from "real life" observations of preschool children and their families at home. These authors confirm that the total time spent on "social tasks" (a rather widely defined category, including such activities as "enjoying pets") takes up only a small proportion of the children's daily lives, i.e. 10% in the 12 to 15 months age range (though significantly children who developed the greatest degree of psychological competence subsequently were those who had nearly twice as much social experience as those who did not do as well). In the majority of cases it was the child rather than the mother (or any other adult) who initiated the experience, indicating that the mothers did not by any means spend the bulk of their day focussing exclusively on their children. More often than not the interactive episodes were very brief, generally lasting between 10 and 40 seconds at a time (an average of 16 seconds for child-initiated and 26 seconds for adult-initiated episodes). They usually occurred in the course of the mother's other activities in the house which were merely interrupted for a moment and then resumed.

Table 11. *Average daily time in minutes spent interacting with all individuals encountered, according to context and interaction level.*

	Play Contexts	Basic Care Contexts
Concentrated	46	43
Continuous	150	60
Available	169	17

(Adapted from Douglas *et al.*, 1968)

Such observations help to put the data on dyadic interaction into perspective. A parent's contacts with her child occur in the context of other commitments and other relationships. Paying undivided and continuous attention to one individual child is hardly possible in the light of competing demands from siblings, spouse, visitors, household duties or any of the many other activities in which a particular dyadic exchange is likely to be embedded. In settings such as daycare or nursery establishments, where one adult must divide her attention among a large group of children, such considerations become even more important. Sensitivity and the ability to be attuned to the child's interests and goals, which we have repeatedly emphasized as highly significant aspects of the adult's relationship with the child, clearly become much more difficult to sustain under such circumstances.

It becomes important therefore to investigate the way in which influences outside the dyad affect the interaction. In particular, the influence of third parties needs to be ascertained: as Hinde (1979) has stressed, every dyadic relationship exists in a social setting where individual partners have relationships with other individuals that mutually influence each other. Thus the child lives in a polyadic, not a dyadic world; he is part of an interlocking system of relationships in which he is exposed to a multiplicity of forces that require description. What is more, the child himself must develop skills that will enable him to interact not just with one person at a time but with several simultaneously in the various multi-person situations that he will frequently encounter — whether it be in the context of the family, the playgroup, the nursery or some other such group setting. The development of social competence thus turns out to be a rather more complex affair than studies of dyadic interaction alone might suggest.

Multiple interactions in family settings

The nature of the child's social interactions tends to vary with the identity of the partner even within the context of the same family. This has been illustrated by the many comparisons of the mother–child system with the father–child system (e.g. Cohen and Campos, 1974; Parke and O'Leary, 1976; Lamb, 1977; Clarke-Stewart, 1978), which show how the child's experiences vary in form and quality when confronted by different partners. It is highly unlikely that differences found (as seen, for example, in the more vigorous and more physical play style of father) reflect patterns so general as to be invariably associated with the sex of the parent; Field's (1978) comparisons of fathers acting as primary or as secondary caretakers throw doubt on such sweeping generalizations and suggest the specific role and personality of individual parents may be of greater significance. Nevertheless, these studies do indicate the diversity of the child's social environment and show how early he must develop different sets of skills and expectations with regard to the various individuals that he encounters.

Comparisons of the mother–child with the father–child relationship, such as those quoted above, involve splitting up the family into its component dyads, treating each dyad as a separate unit. But as Belsky (1981) points out, it may well be the *joint* influence of the parents that should be examined if one is to understand their contribution to the child's development, and that both mother *and* father should therefore be treated as the unit of analysis. To illustrate, Belsky quotes some findings by Clarke-Stewart, who determined the differences between parents and related these to indices of children's development. The extent of differences in their behaviour towards the child were found to be positively associated with developmental progress (presumably because of the beneficial effect of a wide variety of stimuli available); attitudinal differences, on the other hand, appeared to have a negative impact, being an expression of inconsistent child rearing policies held by the parents. Such findings show well how mother and father do not impinge on the child separately, with additive effects, but have a combined influence to which the child responds.

(1) Second-order effects: mother–father–child triads

Adding another individual to a dyad does not, of course, just increase the number of relationships to be investigated; it transforms one system into another, the properties of which may not be those of the former. Thus taking account of the father's presence when describing mother–child interaction is not merely a matter of adding another influence: the dyad has become a triadic family group the characteristics of which are more than the sum total of its component dyads. Just how complex and varied these characteristics may be in even so limited a group such as a triadic family of mother, father and child is well illustrated by Parke *et al.* (1979), who have contributed a detailed analysis and classification of the various types of interactive influences that can be distinguished in such a group.

The type of influence to which most attention has so far been given is that generally designated as second-order (or indirect) effect, referring to the changes in a dyadic interaction brought about by the presence of a third individual. As Bronfenbrenner (1974) originally pointed out, existing models of human development appear to assume a two-person system only (generally of mother and child), treating such a system in isolation from its social context and paying no attention to the effects upon it of other parties (e.g. the father). Yet a dyadic relationship cannot be fully understood until one can specify the various factors which influence each member separately, for these in turn may affect how that individual behaves within the dyad. What transpires between mother and child is thus affected by the relationship the mother has with her husband as well as by the child's relationship with the father; his mere presence during the interaction may well have a marked influence on the mother–child dyad.

There is indeed considerable evidence that interactions between a parent and the child differ according to the presence or absence of the other parent, and that this effect can be seen in the behaviour of both child and adult. The research design generally adopted involves comparing the behaviour of individual participants within a particular dyad with their behaviour in the triadic group; any differences may then be taken to indicate the modifying influence on a dyad exerted by the third individual. The overall conclusion which a number of studies (Lamb, 1976, 1977; Parke and O'Leary, 1976; Clarke-Stewart, 1978; Belsky, 1979; Pederson *et al.*, 1981) have drawn from such comparisons is that the presence of the other parent markedly depresses the interaction rate within each dyad: mother–child interaction is reduced when the father is present, and equally father–child interaction is reduced in the mother's presence. In some respects such a finding is not surprising. In the presence of several partners an individual's attention is distributed among all of them rather than focussed solely on one; there are thus competing sources of interest which will dilute each dyadic interchange. Moreover, when any pair of partners is interacting they may be too involved with one another to include the third individual, leaving him to his own devices and giving him little chance to join in with the others. This is seen in a finding by Pederson *et al.* (1981), according to which the dilution of parent–child behaviour rates occurring in the three-person situation was seen mainly during those periods when husband and wife were talking with each other. Their mutual involvement at those times was clearly incompatible with also interacting with the child—or at any rate with directing such focussed interactive responses to him as smiling, mutual gaze and talking; various other kinds of behaviour of a more routine nature (e.g. holding, cuddling and feeding) could still be carried out during those periods because they did not involve any incompatibility with simultaneously communicating with the spouse.

Two important points arise from this last observation. The first is that it is essential to study what goes on simultaneously between *all* the dyads in the triadic system. It is insufficient to conclude, by examining one or two pairs, that dyadic interactive rates are affected by the presence of a third individual; if one is to understand why this occurs the totality of events in the system needs to be investigated. For instance, Parke and O'Leary (1976) found that the amount of each parent's visual attention to the child in the triadic situation was just as great as in the dyadic situation; Belsky (1979), on the other hand, found it to be significantly reduced. Neither study provides data about mother–father interaction; it may well be, however, that this was minimal in the former study because here the children were newborns and hence presumably totally fascinating to their parents, whereas in the latter study the children were 15 months old and thus not quite so absorbing, leaving the parents free to pay attention to each other as well. The over-all meaning of the situation is thus different in the two cases, the difference between them in parent–child interaction being explained by the difference between the parent–parent interactions.

The other point is that different measures are affected in different ways when a dyad is converted into a triad—indeed the generalization that dyadic interaction rates drop in the presence of a third person turns out on closer inspection to be much too sweeping a generalization. The above quoted data from the Pederson *et al.* study makes this clear: some types of behaviour can be maintained at the same level in triadic exchanges because they are not incompatible with other simultaneously occurring behaviours by that parent: a mother can cuddle her child and talk to the father at the same time. Or take Parke and O'Leary's (1976) findings: as Table 12 shows, various patterns emerge in the comparison of dyads and triads according to which responses one examines. The amount of touching the baby by each parent is *reduced* in the triadic situation, as is rocking; smiling, on the other hand, is *increased*. Looking (as already mentioned) remains at the *same* level. And just to complicate matters still further, vocalizing shows a reduction by the mother but not by the father. Such inconsistencies can only be resolved if all interactive events in the situation are taken into account; it may well be, for instance, that the increase of smiling in the triad is due to the effect that mother and father have on each other when they share their excitement about the new baby; rocking, on the other hand, will be reduced because a one-person-at-a-time rule holds for this type of interaction.

Table 12. *Mean frequency of parent behaviour in two-person (mother or father and infant) and three-person (both parents and infant) situations.*

	Two-person:		Three-person:	
	Mother	Father	Mother	Father
Touch	17·7	17·6	9·2	12·3
Rock	7·4	13·7	1·6	5·6
Smile	3·7	4·8	9·2	7·7
Look	38·0	38·6	38·7	39·3
Vocalize	10·4	12·8	4·0	11·9

(Adapted from Parke and O'Leary, 1976)

(2) Second-order effects: mother–child–child triads

When we turn to other kinds of triads it becomes even clearer that there is nothing automatic about the reduction of behavioural rates with an increase in the number of participants. This is particularly well illustrated by the studies of Dunn and Kendrick (1982) on the effects of a new baby on the interaction between mother and first born child.

In a follow-up of 40 families these authors found a general *decrease* in measures of maternal attention to the older child following the birth of the younger; at the same time there was an *increase* in confrontation, restraint and prohibition when comparing pre-birth with post-birth observations. It is, of course, possible that such a difference might have arisen anyway because of the child's increasing age. However, comparisons were also made for one particular age point (during the second and third weeks after the baby's birth) between mother–child interactions occurring during periods when the mother was attending to the baby and those when she was not attending. The findings show that in the triadic situation a general *increase* took place in measures reflecting positive interaction of a mother and child, e.g. in joint attention, mutual looking and "highlighting" suggestions made by the mother. At the same time there was also an increase in negative interactions, as reflected by the frequency of prohibitions and the time spent in confrontation. Thus, far from ignoring the older child while attending to the baby the mother in fact was involved in a more intense interaction with the former; the general decrease of her attentiveness compared with the pre-birth period appeared to be due to those times when the mother was *not* involved with the baby. In this instance therefore the particular triadic combination investigated produced a pattern of social interactions distinctive from those described for mother–father–child combinations.

Second-order effects among yet another set of individuals have been described by Rubenstein *et al.* (1982). In this study the interactions of mothers and their 19-month-old toddlers were examined when joined by another toddler and/or his mother. These two individuals exerted very different effects on the mother–child pair. The presence of the peer tended to promote independent, autonomous behaviour in the toddlers, in that they made fewer demands for help and attention on the mother than in situations without the other child. On the other hand the presence of the peer's mother (but without her own child) brought about more dependent and regressed behaviour. Thus the way in which a third individual influences mother–child interaction differs according to the identity of that individual, and even quite young children already respond selectively.

One must conclude that any statement about the way in which second-order effects operate needs to take into account the following:

(1) The aspect of interactive behaviour examined. Not all responses are similarly affected; even where total interactive rates within a dyad are reduced in the presence of a third individual the effect does not apply equally to every type of response.

(2) The identity of the individuals involved. Thus it is apparent that making generalizations about the effects on the mother–child interaction without taking account of the identity of the third individual (e.g. father, another adult, peer or sibling) is not justified; no doubt the same applies to other combinations of persons.

(3) The participation of the third party in the interchange. In particular, if that individual engages one of the others in some communicative exchange the interaction between the latter and the remaining member will (as Pederson *et al.*, 1981, showed) be much reduced.

Thus the mechanisms whereby second-order effects play a part in determining the nature and quantity of interactive behaviour are unlikely to be identical in all instances; they can only be understood by considering in full the various circumstances that prevail in each case.

(3) Polyads and networks

The investigation of second-order effects represents a welcome extension of the customary focus on isolated dyads. Yet even here the interest is still centred on the dyad as such, in that questions are asked about the way in which an interacting couple is affected by an extraneous condition, i.e. the presence or absence of a third person. Nothing is said about the nature of triadic interactions, i.e. about those periods when all three partners are simultaneously engaged with one another in the pursuit of some joint goal. Treatment in terms of second-order effects thus implies various simplifying assumptions; the basic point made by this line of enquiry, namely that component dyads functioning within a larger group are not independent of each other, is an important one; by itself, however, it fails to do justice to the full complexity of "real" social life. How to handle triads, let alone larger polyads, as unitary entities while at the same time recognizing the various component relationships within the group is a problem to which no satisfactory solution has yet been found. The complexity of the task is indicated by the fact that as the number of participants in a group increases so the number of direct relationships between them rises in geometrical proportion; add to that second-order and triadic (plus other polyadic) relationships and the task of describing what goes on becomes a daunting one indeed.

The complexity of explaining a polyadic family group becomes even greater when one extends the focus still further and considers the effects of extra-familial influences. Each family is, after all, part of various wider social groupings that may affect the behaviour of any one or more individual members and hence their relationships with each other. For example, Bott (1957) showed that systematic associations can be found between the nature of husband–wife relationships and the involvement of each spouse in external social networks: the more close-knit the network of relatives and friends to which each belongs the greater the degree of role segregation of the married couple is likely to be.

Cochran and Brassard (1979) have discussed the various ways in which people outside the family influence the rearing of children. They propose that the influence may take two forms, directly on the child or indirectly through the parents. The former occurs by means of the child's contacts with extra-family individuals: peers, teachers, relatives, neighbours, etc. These give the child an opportunity to experience a variety of interactive styles and are therefore valuable in differentiating and extending his social repertoire. It does seem, however, that the quality of the relationships within the family itself can affect the nature of the child's relationships with these outsiders; thus comparisons of mother–child attachment with the child's sociability vis à vis peers indicate that earlier positive social relationships may well generalize to later ones (Waters *et al.*, 1979; Pastor, 1981). As far as indirect influences are concerned, these operate through the parents' access to emotional and material assistance from official and unofficial agencies, through observing the child rearing practices of other people, through the availability in crises of friends and relatives, and so forth. As Crockenberg (1981) showed, the more a mother receives support from such sources the more satisfactory the relationship with her child is likely to be, and this holds in particular when the child is "difficult" and the mother therefore especially in need of help.

Group care

Most studies of polyadic interactions have taken place in family settings. There is, however, another context in which this issue assumes importance, namely in group care situations where one adult is responsible for several children simultaneously. Large numbers of young children spend appreciable portions of their lives in some form of daycare; in so far as daycare generally involves group care we have here yet another setting where a focus wider than that of the dyad needs to be adopted.

There has been a great deal of research in recent years into the topic of daycare. However, as becomes apparent from reviews of this literature (e.g. Belsky and Steinberg, 1978), most studies have concerned themselves with products rather than with processes; interest, that is, has focussed on outcome: is daycare good or bad? What are the implications for intellectual development? Does such an experience adversely affect the child's attachment to the mother? With a few notable exceptions investigators have not usually asked about the precise conditions prevailing in daycare settings that bring about whatever consequences can be detected in children's development. Above all, we know relatively little about the day to day experiences of children in such places or about the nature of their social interactions with the adults who staff these centres, and virtually nothing about what these adults actually do and what the nature of the child care task is that confronts them in such settings.

The latter point is particularly important, in that it is largely through adult action that children's experiences are structured. One must therefore examine more closely the particular demands made on an adult charged with caring for a group of children — as opposed to having responsibility for just one child, the situation normally discussed in the social development literature. That literature, as we have seen, places special emphasis on the role of sensitive responsiveness on the part of caretakers, in that it brings about the joint involvement of adult and child, both paying attention to the same topic and becoming mutually engaged in the same course of action. Such joint involvement, it has been argued (e.g. by Bruner, 1980, and by Wood *et al.*, 1980) provides a context rich in opportunities for adults to further children's development. Sustained interactions, where the adult is sensitive to the ongoing interests of the child, may thus exert a positive effect on the latter's growing competence; as Wachs and Gruen's (1982) review shows, sensitive responsiveness on the part of adult caretakers has indeed manifold implications for children's social and cognitive development.

In a dyadic situation, where an adult is shielded from distractions and other commitments, she is free to pay undivided attention to the child and sensitive responsiveness is thus relatively easily achieved. But what of those situations where any one interaction occurs against a constant background of competing demands and where it is therefore necessary for the adult to split her attention? This applies, of course, to any group care situation; the question thus arises as to how a caretaker's behaviour changes when she is responsible for several children as opposed to a single child, and in what way the quality of interaction is affected thereby. Do children lose out under such circumstances?

In a study concerned with these issues Schaffer and Liddell (1984) asked staff members in day nurseries to participate in a specially set-up joint play session with some of the 2-year-old children in their charge. Each adult was requested to help the children with some simple construction tasks, and to do so in both a dyadic and a polyadic setting, i.e. with just one child or with four children present. The group of four always included the child from the dyadic setting (referred to as the "focal child"), so that it was possible to compare the experience of one child under the two conditions as well as the behaviour of the same adult.

Not surprisingly, quantitative differences were found in the sheer amount of attention children received in the two kinds of setting. Take the adults' talk to the children: with four children present adults spoke somewhat more than they did with one child, yet by no means four times as much (the mean numbers of utterances were 161·95 and 141·32 respectively). However, for any one child this meant a considerable reduction in the amount of speech specifically addressed to him when participating in the larger group: a mean of 41·19 utterances were directed to focal children in the polyads as compared with 141·32 utterances under dyadic conditions. In similar vein, other studies have shown that, however busy a particular adult may be in a nursery and however much she may actually be talking altogether, the amount specifically addressed to any one individual child may be extremely limited (according to the findings of one study, i.e. Sylva *et al.*, 1980, an average of only 3 minutes per hour).

But over and above such quantitative differences there are also stylistic differences in the way in which adults behave in the two kinds of setting. Thus, with four children present, Schaffer and Liddell found the adults to engage in far more "management" talk: their speech, that is, was more concerned with such extraneous matters as keeping the children from wandering away, preventing them from fighting and snatching each other's toys, and so forth. With only one child present, on the other hand, distractions were minimal and talk was consequently almost exclusively devoted to the task in hand. There was, for that matter, frequently a somewhat harrassed air about the staff in the polyadic group: they were, for instance, somewhat more inclined to use prohibitive expressions and to put their requests in the rather more peremptory, briefer imperative mood than in the more relaxed interrogative or declarative mood.

Of most significance, however, is the way in which the adults responded to the extra demands placed on them in the larger group setting. The main strategy adopted was to ignore: plotting the incidence of adult responsiveness to children's bids for attention shows that ignoring was more than three times as high in polyads as compared with dyads (Table 13). Thus nearly half of all children's bids failed to elicit a response from the adult when made in the larger group, though when she did respond it was nearly always in an appropriate manner. The basic problem appears therefore to concern the initial reception of the child's messages: where the adult has to divide her attention among several children she is just not available to any one child for a large part of the session and is often unaware of an approach made to her. What is more, when the adults did respond the resulting bout of joint involvement tended to be far briefer than in dyadic settings; seen from the child's point of view, the interaction tended consequently to be of a continuously fluctuating, on–off nature: not only was the adult often unavailable but when she did respond she showed none of the concentrated interest in the child's activity that she showed in the dyadic situation.

Whether an increase in the number of children in an adult's care must inevitably lead to a reduction in her availability is an open question. A mother looking after several children at home may well show a much higher level of responsiveness than that described above; however, the likelihood that the children will be at different developmental levels and thus have different requirements may make it easier for the mother to distribute her attention among them and to do justice to all. It is nevertheless suggestive that, according to the home observations reported by White *et al.* (1979), mothers' responsiveness to first born (and at the time only) children was at a consistently higher level than to subsequent children. Thus one might expect that the greater the number of children, and possibly also the more closely spaced they are, the more difficult will be the task of the adult to meet their demands in a sensitive and contingent fashion. Variations in sensitivity, it must be concluded, are not merely a function of individuals' personality make-up but also of the particular conditions under which they operate. As we have just seen, an individual may change markedly in responsiveness to particular children when observed under polyadic and under dyadic conditions; the demand characteristics of the former are such that quite different patterns of behaviour can emerge compared with those found in the latter condition.

Table 13. *Adults responsiveness to children's bids*

	In dyad to focal child (1)	In polyad to focal child (2)	In polyad to all children (3)	p (1) vs. (2)	p (1) vs. (3)
Responsiveness (as % of children's bids):					
Responds	86·27	55·06	59·24	<0·05	<0·001
Ignores	13·73	44·94	40·74	<0·05	<0·001
Appropriateness (as % of responsiveness):					
Appropriate	88·52	94·14	91·29	n.s.	n.s.
Inappropriate	11·48	5·86	8·72	n.s.	n.s.

(From Schaffer and Liddell, 1984); n.s. = not significant

Yet it is also noteworthy that these adults did not altogether abandon attempts to individualize their interactions with the children and that they did not simply adopt a strategy of treating the children as though constituting a homogeneous group. Thus in the polyadic setting only 6·9% of their utterances were addressed to the group as a whole, all others being directed to specific children; the constant use of children's names in the polyads (found in about one in every five utterances, as compared with just 2% in dyads where, of course, the identity of the addressee did not have to be emphasized) is further indication that the adults continued to treat the group as a series of dyads. It may well be, of course, that as group size increases such a strategy will break down at some point. The polyads referred to here contained only four children; although the quality of interaction with each child changed as a result of fragmentation the adults were clearly still attempting to relate to children as individuals, and dyadic principles were therefore still applicable to events in these groups. With greater numbers of children present it seems likely that, given the same task situation, the adult will no longer be able to maintain this mode of interaction and will instead increasingly treat the children as a homogeneous group. One can therefore hypothesize a progression according to group size: in the dyadic situation the adult is able to devote herself wholly to the one child and maintain a more or less continuous interaction; in a small polyad the same individual-based strategy is applied, albeit at the cost of no longer sustaining a high level of responsiveness; while in a still larger group it might be expected that overload on the adult's attentional capacity would result from any attempt to respond to individual children and a group-based strategy is thus adopted instead.

Do children lose out in group care settings? If the responsiveness of adult caretakers and the opportunity to become jointly involved with them in activities of mutual interest are indeed as important to children's developmental progress as has been suggested, then one might well regard such settings as hazardous. But there are a number of other considerations. For one thing, we have already made the point that group care does not necessarily involve de-individualizing: by such means as the careful scheduling of attention and the construction of mixed-age rather than same-age groups it may well be possible to maintain high levels of responsiveness. And for another, any disadvantage must be examined in the light of the undoubted advantages that can accrue from group care: above all the opportunity for peer interaction and the consequent diversification of social skills, but perhaps also the lesson that an adult cannot always be available and that the child therefore needs to ration his demands and slot them in at appropriate moments. Whether advantages such as these outweigh the disadvantages cannot be said at present; reviews of the effects of daycare (Belsky and Steinberg, 1978; Clarke-Stewart, 1982) suggest by and large that children do appear to benefit, though with the important proviso that this applies only to those better quality nurseries that have been almost the sole subject of research so far. Clearly more work of a process-oriented nature is required to identify the specific conditions that bring about particular kinds of effects in different types of social setting; only then can one take steps to maximize those conditions that lead to beneficial consequences and minimize the rest.

Children's polyadic skills

The development of children's social skills has been studied almost exclusively in relation to dyadic situations, where the questions asked deal with children's communicative competence vis à vis one other individual. However, children live in a multi-person world; not only must they establish a battery of relationships with diverse individual partners, but they must also learn to interact with several people simultaneously, i.e. to develop skills specific to polyadic groups.

It is true, of course, that groups may break up into dyads, and there is some evidence that the younger the children the more likely this will occur. According to Smith (1977), "early play sequences are almost invariably dyadic". The children he observed in playgroups spontaneously aggregated in groups of two on 58% of occasions in the 2½ to 3½ year range, 50% at 3½ to 4½ years, and 35% at 4½ to 5. The proportion of dyadic encounters thus decreased with age, though a grouping of two remained more frequent than any other group size throughout the age range. The still younger children (13 to 15 months old at the beginning of the study) observed by Mueller and Rich (1976) rarely formed clusters of 3 or more: observations of their 2½-hour playgroup meetings held twice weekly yielded an average rate for clusters of such size of only once every 15 minutes—a rate, moreover, that did not vary over the 3 months follow-up period of this study. It may be that skills for dyadic interaction are more readily acquired than skills for polyadic interaction, that the former are "easier" than the latter and thus appear earlier. What is certain is that interacting with more than a single other person places demands on an individual that are of a different order to those present in dyadic situations. For instance, in a polyad a child may relate not only to particular individuals but also to exchanges between individuals, i.e. he interacts with interactions (Collis, 1982). In the large group the child has to make decisions as to how to distribute his attention over several individuals; in the dyad he merely has the option of attending or not attending to the partner. Thus the different demands on attentional capacity may well account for the prevalence of dyadic clustering found at younger ages; children then may simply not be capable of the attentional flexibility that dealing with several individuals at the same time requires.

The following are some examples of skills specific to polyadic groups:

(1) *Addressing*. The necessity to mark messages as being intended for particular individuals is clearly of far greater importance in polyads than in dyads. In the latter anything one person says can be assumed to be directed to the other; in the larger group devices are required to clarify for whom the message is intended. Looking and physical contact may be employed for

this purpose and are apparent from an early age on; addressing the other person by name is likely to appear much later. Verbal means in particular may, of course, also be used in order to indicate that the message is addressed to the group as a whole rather than to any one individual.

(2) *Monitoring.* Complementary to addressing, which involves the selective marking of the child's outgoing messages, there is the selection of incoming messages from the other members of the group. The monitoring of more than one other person requires a splitting of attention—a difficult achievement for young children, as we have repeatedly seen. The basis on which attention is allocated in a group deserves study: it may well change with age, initially being determined by such crude factors as "whoever shouts the loudest" but gradually becoming more sophisticated and based more on whatever is meaningful to the child in particular communicative exchanges.

(3) *Sequencing.* In dyadic interactions it is necessary for an individual's communicative acts to be timed appropriately in relation to one other person's behaviour. Turn taking will thus take a simple ABAB form; A's silence can then usually be regarded as a sign to B that the floor is his. In polyadic settings this is not necessarily so; sequencing is of a much more complex form, depending largely on the number of participants. Whether to join in or not at a specific point of the exchange will depend on many factors: the relative status of the participants, the nature of the activity in which each is engaged, and so forth. Precisely what these factors are and the part they play in young children's polyadic interactions have yet to be determined; the point emphasized here is that a skill of a different order of complexity, specific to multi-person groups, is implicated. Whether such a skill is developmentally related to dyadic turn taking, in the sense that the latter inevitably precedes the former and is a prerequisite for it, is another problem to be investigated.

Thus, in so far as polyadic processes are not just reducible to processes found in dyadic exchanges, children need to acquire skills that will do justice to these additional complexities. To identify these skills and to trace their development over age is a task for future research.

Conclusions

Children live in a multi-person world, where each individual child is simultaneously embedded in a number of relationships with other people, each of whom in turn is similarly embedded in a network of relationships. It is only comparatively recently that this facet has been acknowledged; the amount of research available for review is therefore still extremely limited. This approach, however, heralds a new phase in the study of social development;

thus in a comparatively short time we have widened our focus from the individual to the dyad and now to the polyad. Individual-based statements treated social behaviour as characteristics inherent in persons; they were based on such features as age at onset, intensity and frequency, and they made possible the plotting of developmental norms and ascertainment of individual differences. Such statements were valuable; they missed out, however, what to most people is the hallmark of social behaviour, namely the to-and-fro of interaction — hence the adoption of the dyadic approach, which aimed to do justice to the specifically interactive aspect of social behaviour.

The dyadic approach has in many respects been a profitable one. It has, in particular, thrown light on the "meshing" process, showing how it is manifested in the early years and how it changes over age. It has enabled us to make statements about the respective roles played by child and adult in their encounters with one another: about the developing skills brought by the child to social interactions and the supportive techniques employed by the adult to make up for the child's deficiencies. However, there are three reservations that need to be borne in mind:

(1) In the first place there is the concern that confining oneself to dyadic settings does not tell one everything about children's social behaviour. An example is the various social skills that we have described as specific to polyadic groupings; qualitatively different behaviour patterns may thus appear in these settings which are not found under dyadic conditions. Similarly, the very fact that a child is confronted by a number of individuals simultaneously may lead to experiences that he would not encounter with only one person present, providing him, for example, with the opportunity to monitor the exchanges of other dyads and profiting accordingly. Thus certain things happen that are *unique* to multi-person situations which are not illuminated by the study of dyads.

(2) Another reservation is the fear that observations in dyadic settings may give rise to results that in certain respects are *misleading*. An example is the totally absorbed attention mothers are said to give their infants in face-to-face encounters — a picture derived solely from dyadic situations, usually conducted in laboratories where the mother is sheltered from all distractions and indeed has little to attend to but the child. As home observations have shown, this is a highly unusual pattern; in the presence of such competing demands as siblings clamouring for attention and other adults attempting to engage the mother in conversation a very different pattern emerges, i.e. one involving short though intense episodes of interaction with the child. To generalize from dyadic settings may therefore be unjustified in certain respects.

(3) A further point to take into account is the possibility that experience

in polyadic settings may lead to different developmental outcomes for the child compared with experiences in dyadic settings. For instance, we have repeatedly drawn attention to the role which the adult's sensitive responsiveness plays in furthering developmental progress (e.g. in language acquisition) and in fostering emotional security—an effect allegedly possible only in one-to-one encounters where the adult can devote herself wholly to the child and thus be appropriately responsive to his overtures. But what of children who are reared in group care settings, whether continuously as in the traditional kibbutz or intermittently as in daycare? Under such circumstances they will receive far less one-to-one interaction with interested adults; if such encounters are indeed necessary for developmental progress they might well lose out. It may, of course, be possible that there are compensating gains achieved through, for example, the opportunity for peer interaction in group care environments; the point must nevertheless be made that polyadic settings can have effects on children's development that are not produced by dyadic settings. Again the need to examine what goes on in polyads becomes apparent.

One way in which recognition has been given to the multi-person nature of the child's world is by studying the various dyadic relationships formed by him (with the mother, the father, a peer or a sibling, and so forth) and comparing these relationships with one another. While this approach goes beyond the previous preoccupation with the mother–child relationship in that it acknowledges that children have meaningful contacts with people other than the one caretaker, it nevertheless maintains a basically dyadic orientation. To compare the child's behaviour across these relationships and to analyse the demand characteristics of each in turn is useful but insufficient; it is also necessary to understand how the *aggregate* of these various relationships impinges on the child—not in some simple additive way but by, for example, examining the implications which varying kinds and degrees of difference between relationships have for his development. There have been many attempts in the past to predict aspects of child behaviour from knowledge of parental characteristics; their poor success rate has various causes, methodological and conceptual, to which we have already referred, but above all they have foundered because of their assumption that a child's social experience can be defined in terms of a single interpersonal relationship (usually that with the mother) and the belief that predictive statements can be based entirely on that. The *joint* influence of the child's diverse experiences must be taken into account rather than merely studying one relationship at a time.

For heuristic purposes it is useful to consider polyadic processes under the following headings:

(1) The implications for *individuals* of being involved in polyads. Thus,

as far as children are concerned, one can ask questions about the social skills or interactive styles that they must develop in order to participate in multi-person settings; or one can ask about the effects of polyads on such individual functions as play constructiveness or aggressiveness; or one can examine the developmental implications of polyadic experience for social maturity, language growth, etc. As far as the implications for adults are concerned, we have seen that their behaviour may change markedly in certain respects when confronted by several children simultaneously as compared with one-to-one situations, and though this in turn creates a different environment for the child to respond to, the statements made are basically about the behaviour of the adult as an individual.

(2) The implications for *dyads* of being incorporated in a polyad. Much of the literature on second-order effects is allegedly at this level, though in fact it mostly presents findings about individual rather than dyadic functions. However, questions can be asked about such genuinely dyadic phenomena as the joint involvement of adult and child in the presence of others; about conversational exchanges and their characteristics in polyadic settings; or about two-person friendship patterns when other children are also available.

(3) Statements about *polyads* as such, i.e. about the group as a whole rather than about its component individuals or dyads. Apart from Systems Theory there is little as yet to provide understanding at this level; it may well be that just as the progression from an individual-based to a dyadic level necessitated new methods and concepts, so the transition from dyad to polyad will require different tools for descriptive and analytic purposes. A dyad, it has become apparent, cannot be understood as the sum of the two sets of individual characteristics; similarly polyads cannot be merely reduced to their constituent dyads but must be considered as having their own unique properties. Just what these properties are, and the way they vary with the number of participants and the identity, interrelationships and concurrent activities of these individuals, remains to be determined. And above all methods must still be found to combine the various levels of analysis—individual, dyadic and polyadic—in ways that do justice to the system as a whole.

References

Adamson, L., Als, H., Tronick, E. and Brazelton, T. B. (1977). The development of social reciprocity between a sighted infant and her blind parents. *Journal of the American Academy of Child Psychiatry* **16**, 194-207.

Ainsworth, M. D. S., Blehar, M. C., Waters, E. and Wall, S. (1977). "Patterns of Attachment". Lawrence Erlbaum, Hillsdale, New Jersey.

Alberts, E., Kalverboer, A. F. and Hopkins, B. (1983). Mother-infant dialogue in the first days of life: an observational study during breast-feeding. *Journal of Child Psychology and Psychiatry* **24**, 145-162.

Als, H. (1979). Social interaction: dynamic matrix for developing behavioral organization. *In:* "Social Interaction and Communication During Infancy", (I. C. Uzgiris, ed.). Jossey-Bass, San Francisco.

Anderson, B. J. and Vietze, P. M. (1977). Early dialogues: the structure of reciprocal infant-mother vocalization. *In:* "Child Development: A Study of Growth Processes" (2nd edition), (S. Cohen and T. J. Comiskey, eds). Itaska, Peacock Publishers, Illinois.

Anderson, B., Vietze, P. and Dobeck, P. R. (1978). Interpersonal distance and vocal behavior in the mother-infant dyad. *Infant Behavior and Development* **1**, 381-391.

Appleton, T., Clifton, R. and Goldberg, S. (1975). The development of behavioral competence in infancy. *In:* "Review of Child Development Research, Vol.4", (F. D. Horowitz, ed.). University of Chicago Press, Chicago.

Argyle, M. (1972). "The Psychology of Interpersonal Behaviour" (2nd edition). Penguin, Harmondsworth.

Argyle, M. and Cook, M. (1976). "Gaze and Mutual Gaze". Cambridge University Press, Cambridge.

Aronson, E. and Rosenblum, S. (1971). Space perception in early infancy: perception within a common auditory-visual space. *Science* **171**, 818-820.

Bakeman, R. and Brown, J. V. (1980). Early interaction: consequences for social and mental development at three years. *Child Development* **51**, 437-447.

Barrera, M. E. and Maurer, D. (1981). Discrimination of strangers by the three-month-old. *Child Development* **52**, 558-563.

Barrett-Goldfarb, M. S. and Whitehurst, G. J. (1973). Infant vocalizations as a function of parental voice selection. *Developmental Psychology* **8**, 273-276.

Bates, E., Camaioni, L. and Volterra, V. (1975). The acquisition of performatives prior to speech. *Merrill-Palmer Quarterly* **21**, 205-226.

Bates, E., Benigni, L., Bretherton, I., Camaioni, L. and Volterra, V. (1979). From gesture to the first word: on cognitive and social prerequisites. *In:* "Origins of Behavior: Communication and Language", (M. Lewis, and L. Rosenblum, Eds). Wiley, New York.

Bateson, M. C. (1975). Mother–infant exchanges: the epigenesis of conversation interaction. *Annals of the New York Academy of Science* **263**, 101–113.

Becker, W. C. and Krug, R. S. (1965). The Parent Attitude Research Instrument: a research review. *Child Development* **36**, 329–366.

Beckwith, S. E., Kopp, C. B., Parmelee, A. H. and Marcy, T. G. (1976). Caregiver–infant interaction and early cognitive development in preterm infants. *Child Development* **47**, 579–587.

Beebe, B. and Stern, D. N. (1977). Engagement–disengagement and early object experiences. *In:* "Communicative Structures and Psychic Structures", (N. Freedman and S. Grant, eds). Plenum, New York.

Bell, R. Q. (1968). A reinterpretation of the direction of effects in studies of socialization. *Psychological Review* **75**, 81–95.

Bellinger, D. (1980). Consistency in the pattern of change in mothers' speech: some discriminant analyses. *Journal of Child Language* **7**, 469–487.

Bellugi-Klima, U. (1969). Language acquisition. Paper presented at the Wenner-Gren Foundation for Anthropological Research Symposium on Cognitive Studies and Artificial Intelligence Research, Chicago.

Belsky, J. (1979). Mother–father–infant interaction: a naturalistic observational study. *Developmental Psychology* **15**, 601–607.

Belsky, J. (1981). Early human experience: a family perspective. *Developmental Psychology* **17**, 3–23.

Belsky, J. and Steinberg, L. D. (1978). The effects of daycare: a critical review. *Child Development* **49**, 929–949.

Belsky, J., Goode, M. K. and Most, R. K. (1980). Maternal stimulation and infant exploratory competence: cross-sectional correlational, and experimental analyses. *Child Development* **51**, 1168–1178.

Berg, W. K. and Berg, K. M. (1979). Psychophysiological development in infancy: state, sensory function and attention. *In:* "Handbook of Infant Development", (J. D. Osofsky, ed.). Wiley, New York.

Berko Gleason, J. (1973). Code-switching in children's language. *In:* "Cognitive Development and the Acquisition of Language", (T. E. Moore, ed.). Academic Press, New York.

Berman, P. W. (1980). Are women more responsive than men to the young? A review of developmental and situational variables. *Psychological Bulletin* **88**, 668–695.

Bijou, S. W. (1970). Reinforcement history and socialization. *In:* "Early Experiences and the Processes of Socialization", (R. A. Hoppe, G. A. Milton and E. C. Simmel, eds). Academic Press, New York.

Bijou, S. W. and Baer, D. M. (1962). "Child Development". Appleton-Century-Crofts, New York.

Blauvelt, H. and McKenna, J. (1961). Mother–neonate interaction: capacity of the human newborn for orientation. *In:* "Determinants of Infant Behaviour", (B. M. Foss, ed.). Methuen, London.

Blehar, M. C., Lieberman, A. F. and Ainsworth, M. D. S. (1977). Early face-to-face interaction and its relation to later infant–mother attachment. *Child Development* **48**, 182–194.

Bloom, K. (1974). Eye contact as a setting event for infant learning. *Journal of Experimental Child Psychology* **17**, 250–263.

Bloom, K. and Esposito, A. (1975). Social conditioning and its proper control procedures. *Journal of Experimental Child Psychology* **19**, 209–222.

Bloom, L. (1973). Talking, understanding and thinking. *In:* "Language Perspectives: Acquisition, Retardation and Intervention", (R. Schiefelbush and L. Lloyd, eds). Macmillan, New York.

Bloom, L., Hood, L. and Lightbown, P. (1974). Imitation in language development: If, when, and why. *Cognitive Psychology* **6**, 380–420.

Blount, B. G. (1973). Aspects of Luo socialization. *Language and Society* **1**, 235–248.

Borke, H. (1971). Interpersonal perception of young children: egocentrism or empathy? *Developmental Psychology* **5**, 263–269.

Bott, E. (1957). "Family and Social Network". Tavistock, London.

Bower, T. G. R. (1974). "Development in Infancy". W. H. Freeman, San Francisco.

Bowerman, M. (1978). The acquisition of word meaning: an investigation into some current conflicts. *In:* "The Development of Communication", (N. Waterson and C. Snow, eds). Wiley, Chichester.

Bowlby, J. (1969). "Attachment and Loss. Vol.1: Attachment". Hogarth Press, London.

Brazelton, T. B. (1977). Implications of infant development among the Mayan Indians of Mexico. *In:* "Culture and Infancy", (P. H. Liederman, S. R. Tulkin and A. Rosenfeld, eds). Academic Press, New York.

Brazelton, T. B., Koslowski, B. and Main, M. (1974). The origins of reciprocity: the early mother–infant interaction. *In:* "The Effect of the Infant on its Caregiver", (M. Lewis and L. A. Rosenblum, eds). Wiley, New York.

Bretherton, I. and Bates, E. (1979). The emergence of intentional communication. *In:* "Social Interaction and Communication During Infancy", (I. C. Uzgiris, ed.). Jossey-Bass, San Francisco.

Bretherton, I., McNew, S. and Beeghly-Smith, M. (1981). Early person knowledge as expressed in gestural and verbal communication: When do infants acquire a "Theory of Mind"? *In:* "Infant Social Cognition", (M. E. Lamb and L. R. Sherrod, eds). Lawrence Erlbaum, Hillsdale, New Jersey.

Broen, P. (1972) "The verbal environment of the language-learning child". American Speech and Hearing Association Monograph no.17.

Bronfenbrenner, U. (1974). Developmental research, public policy, and the ecology of childhood. *Child Development* **45**, 1–5.

Bronson, G. (1974). The postnatal growth of visual capacity. *Child Development* **45**, 873–890.

Bronson, W. C. (1981). Toddlers' behaviors with agemates: issues of interaction, cognition and affect. "Monographs on Infancy, Vol.1". Ablex, Norwood, New Jersey.

Brooks-Gunn, J. and Lewis, M. (1978). Early social knowledge: the development of knowledge about others. *In:* "Issues in Childhood Social Development", (H. McGurk, ed.). Methuen, London.

Brown, J. V. and Bakeman, R. (1979). Relationship of human mothers with their infants during the first year of life: effects of prematurity. *In:* "Maternal Influences and Early Behavior", (R. W. Bell and W. P. Smotherman, eds). Spectrum, Holliswood, New York.

Brown, R. (1973). "A First Language". Harvard University Press, Cambridge, Mass.

Brown, R. and Hanlon, C. (1970). Derivational complexity and order of acquisition in child speech. *In:* "Cognition and the Development of Language", (J. R. Hayes, ed.). Wiley, New York.

Bruner, J. S. (1973). Organization of early skilled action. *Child Development* **44**, 1–11.

Bruner, J. S. (1977). Early social interaction and language acquisition. *In:* "Studies in Mother–infant Interaction", (H. R. Schaffer, ed.). Academic Press, London.

Bruner, J. S. (1980). Under Five in Britain. Grant McIntyre, London.

Bruner, J. S. and Sherwood, V. (1976). Early rule structure: the case of "peekaboo". *In:* "Life Sentences", (R. Harre, ed.). Wiley, London.

Butterworth, G. E. and Cochran, E. (1980). Towards a mechanism of joint visual attention in human infancy. *International Journal of Behavioural Development* **4**, 253–272.

Byers, P. (1975). Rhythms, information processing and human relations: toward a typology of communication. *In:* "Perspectives in Ethology, Vol.2", (P. Klopper and P. Bateson, eds). Plenum Press, New York.

Call, J. D. (1964). Newborn approach behaviour and early ego development. *International Journal of Psychoanalysis* **45**, 286–294.

Campos, J. J. and Stenberg, C. R. (1981). Perception, appraisal and emotion: the onset of social referencing. *In:* "Infant Social Cognition: Empirical and Theoretical Considerations", (M. E. Lamb and L. R. Sherrod, eds). Lawrence Erlbaum, Hillsdale, New Jersey.

Carlsson, S. G., Fagerberg, H., Horneman, G., Hwang, C. P., Larsson, K., Rodholm, M. and Schaller, J. (1978). Effects of amount of contact between mother and child on the mother's behavior. *Developmental Psychobiology* **11**, 143–150.

Carlsson, S. G., Fagerberg, H., Horneman, G., Hwang, C. P., Larsson, K., Rodholm, M. and Schaller, J. (1979). Effects of various amounts of contact between mother and child on the mother's nursing behavior. *Infant Behavior and Development* **2**, 209–214.

Carpenter, G. C. (1974). Visual regard of moving and stationary faces in early infancy. *Merrill-Palmer Quarterly* **20**, 181–194.

Carpenter, G. C., Tecce, J. J., Stechler, G. and Friedman, S. (1970). Differential visual behavior to human and humanoid faces in early infancy. *Merrill-Palmer Quarterly* **16**, 91–108.

Carter, A. L. (1978). From sensorimotor vocalizations to words: a case study of the evolution of attention-directing communication in the second year. *In:* "Action, Gesture and Symbol", (A. Lock, ed.). Academic Press, London:

Caudill, W. A. and Schooler, C. (1973). Child behavior and child rearing in Japan and the United States: An interim report. *Journal of Nervous and Mental Disease* **157**, 323–338.

Caudill, W. and Weinstein, H. (1969). Maternal care and infant behavior in Japan and America. *Psychiatry* **32**, 12–43.

Cazden, C. (1965). Environmental assistance to the child's acquisition of grammar. Unpublished doctoral dissertation. Harvard University, Cambridge, Mass.

Chandler, M. J. and Greenspan, S. (1972). Ersatz egocentrism: a reply to H. Borke. *Developmental Psychology* **7**, 104–106.

Circourel, A. V. and Boose, R. J. (1972). Sign language acquisition and the teaching of deaf children. *In:* "Functions of language in the Classroom", (C. Cazden and D. Hymes, eds). Teacher's College Press, New York.

Clark, E. V. (1973). What's in a word? On the child's acquisition of semantics in his first language. *In:* "Cognitive Development and the Acquisition of Language", (T. E. Moore, ed.). Academic Press, New York.

Clark, E. V. (1978). From gesture to word: the natural history of deixis in language acquisition. *In:* "Human Growth and Development", (J. S. Bruner and A. Garton, eds). Oxford University Press, London.

Clarke, A. M. and Clarke, A. D. B. (1976). Early Experience: Myth and Evidence. Open Books, London.

Clarke-Stewart, K. A. (1978). And daddy makes three: the father's impact on mother and young child. *Child Development* 49, 466–478.

Clarke-Stewart, K. A. (1982). Daycare. Fontana, London; Harvard University Press, Cambridge, Mass.

Cochran, M. M. and Brassard, J. A. (1979). Child development and social network. *Child Development* 50, 601–616.

Cohen, L. J. and Campos, J. J. (1974). Father, mother and stranger as elicitors of attachment behaviors in infancy. *Developmental Psychology* 10, 146–154.

Collis, G. M. (1977). Visual coorientation and maternal speech. *In:* "Studies in Mother–Infant Interaction", (H. R. Schaffer ed.). Academic Press, London.

Collis, G. M. (1982). Beyond dyadic interaction. *Bulletin of the British Psychological Society* 35, A82.

Collis, G. M. and Bryant, C. A. (1981). Interactions between blind parents and their young children. *Child: Care, Health and Development* 7, 41–50.

Collis, G. M. and Schaffer, H. R. (1975). Synchronization of visual attention in mother–infant pairs. *Journal of Child Psychology and Psychiatry* 16, 315–320.

Condon, W. S. (1977). A primary phase in the organization of infant responding behavior? *In:* "Studies in Mother–Infant Interaction", (H. R. Schaffer, ed.). Academic Press, London.

Condon, W. S. and Sander, L. W. (1974). Neonate movement is synchronized with adult speech: interactional participation and language acquisition. *Science* 183, 99–101.

Condry, S. M., Haltom, M. and Neisser, U. (1977). Infant sensitivity to audio-visual discrepancy. *Bulletin of the Psychonomic Society* 9, 431–432.

Connolly, K. (1973). Factors influencing the learning of manual skills by young children. *In:* "Constraints on Learning", (R. A. Hinde and J. Stevenson-Hinde, eds). Academic Press, London.

Contole, J. and Over, R. (1979). Signal detection analysis of infant social behavior. *Infant Behavior and Development* 2, 189–200.

Crockenberg, S. B. (1981). Infant irritability, mother responsiveness, and social support influences on the security of infant–mother attachment. *Child Development* 52, 857–865.

Cross, T. (1977). Mothers' speech adjustment: the contribution of selected child listener variables. *In:* "Talking to Children: Language Input and Acquisition", (C. E. Snow and C. A. Ferguson, eds). Cambridge University Press, Cambridge.

Cross, T. (1978). Mothers' speech and its association with rate of linguistic development in young children. *In:* "The Development of Communication", (N. Waterson and C. Snow, eds). John Wiley, Chichester.

Davis, H. (1978). A description of aspects of mother–infant vocal interaction. *Journal of Child Psychology and Psychiatry* 19, 379–386.

DeCasper, A. J. and Fifer, W. P. (1980). Of human bonding: newborns prefer their mothers' voices. *Science* 208, 1174–1176.

Demany, L., McKenzie, B. and Vurpillot, E. (1977). Rhythm perception in early infancy. *Nature* **266**, 718-719.

DeMauser, L. (ed.). (1976). "The History of Childhood". Souvenir Press, London.

Dennis, W. (1973). "Children of the Creche". Appleton-Century-Crofts, New York.

DeVilliers, J. and DeVilliers, P. (1978). "Language Acquisition". Harvard University Press, Cambridge Mass.

Dodd, B. (1979). Lip reading in infants: attention to speech presented in and out-of-synchrony. *Cognitive Psychology* **11**, 478-484.

Douglas, J. W. B., Lawson, A., Cooper, J.E. and Cooper, E. (1968). Family inter-action and the activities of young children: method of assessment. *Journal of Child Psychology and Psychiatry* **9**, 157-172.

Duncan, S. (1972). Some signals and rules for taking speaking turns in conversations. *Journal of Personality and Social Psychology* **23**, 283-292.

Dunn, J. and Kendrick, C. (1982). "Siblings: Love, Envy and Understanding". Harvard University Press, Cambridge, Mass.

Eckerman, C. O., Whatley, J. L. and Kutz, S. L. (1975) Growth of social play with peers during the second year of life. *Developmental Psychology* **11**, 42-49.

Eckerman, C. O., Whatley, J. L. and McGhee, L. J. (1979). Approaching and contacting the object another manipulates: a social skill of the 1-year-old. *Developmental Psychology* **15**, 585-593.

Edwards, D. (1978). The sources of children's early meanings. *In:* "The Social Context of Language", (I. Markova, ed.). Wiley, Chichester.

Eimas, P. D. (1975). Speech perception in early infancy. *In:* "Infant Perception: From Sensation to Cognition", Vol.2, (L. B. Cohen and P. Salapatek, eds). Academic Press, New York.

Eimas, P. D., Siqueland, E. R., Jusczyk, P. and Vigorito, J. (1971). Speech perception in infants. *Science* **171**, 303-306.

Ellis, R. and Wells, C. G. (1980). Enabling factors in adult–child discourse. *First Language* **1**, 46-62.

Emde, R. N., Gaensbauer, T. J. and Harmon, R. J. (1976). Emotional expression in infancy: a behavioral study. *Psychological Issues* **10**, (1, Whole no.37).

Exline, R. V. and Winters, L. C. (1965). Affective relations and mutual glances in dyads. *In:* "Affect, Cognition and Personality", (S. S. Tomkins and C. Izard, eds). Tavistock, London

Eysenck, H. J. (1977). "Crime and Personality". Routledge and Kegan Paul, London.

Fantz, R. L. (1963). Pattern vision in newborn infants. *Science* **140**, 296-297.

Fantz, R. L. (1966). Pattern discrimination and selective attention as determinants of perceptual development from birth. *In:* "Perceptual Development in Children", (A. H. Kidd and J. L. Rivoire, eds). International Universities Press, New York.

Fenson, L., Kagan, J., Kearsley, R. B. and Zelazo, P. R. (1976). The developmental progression of manipulative play in the first two years. *Child Development* **47**, 232-236.

Field, T. M. (1977a). Maternal stimulation during infant feeding. *Developmental Psychology* **14**, 539-540.

Field, T. M. (1977b). Effects of early separation, interactive deficits, and experimental manipulations on infant–mother face-to-face interaction. *Child Development* **48**, 763-771.

Field, T. M. (1978). Interaction behaviors of primary versus secondary caretaker fathers. *Developmental Psychology* **14**, 183-184.

Field, T. M. (1979a). Infant behaviors directed towards peers and adults in the presence and absence of mother. *Infant Behavior and Development* **2**, 47–54.

Field, T. M. (1979b). Visual and cardiac responses to animate and inanimate faces by young and preterm infants. *Child Development* **50**, 188–194.

Field, T. M. (1980). Interactions of preterm and term infants with their lower- and middle-class teenage and adult mothers. *In:* "High-Risk Infants and Children", (T. M. Field ed.). Academic Press, New York.

Flavell, J. H. (1977). "Cognitive Development". Prentice-Hall, Englewood Cliffs, New Jersey.

Flavell, J. H. (1979). Metacognition and cognitive monitoring. *American Psychologist* **34**, 906–911.

Fogel, A. (1977). Temporal organization in mother–infant face-to-face interaction. *In:* "Studies in Mother–Infant Interaction", (H. R. Schaffer, ed.). Academic Press, London.

Fogel, A. (1979). Peer vs. mother-directed behavior in one- to three-month-old infants. *Infant Behavior and Development* **2**, 215–226.

Fraiberg, S. H. (1977). "Insights from the Blind". Basic Books, New York.

Fraser, C. and Roberts, N. (1975). Mothers' speech to children of four different ages. *Journal of Psycholinguistic Research* **4**, 9–16.

Freedle, R. and Lewis, M. (1977). Prelinguistic conversations. *In:* "Interaction, Conversation and the Development of Language", (M. Lewis and L. A. Rosenblum, eds). Wiley, New York.

Freud, S. (1963). "Civilization and its Discontents". Hogarth Press, London.

Friedlander, K. (1947). "The Psychoanalytic Approach to Juvenile Delinquency". Routledge and Kegan Paul, London.

Frye, D., Rawling, P., Moore, C. and Myers, I. (1983). Object–person discrimination and communication at 3 and 10 months. *Developmental Psychology* **19**, 303–309.

Furrow, D., Nelson, K. and Benedict, H. (1979). Mothers' speech to children and syntactic development: some simple relationships. *Journal of Child Language* **6**, 423–442.

Garvey, C. and Berninger, G. (1981). Timing and turn taking in children's conversations. *Discourse Processes* **4**, 27–57.

Garvey, C. and Hogan, R. (1973). Social speech and social interaction: egocentrism revisited. *Child Development* **44**, 562–568.

Gentner, D. (1978). On relational meaning: the acquisition of verb meaning. *Child Development* **49**, 988–998.

Gesell, A. (1940). "The First Five Years of Life". Harper, New York.

Girton, M. C. (1979). Infants' attention to intrastimulus motion. *Journal of Experimental Child Psychology* **28**, 416–423.

Glucksberg, S., Krauss, R. and Higgins, E. T. (1975). The development of referential communication skills. *In:* "Review of Child Development Research Vol.4", (F. D. Horowitz, ed). University of Chicago Press, Chicago.

Goldberg, S., Brachfeld, S. and Divitto, B. (1980). Feeding, fussing and play: parent–infant interaction in the first year as a function of prematurity and perinatal medical problems. *In:* "High-Risk Infants and Children", (T. M. Field, ed.). Academic Press, New York.

Goslin, D. A. (1969). "Handbook of Socialization Theory and Research". Rand McNally, New York.

Gray, H. (1978). Learning to take an object from the mother. *In:* "Action, Gesture and Symbol", (A. Lock ed.). Academic Press, London.

Grossman, K., Thane, K. and Grossman, K. E. (1981). Maternal tactual contact of the newborn after various postpartum conditions of mother–infant contact. *Developmental Psychology* 17, 158–169.

Gustafson, G. E., Green, J. A. and West, M. J. (1979). The infant's changing role in mother–infant games: the growth of social skills. *Infant Behavior and Development* 2, 301–308.

Haaf, R. A. (1974). Complexity and facial resemblance as determinants of response to facelike stimuli by 5- and 10-week-old infants. *Journal of Experimental Child Psychology* 18, 480–487.

Haith, M. M. (1979). Visual cognition in early infancy. *In:* "Infants At Risk: Assessment of Cognitive Functioning", (R. B. Kearsley and I. E. Sigel, eds). Lawrence Erlbaum, Hillsdale, New Jersey.

Halliday, M. A. K. (1975). "Learning How to Mean". Arnold, London.

Harding, C. G. and Golinkoff, R. M. (1979). The origins of intentional vocalizations in prelinguistic infants. *Child Development*, 50, 33–40.

Hay, D. S., Ross, H. S. and Goldman, B. D. (1979). Social games in infancy. *In:* "Play and Learning", (B. Sutton-Smith, ed.). Gardner Press, New York.

Hayes, A. and Elliott, T. (1979). Gaze and vocalization in mother–infant dyads: conversation or coincidence? Paper to Society for Research in Child Development, San Francisco.

Hayes, L. A. and Watson, J. S. (1981). Neonatal imitation: fact or artifact? *Developmental Psychology* 17, 655–660.

Hellbrugge, T., Lauge, J. E., Rutenfrauz, J. and Stehr, K. (1964). Circadian periodicity of physiological functions in different stages of infancy and childhood. *Annals of the New York Academy of Sciences* 117, 361–373.

Hepburn, A. and Schaffer, H. R. (1983). Les controles maternels dans la prime enfance. *Enfance* 1–2, 117–127.

Hillman, D. and Bruner, J. S. (1972). Infant sucking in response to variations in schedules of feeding reinforcement. *Journal of Experimental Child Psychology* 13, 240–247.

Hinde, R. A. (1979). "Towards Understanding Relationships". Academic Press, London.

Hinde, R. A. (1982). Attachment: some conceptual and biological issues. *In:* "The Place of Attachment in Human Behavior", (C. M. Parkes and J. Stevenson-Hinde, eds). Basic Books, New York.

Hinde, R. A. and Stevenson-Hinde, J. (eds). (1983). "Constraints on Learning". Academic Press, London.

Hoffman, M. L. (1977). Moral internalization: current theory and research. *In:* "Advances in Experimental Social Psychology, Vol.10", (L. Berkowitz, ed.). Academic Press, New York.

Holmberg, M. C. (1980). "The development of social interchange patterns from 12 to 42 months. *Child Development* 51, 448–456.

Howe, C. (1981). "Acquiring Language in a Conversational Context". Academic Press, London.

Hunt, J. McV. (1961). "Intelligence and Experience". Ronald Press, New York.

Hutt, S. J., Hutt, C., Lenard, H. G., Bernuth, H. V. and Muntjewerff, W. J. (1968). Auditory responsivity in the human neonate. *Nature* 218, 888–890.

Hutt, S. J., Lenard, H. G. and Prechtl, H. F. R. (1969). Psychophysiological studies in newborn infants. *In:* "Advances in Child Development and Behavior, Vol.4", (L. P. Lipsitt and H. W. Reese, eds). Academic Press, New York.

Ingram, D. (1978). Sensorimotor intelligence and language development. *In:* "Action, Gesture and Symbol", (A. Lock ed.). Academic Press, London.

Jaffe, J. and Feldstein, S. (1970). "Rhythms of Dialogue". Academic Press, New York.

Jaffe, J., Stern, D. N. and Peery, J. C. (1973). "Conversational" coupling of gaze behavior in pre-linguistic human development. *Journal of Psycholinguistic Research* 2, 321-330.

Jancovic, M. A., Devoe, S., and Weiner, M. (1975). Age-related changes in hand and arm movements as nonverbal communication: some conceptualizations and an empirical exploration. *Child Development* 46, 922-928.

Jones, O. H. M. (1977). Mother–child communication with pre-linguistic Down's Syndrome and normal infants. *In:* "Studies in Mother–Infant Interaction", (H. R. Schaffer, ed.). Academic Press, London.

Jones, S. J. and Moss, H. A. (1971). Age, state and maternal behavior associated with infant vocalizations. *Child Development* 42, 1039-1052.

Kagan, J. (1981). "The Second Year: The Emergence of Self-Awareness". Harvard University Press, Cambridge.

Kagan, J. and Tulkin, S. (1971). Social class differences in child rearing during the first year. *In:* "The Origins of Human Social Relations", (H. R. Schaffer, ed.). Academic Press, London.

Kaplan, E. and Kaplan, G. (1971). The prelinguistic child. *In:* "Human Development and Cognitive Processes", (J. Eliot, ed.). Holt, Rinehart and Winston, New York.

Kaye, K. (1977). Toward the origin of dialogue. *In:* "Studies in Mother–Infant Interaction", (H. R. Schaffer, ed.). Academic Press, London.

Kaye, K. and Fogel, A. (1980). The temporal structure of face-to-face communication between mothers and infants. *Developmental Psychology* 16, 454-464.

Keenan, E. O. (1974). Conversational competence in children. *Journal of Child Language* 1, 163-183.

Kendon, A. (1967). Some functions of gaze-direction in social interaction. *Acta Psychologica* 26, 22-63.

Klaus, M. H. and Kennell, J. H. (1976). "Parent-Infant Bonding". Mosby, St. Louis.

Koepke, J. E., Hamm, M., Legerstee, M. and Russell, M. (1983). Neonatal imitation: two failures to replicate. *Infant Behavior and Development* 6, 97-102.

Kopp, C. B. (1982). Antecedents of self-regulation: a developmental perspective. *Developmental Psychology* 18, 199-214.

Korner, A. F. and Thoman, E. B. (1972). The relative efficacy of contact and vestibular-proprioceptive stimulation in soothing neonates. *Child Development* 43, 443-453.

Kramer, P. E. (1977). Young children's free responses to anomalous commands. *Journal of Experimental Child Psychology* 24, 219-234.

Kubicek, L. F. (1980). Organization in two mother–infant interactions involving a normal infant and his fraternal twin brother who was later diagnosed as autistic. *In:* "High-Risk Infants and Children", (T. M. Field, ed.). Academic Press, New York.

Lamb, M. E. (1976). The role of the father: an overview. *In:* "The Role of the Father in Child Development", (M. E. Lamb, ed.). Wiley, New York.

Lamb, M. E. (1977). Father–infant and mother–infant interaction in the first year of life. *Child Development* 48, 167-181.

Lamb, M. E., Thompson, R. M., Gardner, W., Charnov, E. L. and Estes, D. (1984).

Security of infantile attachment as assessed in the "Strange Situation": its study and biological interpretation. Behavioral and Brain Sciences, in press.

Lashley, K. S. (1951). The problem of serial order in behavior. *In:* "Cerebral Mechanisms in Behavior", (L. A. Jeffress, ed.). Wiley, New York.

Leiderman, P. H., Tulkin, S. R. and Rosenfeld, A. (eds). (1979). "Culture and Infancy". Academic Press, New York.

Lempers, J. D. (1979). Young children's production and comprehension of nonverbal diectic behaviors. *Journal of Genetic Psychology* **135**, 93–102.

Lempers, J., Flavell, E. and Flavell, J. H. (1977). The development in very young children of tacit knowledge concerning visual perception. *Genetic Psychology Monographs* **95**, 3–53.

Lenneberg, E. (1967). "Biological Foundations of Language". Wiley, New York.

Leung, E. H. L. and Rheingold, H. L. (1981). Development of pointing as a social gesture. *Developmental Psychology* **17**, 215–220.

LeVine, R. A. (1969). Culture, personality and socialization: an evolutionary view. *In:* "Handbook of Socialization Theory and Research", (D. A. Goslin, ed.). Rand McNally, Chicago.

LeVine, R. A. (1970). Cross-cultural study in child psychology. *In:* "Manual of Child Psychology", (P. H. Mussen, ed.). Wiley, New York.

Lewis, M. and Brooks-Gunn, J. (1979). "Social Cognition and the Acquisition of Self". Plenum, New York.

Lewis, M. and Lee-Painter, S. (1974). An interactional approach to the mother–infant dyad. *In:* "The Effect of the Infant on its Caregiver", (M. Lewis and L. A. Rosenblum, eds). Wiley, New York.

Lewis, M., Young, G., Brooks, J. and Michalson, L. (1975). The beginning of friendship. *In:* "Friendship and Peer Relations", (M. Lewis and L. A. Rosenblum eds). Wiley, New York.

Lewis, M. M. (1959). "How Children Learn to Speak". Basic Books, New York.

Lieberman, A. F. and Garvey, C. (1977). Interpersonal pauses in preschoolers' verbal exchanges. Paper presented at the Meeting of the Society for Research in Child Development, New Orleans.

Lieven, E. V. M. (1978). Conversations between mothers and young children: individual differences and their possible implication for the study of language learning. *In:* "The Development of Communication", (N. Waterson and C. Snow, eds). Wiley, London.

Londerville, S. and Main, M. (1981). Security of attachment, compliance and maternal training methods in the second year of life. *Developmental Psychology* **17**, 289–299.

Lytton, H. (1980). "Parent–Child Interaction: The Socialization Process Observed in Twin and Singleton Families", Plenum, New York.

McCall, R. B., Eichorn, D. H. and Hogarty, P. S. (1977). Transitions in early development. *Monographs of the Society for Research in Child Development* **42**, No.3, (Serial No. 171).

McGurk, H. and Lewis, M. (1974). Space perception in early infancy: perception within a common auditory–visual space? *Science* **186**, 649–650.

McGurk, H. and Macdonald, J. (1978). Auditory–visual co-ordination in the first year of life. *International Journal of Behavioral Development* **1**, 119–239.

McKenzie, B. and Over, R. (1983). Young infants fail to imitate facial and manual gestures. *Infant Behavior and Development* **6**, 85–96.

McLaughlin, B. (1983). Child compliance to parental control techniques. *Developmental Psychology* **19**, 667–673.

Macnamara, J. (1972). Cognitive basis of language learning in infants. *Psychological Review* **79**, 1–13.

McShane, J. (1979). The development of naming. *Linguistics* **17**, 879–905.

Main, M. and Watson, D. R. (1981). The quality of the toddler's relationship to mother and to father: related to conflict behavior and the readiness to establish new relationships. *Child Development* **52**, 932–940.

Martin, J. A., Maccoby, E. E. and Jacklin, C. N. (1981). Mothers' responsiveness to interactive bidding and nonbidding in boys and girls. *Child Development* **52**, 1064–1067.

Masangkay, Z. A., McCluskey, K. A., McIntyre, C. W., Sims-Knight, J., Vaughn, B. E. and Flavell, J. H. (1974). The early development of inferences about the visual percepts of others. *Child Development* **45**, 357–366.

Matas, L., Arend, R. A. and Stroufe, L. A. (1978). Continuity of adaptation in the second year: the relationship between quality of attachment and later competence. *Child Development* **49**, 547–556.

Maurer, D. and Salapatek, P. (1976). Developmental changes in the scanning of faces by young infants. *Child Development* **47**, 523–527.

Mead, G. H. (1934). "Mind, Self and Society". University of Chicago Press, Chicago.

Mehler, J., Tertoncini, J., Barriere, M. and Jassik-Gerschenfeld, D. (1978). Infant recognition of mother's voice. *Perception* **7**, 499–506.

Meltzoff, A. N. and Moore, M. K. (1977). Imitation of facial and manual gestures by human neonates. *Science* **198**, 75–78.

Messer, D. J. (1978). The integration of mother's referential speech with joint play. *Child Development* **49**, 781–787.

Messer, D. J. (1980). The episodic structure of maternal speech to young children. *Journal of Child Language* **7**, 29–40.

Messer, D. J. (1981). The identification of names in maternal speech to infants. *Journal of Psycholinguistic Research* **10**, 69–77.

Millar, W. S. and Schaffer, H. R. (1972). The influence of spatially displaced feedback on infant operant conditioning. *Journal of Experimental Child Psychology* **14**, 442–453.

Millar, W. S. and Schaffer, H. R. (1973). Visual–manipulative response strategies in infant operant conditioning with spatially displaced feedback. *British Journal of Psychology* **64**, 545–552.

Miller, G. A. (1963). Review of J. H. Greenberg (ed.), Universals of Language. *Contemporary Psychology* **8**, 417–418.

Miller, G. A. (1978). The acquisition of word meaning. *Child Development* **49**, 999–1004.

Mills, M. and Melhuish, E. (1974). Recognition of mother's voice in early infancy. *Nature* **252**, 123–124.

Mischel, W. and Paterson, C. J. (1979). Effective plans for self-control in children. *In:* "Minnesota Symposia on Child Psychology, 11", (W. A. Collins, ed.). Lawrence Erlbaum, Hillsdale, New Jersey.

Moerk, E. L. (1975). Verbal interaction between children and their mothers during the preschool years. *Developmental Psychology* **11**, 788–794.

Moerk, E. L. (1983). "The Mother of Eve—As A First Language Teacher". Ablex, New York.

Molfese, D. L. and Molfese, V. J. (1980). Cortical responses of preterm infants to phonetic and nonphonetic speech stimuli. *Developmental Psychology* **16**, 574–581.

Morse, P. A. (1972). The discrimination of speech and non-speech stimuli in early infancy. *Journal of Experimental Child Psychology* 14, 477–492.

Mueller, E. and Lucas, T. (1975). A developmental analysis of peer interaction among toddlers. *In:* "Friendship and Peer Relations", (M. Lewis and L. A. Rosenblum, eds). Wiley, New York.

Mueller, E. and Rich, A. (1976). Clustering and socially-directed behaviour in a playgroup of 1-year-old boys. *Journal of Child Psychology and Psychiatry* 17, 315–322.

Mueller, E. C. and Vandell, D. (1979). Infant–infant interaction. *In:* "Handbook of Infant Development", (J. S. Osofsky, ed.). Wiley, New York.

Murphy, C. M. (1978). Pointing in the context of a shared activity. *Child Development* 49, 371–380.

Murphy, C. M. and Messer, D. J. (1977). Mothers, infants and pointing: a study of a gesture. *In:* "Studies of Mother–Infant Interaction", (H. R. Schaffer, ed.). Academic Press, London.

Nelson, K. (1973). Structure and strategy in learning to talk. *Monographs of the Society for Research in Child Development* 38, serial no.149.

Nelson, K. (1974). Concept, word and sentence: interrelations in acquisition and development. *Psychological Review* 81, 267–285.

Nelson, K. (1979). The role of language in infant development. *In:* "Psychological Development From Infancy", (M. H. Bornstein and W. Kessen, eds). Lawrence Erlbaum, Hillsdale, New Jersey.

Newport, E. L., Gleitman, H. and Gleitman, L. (1977). Mother, I'd rather do it myself: some effects and non-effects of maternal speech style. *In:* "Talking to Children: Language Input and Acquisition", (C. E. Snow and C. A. Ferguson, eds). Cambridge University Press, Cambridge.

Newson, J. and Newson, E. (1974). Cultural aspects of childrearing in the English-speaking world. *In:* "The Integration of a Child Into a Social World", (M. P. M. Richards, ed.). Cambridge University Press, Cambridge.

Ninio, A. and Bruner, J. (1978). The achievement and antecedents of labelling. *Journal of Child Language* 5, 1–15.

Noirot, E. (1972). The onset of maternal behavior in rats, hamsters and mice: a selective review. *In:* "Advances in the Study of Behavior, Vol.4", (D. Lehrman, R. Hinde and E. Shaw, eds). Academic Press, New York.

Papousek, H. and Papousek, M. (1977). Mothering and the cognitive head start: psycho-biological considerations. *In:* "Studies in Mother–Infant Interaction", (H. R. Schaffer, ed.). Academic Press, London.

Parke, R. D. (1979). Perspectives on father–infant interaction. *In:* "Handbook of Infant Development", (J. Osofsky, ed.). Wiley, New York.

Park, R. D. and O'Leary, S. E. (1976). Father–mother–infant interaction in the newborn period. *In:* "The Developing Individual in a Changing World, Vol.II, Social and Environmental Issues", (K. Riegel and J. MacAdam, eds). Mouton, The Hague.

Parke, R. D., Power, T. G. and Gottman, J. M. (1979). Conceptualizing and qualifying influence patterns in the family triad. *In:* "Social Interaction Analysis", (M. E. Lamb, S. J. Souomi and G. R. Stephenson, eds). University of Wisconsin Press, Wisconsin.

Parmalee, A. H., Wenner, W. H. and Schulz, H. R. (1964). Infant sleep patterns from birth to 16 weeks of age. *Journal of Pediatrics* 65, 576–582.

Pastor, D. L. (1981). The quality of mother–infant attachment and its relationship to toddlers' initial sociability with peers. *Developmental Psychology* 17, 326–335.

Patterson, G. R. (1979). A performance theory for coercive family interaction. *In:* "The Analysis of Social Interactions", (R. B. Cairns, ed.). Lawrence Erlbaum, Hillsdale, New Jersey.

Pawlby, S. J. (1977). Imitative interaction. *In:* "Studies in Mother–Infant Interaction", (H. R. Schaffer, ed.). Academic Press, London.

Pederson, F., Cain, R. and Anderson, B. (1981). Second-order effects involving interactions among mother, father and infant. Paper presented at the meeting of the Society for Research in Child Development, Boston.

Phillips, J. R. (1973). Syntax and vocabulary of mothers' speech to young children: age and sex comparisons. *Child Development* 44, 182–185.

Piaget, J. (1926). "The Language and Thought of the Child". Harcourt Brace, New York.

Piaget, J. (1950). "The Psychology of Intelligence". Routledge and Kegan Paul, London.

Piaget, J. (1954). "The Child's Construction of Reality". Routledge and Kegan Paul, London.

Poindrou, P. and Neindre, P. (1980). Endocrine and sensory regulation of maternal behavior in the ewe. *In:* "Advances in the Study of Behavior, Vol.11", (J. S. Rosenblatt, R. A. Hinde, C. Beer and M-C Busnel, eds). Academic Press, New York.

Power, T. G. and Parke, R. D. (1982). Play as a context for early learning: lab. and home analyses. *In:* "The Family as a Learning Environment", (I. E. Sigel and L. M. Laosa, eds). Plenum, New York.

Prawat, R. S. and Wildfong, S. (1980). The Influence of Functional Context on Children's Labelling Responses. *Child Development* 51, 1057–1060.

Prechtl, H. F. R. (1958). The directed head turning response and allied movements of the human baby. *Behaviour* 13, 212–242.

Provence, S. and Lipton, R. C. (1962). "Infants in Institutions". International Universities Press, New York.

Ramey, C. T., Farran, D. C. and Campbell, F. A. (1979). Predicting IQ from mother–infant interactions. *Child Development* 50, 804–814.

Ratner, N. and Bruner, J. S. (1978). Games, social exchange, and the acquisition of language. *Journal of Child Language* 5, 391–401.

Rheingold, H. L. (1982). Little children's participation in the work of adults, a nascent prosocial behaviour. *Child Development* 53, 114–125.

Rheingold, H. L. and Adams, J. L. (1980). The significance of speech to newborns. *Developmental Psychology* 16, 397–403.

Rheingold, H. L., Gewirtz, J. L. and Ross, H. W. (1959). Social conditioning of vocalizations in the infant. *Journal of Comparative and Physiological Psychology* 52, 68–73.

Richards, M. P. M. (ed.). (1974). "The Integration of a Child into a Social World". Cambridge University Press, London.

Robinson, E. J. (1981). Conversational tactics and the advancement of the child's understanding about referential communication. *In:* "Communication in Development", (W. P. Robinson, Ed.). Academic Press, London.

Rodholm, M. and Larsson, K. (1979). Father–infant interaction at the first contact after delivery. *Early Human Development* 3, 21–27.

Roe, K. V. (1975). Amount of infant vocalization as a function of age: some cognitive implications. *Child Development* **46**, No.4, 936-941.

Rogosa, D. (1980). A critique of cross-lagged correlation. *Psychological Bulletin* **88**, 245-258.

Ross, H. S. and Goldman, B. M. (1976). Establishing new social relations in infancy. *In:* "Advances in Communication and Affect, Vol.4", (T. Alloway, L. Krames and P. Pliner, eds). Plenum Press, New York.

Rossetti Ferreira, M. C. (1978). Malnutrition and mother–infant asynchrony: slow mental development. *International Journal of Behavioural Development* **1**, 207-219.

Rubenstein, J. L. and Howes, C. (1979). Caregiving and infant behavior in day care and in homes. *Developmental Psychology* **15**, 1-24.

Rubenstein, J. L., Howes, C. and Pederson, F. A. (1982). Second order effects of peers on mother–toddler interaction. *Infant Behavior and Development* **5**, 185-194.

Ruddy, M. C. and Bornstein, M. H. (1982). Cognitive correlates of infant attention and maternal stimulation over the first year of life. *Child Development* **53**, 183-188.

Rutter, M. and Madge, N. (1976). "Cycles of Disadvantage". Heinemann, London.

Ryan, M. L. (1976). "Baby talk and intonation in adult speech to preverbal infants". Unpublished Ph.D. thesis, University of Strathclyde.

Sachs, J. and Devin, J. (1976). Young children's use of age-appropriate speech styles in social interaction and role playing. *Journal of Child Language* **3**, 81-98.

Sachs, J., Brown, R. and Salerno, R. (1972). Adults' speech to children. *In:* "Baby Talk and Infant Speech", (W. von Raffler Engel and Y. Lebrun, eds). Swets and Zeitlinger, Lisse.

Sackett, G. P. (1978). Measurement in observational research. *In:* "Observing Behavior, Vol.II: Data Collection and Analysis Methods", (G. P. Sackett, ed). University Park Press, Baltimore.

Salapatek, P. (1975). Pattern perception in early infancy. *In:* "Infant Perception: From Sensation to Cognition, Vol.1", (L. B. Cohen and P. Salapatek, eds). Academic Press, New York.

Sameroff, A. J. and Chandler, M. J. (1975). Reproductive risk and the continuum of caretaking casualty. *In:* "Review of Child Development Research, Vol.4", (F. D. Horowitz, M. Hetherington, S. Scarr-Salapatek and G. Siegel, eds). University of Chicago Press, Chicago.

Sander, L. W. (1969). The longitudinal course of early mother–child interaction. *In:* "Determinants of Infant Behaviour IV", (B. M. Foss, ed.). Methuen, London.

Sander, L. W., Stechler, G., Burns, P. and Lee, A. (1979). Change in infant and caregiver variables over the first two months of life. *In:* "Origins of the Infant's Social Responsiveness", (E. B. Thoman, ed.). Lawrence Erlbaum, Hillsdale, New Jersey.

Scaife, M. and Bruner, J. S. (1975). The capacity for joint visual attention in the infant. *Nature* **253**, 265-266.

Schaffer, H. R. (1966). The onset of fear of strangers and incongruity hypothesis. *Journal of Child Psychology and Psychiatry* **7**, 95-106.

Schaffer, H. R. (1971). The Growth of Sociability. Penguin, Harmondsworth.

Schaffer, H. R. (1974). Cognitive components of the infant's response to strangeness. *In:* "The Origins of Fear", (M. Lewis and L. A. Rosenblum, eds). Wiley, New York.

Schaffer, H. R. (1977). "Mothering". Open Books/Fontana, London; Harvard University Press, Cambridge, Mass.

Schaffer, H. R. and Crook, C. K. (1979). Maternal control techniques in a directed play situation. *Child Development* 50, 989–998.

Schaffer, H. R. and Crook, C. K. (1980). Child compliance and maternal control techniques. *Developmental Psychology* 16, 54–61.

Schaffer, H. R. and Liddell, C. (1984). Adult–child interaction under dyadic and polyadic conditions. *British Journal of Developmental Psychology* 2, 33–42.

Schaffer, H. R., Collis, G. M. and Parsons, G. (1977). Vocal interchange and visual regard in verbal and preverbal children. *In:* "Studies in Mother–Infant Interaction", (H. R. Schaffer, ed.). Academic Press, London.

Schaffer, H. R., Hepburn, A. and Collis, G. M. (1983). Verbal and nonverbal aspects of mothers' directives. *Journal of Child Language* 10, 337–355.

Searle, J. R. (1969). "Speech Acts: An Essay in the Philosophy of Language", Cambridge University Press, Cambridge.

Sears, R. R., Maccoby, E. E. and Levin, H. (1957). "Patterns of Child Rearing", Row, Peterson, Evanston, Illinois.

Sears, R. R., Rau, L. and Alpert, R. (1966). "Identification and Child Rearing". Tavistock, London.

Shantz, C. U. (1975). The development of social cognition. *In:* "Review of Child Development Research Vol.5", (E. M. Hetherington, ed.). University of Chicago Press, Chicago.

Shatz, M. (1978a). The relationship between cognitive processes and the development of communication skills. *In:* "Nebraska Symposium on Motivation", (C. B. Keasey, (ed.). University of Nebraska Press, Lincoln.

Shatz, M. (1978b). Children's comprehension of their mothers' question-directives. *Journal of Child Language* 5, 39–46.

Shatz, M. and Gelman, R. (1973). The development of communication skills: modifications in the speech of young children as a function of listener. *Monographs of the Society for Research in Child Development* 38, No.5 (Serial no.152).

Sherrod, L. R. (1981). Issues in cognitive perceptual development: the special case of social stimuli. *In:* "Infant Social Cognition: Empirical and Theoretical Considerations", (M. E. Lamb and L. R. Sherrod, eds). Lawrence Erlbaum, Hillsdale, New Jersey.

Shorter, E. (1976). "The Making of the Modern Family". Collins, Glasgow.

Shugar, G. W. (1978). Text analysis as an approach to the study of early linguistic operations. *In:* "The Development of Communication", (N. Waterson and C. Snow, eds). John Wiley, Chichester.

Siegel, G. M. (1963). Adult verbal behaviour with retarded children labelled as "high" or "low" in verbal ability. *American Journal of Mental Deficiency* 3, 417–424.

Siegel, G. M. and Harkins, J. P. (1963). Verbal behavior of adults in two conditions with institutionalized retarded children. *Journal of Speech and Hearing Disorders Monograph Supplement* 10, 39–46.

Smith, P. K. (1977). Social and fantasy play in young children. *In:* "Biology of Play", (B. Tizard and D. Harvey, eds). Heinemann, London.

Smith, P. K. and Connolly, K. J. (1980). "The Ecology of Preschool Behavior". Cambridge University Press, Cambridge.

Snow, C. E. (1972). Mothers' speech to children learning language. *Child Development* 43, 549–565.

Snow, C. E. (1977). The development of conversation between mothers and babies. *Journal of Child Language* 4, 1–22.

Snow, C. E. (1979). Conversations with children. *In:* "Language Acquisition", (P. Fletcher and M. Gorman, eds). Cambridge University Press, Cambridge.

Snow, C. E., DeBlan, A. and VanRoosmalen, G. (1979). Talking and playing with babies: the role of ideologies in child-rearing. *In:* "Before Speech: The Beginning of Interpersonal Communication", (M. Bullowa, ed.). Cambridge University Press, Cambridge.

Sorce, J. F. and Emde, R. N. (1982). The meaning of infant emotional expressions: regularities in caregiving responses in normal and Down's Syndrome infants. *Journal of Child Psychology and Psychiatry* **23**, 145-158.

Sroufe, L. A. (1979). The coherence of individual development. *American Psychologist* **34**, 834-841.

Stayton, D. J., Hogan, R. and Ainsworth, M. D. S. (1971). Infant obedience and maternal behavior: the origins of socialization reconsidered. *Child Development* **42**, 1057-1069.

Stern, D. N. (1971). A micro-analysis of mother–infant interaction: behavior regulating social contact between a mother and her 3½ month-old twins. *Journal of the American Academy of Child Psychiatry* **10**, 501-517.

Stern, D. N. (1974). Mother and infant at play: the dyadic interaction involving facial, vocal and gaze behaviour. *In:* "The Effect of the Infant on its Caregiver", (M. Lewis and L. A. Rosenblum, eds). Wiley, New York.

Stern, D. (1977). "The First Relationship". Open Books/Fontana, London; Harvard University Press, Cambridge, Mass.

Stern, D. N., Jaffe, J., Beebe, B. and Bennet, S. J. (1975). Vocalizing in unison and in alternation: two modes of communication within the mother–infant dyad. *Annals of the New York Academy of Science* **263**, 89-100.

Stern, D. N., Beebe, B., Jaffe, J. and Bennett, S. J. (1977). The infant's stimulus world during social interaction. *In:* "Studies in Mother–Infant Interaction", (H. R. Schaffer, ed.). Academic Press, London.

Sugarman-Bell, S. (1978). Some organizational aspects of pre-verbal communication. *In:* "The Social Context of Language", (I. Markova, ed.). Wiley, Chichester.

Super, C. M. and Harkness, S. (1982). The infant's niche in rural Kenya and metropolitan America. *In:* "Cross-Cultural Research At Issue", (L. K. Adler, ed.). Academic Press, New York.

Svejda, M. J., Campos, J. J. and Emde, R. N. (1980). Mother–Infant "Bonding": Failure to Generalize. *Child Development* **51**, 775-779.

Sylva, K., Roy, C. and Painter, M. (1980). "Childwatching at Playgroup and Nursery School". Grant McIntyre, London.

Thoman, E. B. (ed.). (1979). "Origins of the Infant's Social Responsiveness". Lawrence Erlbaum, Hillside, New Jersey.

Thoman, E. B. and Olson, J. P. (1972). Neonate–mother interaction during breast-feeding. *Developmental Psychology* **6**, 110-118.

Thoman, E. B., Barnett, C., Leiderman, P. H. and Turner, A. (1970) Neonate–mother interaction: effects of parity on feeding behavior. *Child Development* **41**, 1103-1111.

Thoman, E. B., Barnett, C. R. and Leiderman, P. H. (1971). Feeding behaviors of newborn infants as a function of parity of the mother. *Child Development* **42**, 1471-1483.

Thomas, E. A. C. and Martin, J. A. (1976). Analyses of parent–infant interaction. Psychological analyses of parent–infant interaction. *Psychological Review* **83**, 141-156.

Tizard, B. (1978). "Adoption: A Second Chance". Open Books, London.

Tomikawa, S. A. and Dodd, D. H. (1980). Early word meanings: perceptually or functionally based? *Child Development* **51**, 1103–1109.

Trevarthen, C. (1977). Descriptive analyses of infant communicative behaviour. *In:* "Studies in Mother-Infant Interaction", (H. R. Schaffer, ed.). Academic Press, London.

Trevarthen, C. (1979). Communication and cooperation in early infancy: a description of primary intersubjectivity. *In:* "Before Speech: The Beginning of Interpersonal Communication", (M. Bullowa, ed.). Cambridge University Press, Cambridge.

Trevarthen, C. and Hubley, P. (1978). Secondary intersubjectivity. *In:* "Action, Gesture and Symbol", (A. Lock, ed.). Academic Press, London.

Tronick, E., Als, H., Adamson, L., Wise, S. and Brazelton, T. (1978). The infant's responses to entrapment between contradictory messages in face-to-face interaction. *Journal of the American Academy of Child Psychiatry* **17**, 1–13.

Vandell, D. L. and Mueller, E. C. (1980). Peer play and friendships during the first two years. *In:* "Friendship and Social Relations in Children", (H. C. Foot, A. J. Chapman and J. R. Smith, eds). Wiley, Chichester.

van der Geest, T. (1977). Some interactional aspects of language acquisition. *In:* "Talking to Children", (C. E. Snow and C. A. Ferguson, eds). Cambridge University Press, Cambridge.

Vaughn, B., Engeland, B., Sroufe, A. L. and Waters, E. (1979). Individual differences in infant-mother attachment at twelve and eighteen months: stability and change in families under stress. *Child Development* **50**, 971–975.

Vygotsky, L. S. (1962). "Thought and Language". M.I.T. Press, Cambridge, Mass.

Vygotsky, L. S. (1966). Development of the higher mental functions. *In:* "Psychological Research in the USSR". Progress Publishers, Moscow.

Vygotsky, L. S. (1978). "Mind in Society". M.I.T. Press, Cambridge, Mass.

Wachs, T. D. and Gruen, G. E. (1982). "Early Experience and Human Development". Plenum, New York.

Walters, G. C. and Grusec, J. E. (1977). "Punishment". W. H. Freeman, San Francisco.

Waters, E. (1978). The reliability and stability of individual differences in infant-mother attachment. *Child Development* **49**, 483–494.

Waters, E., Whippman, J. and Sroufe, L. A. (1979). Attachment, positive affect and competence in the peer group. *Child Development* **50**, 821–829.

Watson, J. B. (1928). "Psychological Care of Infant and Child". Norton, New York.

Webster, R. L. (1969). Selective suppression of infant vocal response by classes of phonemic stimulation. *Developmental Psychology* **4**, 410–414.

Webster, R. L., Steinhardt, M. H. and Senter, M. G. (1972). Changes in infants' vocalizations as a function of differential acoustic stimulation. *Developmental Psychology* **7**, 39–43.

Weisberg, P. (1963). Social and nonsocial conditioning of infant vocalizations. *Child Development* **34**, 377–388.

Wells, C. G. (1979). Variations in child language. *In:* "Language Acquisition", (P. Fletcher and M. Garman, eds). Cambridge University Press, Cambridge.

Werner, H. and Kaplan, B. (1963). "Symbol Formation: An Organismic-Developmental Approach to Language and the Expression of Thought". Wiley, New York.

Wetstone, J. and Friedlander, B. (1973). The effect of word order on young children's responses to simple questions and commands. *Child Development* **44**, 743–750.

White, B. L. (1971). "Human Infants". Prentice-Hall, Englewood Cliffs, New Jersey.

White, B. L. and Watts, J. C. (1973). "Experience and Environment: Major Influences on the Development of the Young Child". Prentice-Hall, Englewood Cliffs, New Jersey.

White, B. L., Kaban, B., Shapiro, B. and Attanucci, J. (1977). Competence and experience. *In:* "The Structuring of Experience", (I. C. Uzgiris and F. Weizmann, eds). Plenum, New York.

White, B. L., Kaban, B. T. and Attanucci, J. S. (1979). "The Origins of Human Competence". D. C. Heath, Lexington, Mass.

Whiten, A. (1977). Assessing the effects of perinatal events on the success of the mother–infant relationship. *In:* "Studies in Mother–Infant Interaction", (H. R. Schaffer, ed.). Academic Press, London.

Wilson, E. (1975). "Sociobiology: A New Synthesis". Harvard University Press, Cambridge, Mass.

Wolff, P. H. (1963). Observations on the early development of smiling. *In:* "Determinants of Infant Behaviour, Vol.2", (B. M. Foss, ed.). Methuen, London.

Wolff, P. H. (1965). The development of attention in young infants. *Annals of the New York Academy of Science* **118**, 815–830.

Wolff, P. H. (1966). The causes, controls, and organization of behaviour in the neonate. *Psychological Issues* **5**, No.1, Monograph No.17.

Wolff, P. H. (1968). The serial organization of sucking in the young infant. *Pediatrics* **42**, 943–956.

Wood, D., McMahon, L. and Cranstoun, Y. (1980). "Working With Under Fives". Grant McIntyre, London.

Yarrow, L. J., Rubenstein, J. L. and Pederson, F. A. (1975). "Infant and Environment: Early Cognitive and Motivational Development". Hemisphere Publishing Corporation, Washington, D.C.

Yogman, M. W., Dixon, S., Tronick, E., Adamson, L., Als, H. and Brazelton, T. B. (April 1976). Development of infant social interaction with fathers. Paper presented at the meeting of the Eastern Psychological Association, New York.

Zigler, E. F. and Child, I. L., (eds). (1973). "Socialization and Personality Development". Addison-Wesley, Reading, Mass.

Zivin, G., (ed.). (1979). "The Development of Self-Regulation Through Speech". Wiley, New York.

Index